D1012317

SUMMA PUBLICATIONS, INC.

Thomas M. Hines
Publisher

William C. Carter
Editor-in-chief

Editorial Board

Orders:
P.O. Box 660725
Birmingham, AL 35266-0725

Editorial Address:
3601 Westbury Road
Birmingham, AL 35223

France at the Dawn of the Twenty-First Century
Trends and Transformations

La France à l'aube du XXIe siècle
Tendances et mutations

France at the Dawn of the Twenty-First Century
Trends and Transformations

La France à l'aube du XXIe siècle
Tendances et mutations

Marie-Christine Weidmann Koop, Editor

Assisted by Rosalie Vermette

SUMMA PUBLICATIONS, INC.
Birmingham, Alabama
2000

Table of contents - Table des matières

List of Illustrations

Preface

Marie-Christine Weidmann Koop

This volume developed out of a research project that I organized under the auspices of the Commission on Cultural Competence of the American Association of Teachers of French (AATF). The Commission had already published a volume that defined four levels of cultural competence. This volume was titled *Acquiring Cross-Cultural Competence. Four Stages for Students of French* and was edited by Alan Singerman (Lincolnwood, IL: National Textbook Company, 1996). That first effort of the Commission needed to be supplemented by other works, including the present volume that proposes an overview of contemporary France and its recent transformations. The writing of the volume was to be completed by fifteen professors of French culture and civilization in American universities who would first attend a two-week seminar in France to share ideas and initiate their research on a topic of their choice. To round out the volume, other specialists would later be invited to write articles on additional topics of interest.

In 1996, I contacted Alain Kimmel at the Centre International d'Etudes Pédagogiques (CIEP) in Sèvres, France, and described the objectives of the proposed seminar with a list of tentative topics to be covered and visits to be included. The CIEP was selected as the site for the seminar because of its tradition of excellence with respect to French culture and because of the reputation of Alain Kimmel who was Editor-in-Chief of *Echos*, a journal of contemporary French life. Sèvres's location was also a major factor, as proximity to Paris would enable the group to meet with officials in various fields. I also applied for and received a generous grant from the French Cultural Services division of the French Embassy in the United States, thanks to the kind mediation of Candide Soci who was then linguistic attaché at the French consulate in New York. A call for applications was then publicized nationally and candidates were selected. The seminar took place in Sèvres in July 1997. By the fall of that year, we had finalized the table of contents for the present volume.

It is our hope that this volume addresses the major issues that have affected today's France and the French. The book is organized around five main themes — politics, social issues, identity, culture, and perception of France from the United States — and ends with a bibliographical essay on contemporary France. In view of the diversity of the topics, each author was free to use different and even contrasting approaches. But the trends and transformations of French society at the dawn of the twentieth century constitute the unifying theme of this work.

The first section explores the political arena, with five articles on various aspects of the question. The contribution of Douglas J. Daniels offers an overview of the political scene in France. This area was dramatically affected by the 1997 legislative election which marked the third period of "cohabitation" since 1981. Never before had a president dissolved an assembly whose composition gave him a majority. There were many considerations, but the most important reason for President Chirac's action was the coinciding of the elections with the decision to adopt the euro, the new European monetary system, in the spring of 1998. Daniels' study first examines how the rebuilding of the *Parti Socialiste* after the 1993 and 1995 defeats coincided with Prime Minister Juppé's government's growing unpopularity to make possible the third cohabitation. Daniels also evaluates the program of the new government in its beginning months. Finally, the author examines the probable long-term effects of these events on the institution of the French presidency.

The second article, by Christopher Pinet, deals with the French Communist Party. Recently, following a twenty-year decline, French communism has experienced an unexpected resurgence, leading to an increase in Communist seats in the National Assembly following the 1997 legislative elections. Since the socialists do not command an absolute majority, they must now turn to the communists when they need a majority voice. This dramatic electoral upturn, and the appointment of three communists as cabinet-level ministers by Prime Minister Jospin, can be explained in large part, by the shared need of a coalition of *rose, rouge,* and *vert* (the "Greens") to command a majority in the National Assembly. Pinet outlines how the French Communist Party under the leadership of its new Secretary, Robert Hue, has managed to reinvent itself, regain some of its lost credibility with voters, and once again play a significant role in French politics and government.

Michel Gueldry next gives an overview of the evolution of French environmental policy since the 1950s, with an emphasis on the last two decades. As background, he first explains the reasons for the weak state of environmental awareness in the France of the 1950s and 1960s, using nuclear energy policy as a case study. Gueldry then analyzes the crystallization of environmental values in the 1970s, addressing the most important developments. Finally, he explains the relative success of the Green agenda since the 1980s, considering such key factors as the 1981 decentralization bill and the Chernobyl disaster. Gueldry also summarizes the main environmental issues currently facing the French government: the SuperPhenix, the COGEMA safety record, air pollution over Paris, and the hunting polemic. In conclusion, Gueldry considers the future of French environmental policy within the context of the European Union.

The French social protection system is analyzed by Alan Singerman, whose article begins with the crisis of November-December 1995 when France experienced its most traumatic social upheaval since May 1968. This crisis was brought on in part by student strikes at universities throughout France, but more particularly by the announcement in mid-November of the *Plan Juppé*. At the heart of Juppé's plan were revisions in the vast system of *sécurité sociale* whose mounting deficits endangered France's strong desire to participate in the European Union's new monetary system. The social explosion, initiated by angry workers whose retirement plans were threatened, has fueled a broad social debate on the future of several central components of social protection in France, notably medical insurance, family allocations, and retirement. Singerman examines the evolution of the national debate on the future of social payments in France since the 1995 crisis produced by the *Plan Juppé* and compares the French and American systems in this area, particularly with regard to medical insurance and the health industry.

Claud DuVerlie's article addresses the pressing issues of European integration. The European Union is now facing some decisive issues, such as monetary and economic union and the efforts to introduce the euro currency in 1999, to be followed by the use of euro notes and coins in 2002. Meanwhile it will be necessary to fine-tune the Maastricht treaty, solve the Europe-wide unemployment problem, and deal with social issues, as well as answer the challenges that derive from the global market. Europeans will have to agree first on the reforms of economic institutions so as to strengthen the EU's political agenda. DuVerlie provides an update on European integration and analyzes its effects on French society. He also addresses such questions as the degree to which the French are becoming European and whether France is really willing to relinquish its "hexagonal" borders.

The book's second section, on social issues, begins with Alain Kimmel's article on the transformations of the French family. At a time when the media and politicians regularly debate the disintegration if not the end of the family as an institution, it appears that the family has in fact never enjoyed such a high level of popular approval among the French. But the type of family involved needs to be more broadly defined — the traditional family plus the single-parent family plus of course the "blended" family. With a steady decline in the number of marriages and a significant increase in the divorce rate, the family is one of the French social institutions that has gone through the most dramatic changes over the last twenty-five years. These transformations are directly related to the changing role of women, a sharp drop in the birthrate, and a broadening vision of the concept of couple, which has led to the idea of establishing a new family status, the *Pacte civil de solidarité (PACS)*, that would embrace all types of households, not excluding homosexual couples.

Alice J. Strange's contribution to this volume presents an overview of the individual and collective issues raised by France's rapidly aging population. It has been more than thirty years since the upheavals of 1968 and France's postwar generation is now heading towards retirement. Life expectancy continues to rise and the growing number of elderly people strains France's social security system. Strange addresses the economic dilemma that France is currently facing: shall the retirement age be lowered to reduce unemployment or raised to avoid straining retirement funds? Many elderly must deal with a growing lack of social and financial resources. At the same time, France's elderly constitute a growing and important political and economic force.

My own article on education focuses on the issue of equal opportunity. The secondary school system in France was originally conceived to prepare young people from the upper classes to pass the *baccalauréat*, designed to be the gateway to higher education. Only a small number of young people had access to this system. With the new demands created by the arrival of the baby boomers and the economic explosion following World War II, secondary education was gradually modified and other types of *baccalauréats* have been introduced over the years to make this diploma available to more and more students. The number of students who receive the *baccalauréat* has increased tremendously since the 1960s. However, it seems that students continue to select different types of *"bacs"* according not only to their abilities, but to other factors, especially social background and gender. This article shows how students' choices are still determined by their social origins and how all *"bacs"* are not equal in terms of social mobility.

Ann Williams-Gascon analyzes graffiti as a reflection of social issues in contemporary France. Using walls as a medium for communication has been a cultural practice since prehistoric times, and the traces left by the often anonymous scribes give an inkling about what issues were considered important. Such is the case today, especially in places where there is political and social turmoil and where a segment of the population feels powerless, even voiceless, with no means of coping with social issues that go unresolved. At the end of the 1990s, graffiti in their diverse forms (stencils, markers, spray can art, tags) are used for a variety of communicative functions. They present social commentary, demonstrate resistance, indicate frustration, and have even become a forum for dialogue. With photographs to illustrate these functions, Williams-Gascon gives examples of social issues brought to the fore by graffiti in France and shows how these issues reflect an underlying social unrest.

The third section of the book deals with French identity, an issue that is taking on new dimensions through the various debates taking place at the turn of the millennium. Edward C. Knox analyzes French identity at three levels — event, sector, and system. He concentrates on the year 1998, the thirtieth anniversary of *"Mai 68"* and the year of the euphoria of France's World Cup victory. Knox shows that a look at the discourse on France in the French and American press of May-July 1998 suggests that many of the French were taking a more flexible position on national identity in an era of global change, and that Americans were less ready to allow for an evolving image of France. It seems, in fact, that the selection of content for coverage of France in the U.S. press often draws on the spectacular, the picturesque, or the stereotypical.

Jacqueline Thomas looks at France's national identity through the prism of the French press. She first notes that the tone of recent articles about France in the American press has been generally negative, suggesting a national identity crisis and focusing on malaise. After surveying the various factors that have been a threat to "Frenchness," Thomas explores the current situation in France that has led to insecurity and social malaise. Following a brief overview of the French press, focusing especially on *Le Monde*, Thomas's article studies the tone and content of six daily newspapers *(Le Monde, Libération, L'Humanité, Le Figaro, La Croix, and France-Soir)* through an analysis of comments on President Chirac's televised address on Bastille Day 1997, in which he specifically referred to the question of national identity.

Fred Toner next addresses the issue of multiculturalism, showing how the immigrant presence serves as an important social catalyst in contemporary France. Over the last decade, the debate on immigration has widened beyond ethnic and economic concerns. A number of minority populations have proclaimed their solidarity with the immigrant cause and have organized associations proclaiming "le droit à la différence." Toner examines the role of this increased activity, which on the one hand could lead to the development of a more tolerant society ready to assume a place in the new European Union, or on the other hand could signal the beginning of the eventual splintering and destruction of the Republic and republican values. The debate between *assimilationnistes* and *communautaristes* is giving rise to a reexamination of some of the core assumptions of French society and a rethinking of what it means to be French.

The book's fourth section, on culture, explores the representations of social and political concerns through various means of cultural expression. Roland Simon's article on pastimes begins with the stereotypes associated with the way French people spend their free time. A survey provides a summary of the changes that have taken place around work and leisure since 1936, when paid vacations were mandated. Following a brief look at the recent evolution of mass-leisure time, Simon examines the favorite leisure time activities of the French. In addition to, or perhaps instead of, traditional pastimes such as gardening or watching professional sports, Simon looks at new ways of fulfilling one's ideal of the perfect way to spend free time in an increasingly diversified France.

Marc Bertrand's article offers insights into contemporary French life through the medium of the social novel. Bertrand shows that each year at least a dozen well-written novels are published that illuminate important aspects of social life in France today. Rich in descriptions of social and professional activities, of social conflicts, and of the changing urban climate, these novels introduce the reader to recent events and social changes in France. Compared to earlier social novels, these are more varied in the social/ethnic origins of their authors, as well as in the milieus they present. The imagination and the subjectivity introduced by the novelists serve to establish a gap between the social reality described and the frustrations, desires, and the rejection of characters that are so close to the social and material reality being treated that they become part of the social realism of these "fictions." Bertrand's study surveys and comments on recently published social novels, suggests categories and themes for their subject matter, and distinguishes between the novels' centrality or marginality.

Jeri DeBois King's article defines and explores the cosmopolitan tradition in French film. France's cosmopolitan tradition dates back to Montaigne's "Essay on Cannibals," Molière's battle with religious hypocrites, the philosophes' fight against intolerance, and Zola's defense of Dreyfus. France's film industry, second only to the United States' in production, certainly reflects this cosmopolitan tradition. France's generous government subsidies to its film industry and the lengthy list of countries with which France collaborates in film-making prove that France has taken a serious international outlook toward the art of film. King identifies cosmopolitan conventions in French film and examines how they appear and reappear in films of the 1990s. Some of these conventions are: breaking national stereotypes and redefining the concept of "foreigner," revisiting the deportation of Jews during World War II, appealing to the intellectual community's appetite for innovative artistic techniques to gain acceptance for cosmopolitan ideas, and using historical and classical references to create contemporary parables.

Gregg Siewert next examines new cultural spaces in France. Showing that France's leaders have not uncommonly left behind impressive cultural and architectural monuments, Siewert points out that the presidency of François Mitterrand was not all that different. Mitterrand's fourteen-

year presidency produced such headline-grabbing projects as the renovation of the Louvre, the installation of the Musée d'Orsay, the Grande
Arche, the Opéra Bastille, the rebuilding of the Bercy district, and the relocation of France's national library to a reclaimed site next to the Seine.
Siewert traces the histories of these and other monuments, discusses their
impact in France, and assesses their importance as tourist sites. Sites away
from Paris are also discussed, including the World War II Memorial in
Caen, the striking comic-book museum in Angoulême, and the Futuroscope
project in Poitiers.

The book's fifth section explores the perception of France from
across the Atlantic. Michel Sage's essay explores France and America's
changing diplomatic relations as viewed in the American press, noting that
France seems to have become the American press's favorite European target. Most recently it seems that France's international image has suffered
from excessive negative American publicity — too much government
regulation, too much state bureaucracy, too much spending, too much taxation. France's resistance to the global currents of late-century economic
capitalism may have doomed it to bankruptcy and irrelevance, and yet the
country continues to display stubborn pride on an international scale.
Americans are forever puzzled and irritated by the complexity, inaccessi-
bility, and "otherness" of French diplomacy. Such highly respected newspapers as *The Washington Post, The New York Times, and The Los
Angeles Times* have contributed greatly to this negative image not only
through their coverage of events but also in several prominent editorials.
Sage's article addresses the nature of the "great cultural divide" between
the United States and France and the causes of disagreement over diplomatic, economic, and political conflicts. It examines the relationship between France's self-perceived role and its effect on diplomatic relations
with the US, and France's growing alarm at American domination in what it
calls a "unilateral" world and the American conviction that French foreign
policy is systematically challenging the US in international affairs.

In her article on Hollywood remakes of French films, Colette Levin
examines several French films which have been judged by Hollywood to be
particularly well-suited to adaptation for American viewers and the remakes which these films have inspired. A comparative study of individual
practices reveals that, although they use similar plots, the French and

Hollywood versions are noticeably different. The difference lies with the Hollywood filmmakers' response to cultural exigencies: they reject elements perceived as cultural taboos within the American cultural system, substitute others deemed to be acceptable within the same system, and shape their films to meet their viewers' expectations. The comparative analysis of Hollywood remakes and their respective French sources yields an inventory of cultural components pertaining both to the representation of French and American cultures and to the shaping of the films which encapsulate these cultures.

The book concludes with a bibliographic review article by Rosalie Vermette that begins with a synthesis of the various social, political, and cultural changes that mark the end of the twentieth century in France, followed by a critical review of selected studies of contemporary France in order to highlight works beyond those identified in the book's individual essays. Items are annotated and organized by cultural category, reflecting the major divisions of this book. The article ends with a selection of references of a general nature, including a section listing selected newspapers, Web sites, and periodical publications which can help keep the reader current with regard to *l'actualité* in France.

I would like to express my gratitude to Candide Soci and the French Cultural Services whose generous grant made this project possible. My thanks also go to Alain Kimmel who collaborated with me in organizing the 1997 Sèvres seminar. Finally, I am especially grateful to Rosalie Vermette who assisted me with various aspects of this project, including serving on the review committee that selected the participants in the Sèvres seminar, providing many insightful suggestions during the development of the manuscript, and helping to edit this volume.

I. Politics - La vie politique

France on Alternating Power: Cohabitation III

Douglas J. Daniels
Montana State University-Bozeman

On April 21, 1997, with slightly less than one year remaining before the next legislative elections, scheduled normally to take place the
third Sunday of March 1998, Jacques Chirac announced his decision to
dissolve the National Assembly. During his televised address, he informed
viewers that they would be going to the polls on May 25 and June 1, 1997
to elect a new assembly. The strategy was designed to catch the opposition, particularly the socialists, by surprise, unprepared to quickly mount
an effective campaign. On June 1, 1997, however, voters elected a leftist
majority, preponderantly socialist, thereby affirming the national desire for
political alternation. The event was significant. It had the potential to severely weaken the office of President for the next several years. At the
same time, it reanimated the ailing Socialist Party and gave the left new
leadership, filling the vacuum left by Mitterrand. To appreciate the significance of Chirac's blunder, it is important to consider the political climate
and forces leading to his decision as well as the consequences of the event
on the internal dynamics of politics in France.

This new period of cohabitation, the third in eleven years, was
unique on several counts. It was the first juxtaposing a socialist Prime
Minister with a gaullist President. It was the first to result from a dissolution of the National Assembly, the previous periods occurred as the result
of regularly scheduled legislative elections. Above all, it was ironic in that
the dissolution that brought about the new cohabitation was not strategi-
cally necessary. Never before had a president dissolved an assembly

whose composition gave him a majority, let alone as massive a majority as the one that Chirac relinquished.

At the time that Chirac made public his intent, the victory of a right-wing majority seemed to be assured. He knew that the Right would not have the overwhelming majority that the newly dissolved Assembly had enjoyed, but he felt he could easily gain a leaner but more coherent new majority.

One of the major factors in his decision to dissolve the National Assembly was the belief that the opposition, particularly the *Parti socialiste (PS)*, was not prepared to muster a strong campaign. The Elysée considered that the *PS* was weak and unpopular, still hampered by the legacy of Mitterrand's second term which had been marked by a seemingly endless series of scandals involving socialist ministers, their advisers and their friends.

Though corrupt practices were not limited to the *Parti socialiste* and had also occurred while the right was in power, it was the left that experienced the public's outrage in the 1993 legislative elections. The party seemed moribund after the 1993 defeat and appeared leaderless as Mitterrand's term drew to an end.

As the 1995 presidential elections approached, the burning question was who would pick up the party's standard and face the apparently revitalized right. Clearly Mitterrand himself would not run. His favorite *dauphin* during his double *septennat*, Laurent Fabius, did not appear as a strong candidate. Michel Rocard, Mitterrand's perennial opponent within the party, had also lost favor. The only seemingly viable candidate, the architect of French participation in the new Europe, Jacques Delors, after some hesitation, announced that he had decided not to run. The late entrant, Lionel Jospin, a frequent rival of Fabius, made a gallant effort and almost upset the front-runner Jacques Chirac.

One must be careful in interpreting the results of the 1995 Presidential elections. The first round results suggested that the French electorate had not considerably changed since the first cohabitation. The traditional right again held on to somewhat less than 40% of the votes. Since the 1986 legislative election, however, the far right had grown considerably and had become a major obstacle for the traditional right. Jean-Marie Le Pen and Philippe de Villiers combined controlled almost 20% of the ballots. The *PS* had seen its support erode since 1986 but the combined left, including the votes for Robert Hue, Arlette Laguiller and Dominique Voynet with the 23% for Lionel Jospin in the first round totaled slightly more than 40%. While some of the Socialist voters had shifted allegiance since the mid-eighties, the Socialist vote had not disappeared and could return *en masse* in support of a candidate with a compelling program.

Jospin's good showing in the first round and Chirac's victory in the second were also influenced significantly by the presence of a second popular *Rassemblement pour la République (RPR)* candidate in the run up to the election. Edouard Balladur, on the strength of his record as Prime Minister during the cohabitation with the Mitterrand presidency was favored by many to win the first round and be a finalist in the second round. It was no easy task for Chirac to attract the Balladurian voters to support his candidacy during the second round. Old guard Gaullists and christian democrats, they expressed distrust for the promises made by Chirac during the campaign and many remained undecided on the eve of the second round.

Chirac's victory translated as much a desire on the part of the French electorate for change as it did a validation of Chirac's proposed program. In a very real sense, it may be considered as an expression of a will for continued alternation: voters felt that the right of Chirac rather than the left of Jospin or the continuation of the right of Balladur offered the greatest chance for change.

One positive result of the defeat for the Socialists was the strength of Jospin's candidacy when all of the other seemingly viable socialist candidates had failed to face the challenge of a run for the presidency. Jospin now presented a viable focus for the party, which historically needed a strong personal presence to pull together the disparate tendencies of the various groups that compose it. He had given substance and a face to the "New Left." In the second round he was successful in garnering most of the votes of the Communists, Ecologists, and the extreme left (Jarreau 1995). His greatest liability was the association of his image with the Mitterrand regime. The public cried out for change and Chirac made the most attractive promises. Would he be able to deliver?

The months following Chirac's victory would grant the new presidency only the briefest of honeymoons. Things began to go badly for the new regime practically from the start. The choice of Alain Juppé as the new Prime Minister, the creation of a *gouvernement* that did not adequately reflect the composition of the majority coalition, early friction between Juppé and the Finance Minister Alain Madelin, involvement of Juppé in a Parisian rent scandal, the resignation of Madelin in August after less than three months in office, and the international furor created by Chirac's resumption of nuclear testing in the South Pacific in September, all prophesied troubled times for the new regime.

By the beginning of autumn many had run out of patience and began to sharply criticize Chirac for not keeping his campaign promises. On October 10, 1995 France's five million civil servants walked off the job shutting down public transportation, mail distribution, social security and other social services. France had not experienced a strike of this magnitude since the mid-eighties. According to a public opinion poll conducted by the *Institut français d'opinion publique (IFOP)* in early October, scores for both Chirac and Juppé were in steep decline: only 33% held a favorable opinion of Chirac, while 51% were critical of his performance since his election barely four months earlier. Juppé received scores of 37% favorable and 46% unfavorable responses in the same poll.

Two weeks later Chirac appeared before television cameras in an attempt to reassure the nation that he had the situation well in hand. There would be no devaluation of the franc nor did he intend to replace Juppé as prime minister. He asked the public to be patient. He would need two years to reduce the public deficit, a difficult task that needed to be accomplished so that France could join Germany in adopting the *euro*. Reduction of unemployment could only begin after deficit reduction.[1]

While Chirac did not plan to replace his prime minister, Juppé was busy restructuring the various ministries of his *gouvernement*. On November 7, Juppé announced a streamlined, leaner and less feminine *gouvernement*. Only four women were to be found among the 32 members whereas there had been twelve women in the larger 42-member *gouvernement*. The streamlining was justified as a necessary measure to create a more responsive body able to face the challenging task of drafting needed austerity measures. In announcing his new cabinet, Juppé also revealed a project to reform financing of the social security system. One week later as Juppé began presenting the details of this reform plan, the *SNCF* began its strike protesting *le plan Juppé*. The black month was about to begin.

Signs of censure and disapproval that had begun to sprout with the *rentrée* continued throughout the autumn. A student strike at the Mont St. Aignan campus in Rouen immediately spread to other university towns. Toulouse, Metz, and Orléans soon joined the protest. On November 7, Education Minister François Bayrou called for an emergency plan to increase state financial support at the poorest campuses that had borne the brunt of the more than 300% increase in student enrollment of the last few years. Then on 13 November, students at Montpellier, Tarbes, and Auch abandoned classes to demand better conditions. A general mobilization was set for November 21. [2] On November 20 an intercampus memo called for a national student strike of indefinite duration involving not only university students but also those at technical institutes, specialized schools, and lycées. Striking students called for the creation of 6,000 new teaching positions.

Meanwhile the Juppé plan to reform the social security system triggered new protests. On November 28 *Force Ouvrière* and the *CGT (Confédération générale du travail)* urged their members to walk out on their public transportation jobs. The metro and bus systems in Paris became paralyzed and many regions were affected by interrupted traffic on the national railway system. A few days later the transportation strike had hardened to a point that much of the nation was at a standstill. On December 1 the strike had spread to the entire civil service system. The postal workers, telephone employees, and state utilities personnel joined students and transportation workers in what was shaping up to be the worst national shutdowns since 1968.

The Juppé government seemed to turn a deaf ear to these widespread protests. Juppé refused to back away from his plan to reform social security. Opposition leaders naturally exploited the moment to suggest that Juppé did not know how to govern the country. Certain figures who had initially supported the need for social security reform such as Lionel Jospin and Nicole Notat, the chief of the *CFDT (Confédération française et démocratique du travail)*, now began to withdraw their backing. In the street and on campus the strike began to take a more violent turn. Twenty people were injured in protests in Nantes and in Paris. At the Jussieu facility in Paris, police laid siege against thirty students who had set up barricades. By the middle of the first week of December, the crisis had worsened considerably. The paralysis of the public transport system was now well into its second week. Juppé managed to survive a motion of censure raised by the socialist deputies, who in turn, abandoned the *hemicycle* during discussion of the motion.

After three weeks of strikes, just prior to the Christmas holidays, the nation finally went back to work. For many, the holidays promised to be bleak due to wages lost during the walkouts. The first few months of the new year brought some resolution to the crisis. The government had modified some of its proposals without renouncing completely its plan to carry out reform of the social security system. On 24 January the *Conseil des Ministres* approved the first two ordinances authorized by the social security reform law of 20 December 1995.

By May 1996 Chirac's level of approval had risen to 37%, his best score since the previous August but still 22 points lower than his 59% rating immediately following his victory one year earlier. Juppé on the other hand seemed to be stuck in the cellar. His score of 31% approval was only a few points above his 28% score during the strikes of the previous December. In September 1996, Juppé's popularity slipped again to 27% and Chirac was given his worst score (31%) since the previous December. Public perception again seemed to link the two heads of the executive to a single body. "Ce sont deux têtes différentes, mais c'est le même esprit . . . je ne vois pas de différence entre les deux." [3]

Meanwhile, Lionel Jospin was busy girding the *PS* for a battle to regain the majority in 1998. In an interview with *Le Monde* Jospin explained that the Socialists were *calmly* preparing themselves for a cohabitation in 1998. "Nous respecterons les prérogatives constitutionnelles du président de la République et nous appliquerons notre programme." [4]   A few days later in his closing remarks at the Socialist convention on democracy at La Villette, Jospin directly attacked Juppé's competence saying that when one hears Juppé announce that he is going to "'garder le cap', on tremble pour le bateau et on s'inquiète pour le capitaine." Jospin went on to remind his party that they need not prepare to be in the opposition since they were already there. "Ce qui est notre responsabilité, c'est d'être prêts à gouverner, si les Français nous font confiance en 1998. C'est à cela que nous travaillons ensemble." [5]   At the Socialist Party's meeting in La Rochelle at the beginning of September, Jospin attacked the Juppé government for being ineffective, hard and soft at the same time. If the French did not like the government's politics and the government did not want to change them, "ne faut-il pas changer de gouvernement?"[6]

There could be little doubt that Jospin saw himself as a candidate to replace Juppé at Matignon after the next legislative elections. He had become an adept tactician and effectively demonstrated his skill, finely tuned during the presidential race. He refused to be trapped by the legacy of Mitterrand's second term and kept focus on current issues, attacking Juppé and reminding potential voters of the inability of Juppé's government to make good on the promises made by Chirac during the presidential campaign. He suggested that if France was seeking an alternative to Juppé on the right they would not find it in the politics of a Philippe Séguin or a François Léotard any more than they would among the representatives of the far left. The sole alternative lay with the *PS*. But what alternative did that represent? Jospin was reluctant, in the autumn of 1996 to propose a detailed economic program, putting it off until the national convention in December. An editorial in *Le Monde* observed, "Dès à présent, . . . il ne semble guère en passe de trouver les chemins d'une politique économique véritablement différente, non seulement de celle suivie par le gouvernement actuel, mais aussi de celle préconisée, en d'autres temps, par Pierre Bérégovoy."[7] The editorial closed with the observation, "Lionel Jospin se fait fort de préparer l'alternance, mais il n'en a pas encore défini le contenu."

The approaching legislative elections, now only a year-and-a-half away, increased the vulnerability of Juppé and his government. Attacks now came not only from the *PS* but from the right as well. On October 27, 1996, in an appearance on the television program *Sept sur Sept,* François Léotard called on Chirac to consider early legislative elections. "Le Président a trois décisions possibles: La dissolution, le remaniement, le référendum. Je souhaite qu'il appuie sur l'un de ces trois boutons dans les trois à quatre mois qui viennent." (Mano and Birenbaum 51)

A few days later Juppé, in response to Léotard's remarks, told a group of members of the *UDF* (*Union pour la démocratie française*), "Une dissolution correspond à une crise grave, un référendum doit correspondre à une bonne question et un remaniement doit se faire à froid..." (Mano and Birenbaum 53) The remark left unanswered the possibility of a reshuffling of his government. In his televised address to the nation on 12 December, Chirac unequivocally stated his support for Juppé and brushed aside the idea of a change of government, "Pour le moment, le gouverne-

ment est ce qu'il est. Il a un objectif, faire des réformes...Il a une majorité . .
. Le reste c'est de la politique médiatique." (Mano and Birenbaum 56) Immediately following this telecast, Chirac's confidence ratings climbed three
points to a still very low 30% while Juppé's climbed four points to 24%,
a rating considerably lower than his 31% rating in September.[8]

The new year hinted at a more felicitous period for the president.
His ratings in the January public opinion polls maintained the improvement of the previous month. With the debate and the fierce protests
against the Debré law on immigration, Juppé began anew his decline in the
polls. However, he was wounded significantly less than Jospin in public
opinion over the issue. The previous June, Jospin had advanced the basic
tenets for a new socialist policy concerning immigration. His position was
that the party should advocate a law that would be tough on clandestine
immigration but open and flexible on integration. What the press and the
public retained of this proposal, however, was what it failed to state: that
immigrants should be allowed to vote in local elections and that the Pasqua
laws should be repealed (Noblecourt). A few months later, at the beginning of September, Jospin had remained aloof in the protest over the evic-
tion of immigrant squatters from the St. Bernard church in Paris. He
refused to call for regularization for all illegal immigrants. Similarly in the
mobilization against the Debré law in December, Jospin had refused, at
first, to participate in the protests.

Jospin and the *PS* were harmed as well by the debacle in Vitrolles.
The *PS* candidate, Jean-Jacques Anglade, faced the special election handi-
capped by an investigation for fraud and a reputation for mismanagement.
On February 2, Catherine Mégret, the wife of Le Pen's lieutenant, Bruno
Mégret, almost won the election in the first round. The following Sunday,
a "front républicain" effort in which the trailing *UDF* candidate, Roger
Guichard, withdrew in order that his voters might cast their ballots for
Anglade, failed miserably as Cathérine Mégret won 52,5% of the votes.
The *PS* was severely criticized for its inability to react in time and come
forth with a more suitable candidate.

The biggest concern confronting Jospin in the first quarter of 1997
was the challenge of bringing together the diverse elements that existed
within the *PS* and at the same time establishing himself as leader of a more
or less consolidated *gauche*. He faced the predicament squarely, boldly
proposing an initiation of new candidates throughout France, a minimum

of 30% female candidates, and a *pink-red-green* partnership of Socialists, Communists and Ecologists. Such a partnership would not be easy and the negotiations would be extremely delicate. Recent criticism by the *Parti Communiste* of Jospin and the *PS* as "une gauche fadasse" because of their hesitation to protest the Debré law did not promise a very successful endeavor (Noblecourt).

On March 18, Jospin officially inaugurated the *PS* campaign for the 1998 legislative elections. In his press conference he unveiled the long-promised economic and social program which committed to a reduced work-week from 39 to 35 hours, incorporated reform of health insurance, and proposed improved salaries and employment. One week later, Jospin successfully negotiated an electoral pact with *Les Verts* whereby the *PS* promised not to present candidates in 31 electoral districts where there would be a Green party candidate and requested similar consideration from the *Verts* in 75 districts (Chemin and Marre). In spite of this coup, Jospin faced an uphill battle to bring the *PC* into the alliance.

Meanwhile, at the one year mark from the regularly scheduled elections, Chirac was forced to take serious inventory of the chance for a right-wing victory in March 1998. He needed to change something in order to re-launch the economy and attenuate the wide-spread feelings of hopelessness. It was clearly too late to reshuffle the government and asking Juppé to resign was distasteful to him. As the days passed the idea of dissolution and early elections became more and more appealing.

Several considerations weighed in his decision. First of all, the socialists were not scoring highly in the polls, suggesting fairly wide mistrust and disapproval among voters. The scandals that had marked the closing years of the last socialist government, and the revelations that had tarnished the end of Mitterrand's second term were still too fresh to be ignored. Secondly, the Socialists' economic plan, unveiled only a few weeks earlier, had not received the favorable public reaction they had anticipated. Moreover Jospin had not taken a staunch stand against the Debré bill that sought to establish stricter regulation of immigration. Reaction in the media suggested that Jospin was not as decisive as formerly believed. Thirdly, it was clear to Chirac that the *Front National*, in spite of the victory in Vitrolles over the socialist candidate, presented greater problems for the right than for the left. The growing popularity of the movement was unlikely to reverse itself before March 1998. Perhaps the most significant consideration was the realization that the timing of the regularly scheduled elections coincided too closely with the deadline for determining which countries would be qualified to join the first group adopting the new European currency, the euro. The country had mixed feelings about this new stage of development of the European Union, and Chirac's own party was far from united in support of the president's pro-European stand. Moreover the fiscal reforms required to ready France for inclusion in the inaugural group would create painful sacrifices and had already met stiff resistance.

In spite of the illusion of avoiding these obstacles, the decision to dissolve the National Assembly in order to force early and swift elections was clearly a bold and chancy decision. Other less risky options existed. The President could have asked Juppé to form a new *gouvernement* in order to streamline the executive process and introduce new ideas and new energy to work on the difficult issues facing France in the upcoming year. Or he could have asked Juppé to resign as Prime Minister in order to form a more effective *gouvernement* more widely accepted by the public. Of course neither of these solutions would bypass all of the concerns raised by the specter of the legislative elections in the spring of 1998. Of the three choices the dissolution seemed to offer the President the outlook for governing France throughout his entire *septennat* without having to face a cohabitation with a leftist majority.

Chirac's gamble backfired. In the weeks prior to the first round polls showed steady gains for the *PS*. French law prohibits publication of polls about voting intentions in the period immediately preceding the elections, but results were readily available on the Internet. The results of the first round confirmed those predictions. High abstention rates, relatively strong support for *FN* candidates and few clear victors in any of the major contests promised a difficult struggle for the second round. Humiliated by the poor results and seeking to prevent further damage, Juppé announced his resignation as Prime Minister the following day. Many of the contests on June 1, 1997 found candidates thrown into a three-way race, *triangulaires* between *RPR/UDF*, *PS/PC/Vert*, and *FN* candidates. This situation favored the left-wing candidates. In forty-seven of the seventy-six *triangulaires*, the left-wing candidate won (Jarreau 1997).

One may cite several reasons for the surprising defeat of the right. Juppé's steadfast unpopularity and Chirac's refusal to replace him early in his presidency, the general feeling of distrust in the current majority to accomplish necessary changes, the bleak economic situation all weighed heavily on the right. The most significant factor, however was the persistent problem of unemployment. In spite of modest improvement in the month just prior to the elections, the rate of *chômage* remained at 12.8% (Bezat).

In his campaign, Jospin had grasped the importance of this problem in the minds of voters. The *Parti socialiste's* campaign flyer, *Changeons d'avenir: nos engagements pour la France*, listed as its top economic priority the project to create 700,000 jobs. Its second priority was to reduce the work week from 39 to 35 hours without a reduction of salary.[9] Having won the election, Jospin would have to face the reality of these promises in the fall with the beginning of the new legislative session. His first year in office was blessed with substantial good luck. Juppé had forecasted severe austerity measures to overcome more than 100 billion francs of debt if France were to meet the 3% requirement of the Maastricht treaty to adopt the euro. However, when Jospin took over, the economy had begun to experience the benefits of new growth caused largely by the increased strength of the dollar. Consumption of goods and investment increased while unemployment began a downward curve. In July 1997, Finance Minister Dominique Strauss-Kahn presented his economic plan designed to subsidize continued increased consumption without increasing significantly the country's debt. The plan easily passed and in September Strauss-Kahn managed to introduce a favorable 1998 budget which increased state spending by a modest 2% and remained below the Maastricht target of 3% of gross domestic product.[10]

Still, the big task of making good on the campaign promises to increase employment and reduce the work week remained. The new budget included 10 billion francs to create 150,000 jobs for the young, part of Martine Aubry's plan for an eventual 350,000 jobs for those under 26 years old. The more difficult task lay in the promotion of the government's design to reduce the work-week to 35 hours. The project raised a furor with the *Conseil national du patronat français* (*CNPF*) whose leader, Jean Gandois, claiming to have been duped by Aubry, resigned from his position (Aeschimann and Schneider 6). The *CNPF* steadfastly refused to enter into negotiations with the government on the issue, but by the following spring it found little effective support for its position when the bill was approved by the National Assembly.

At the beginning of 1998, Jospin managed to survive the threat that came from protesting *chômeurs* by promising 600 million francs in increased benefits to certain categories of unemployed (Chemin and Monnot 6). During the demonstrations, his rating in public opinion polls plummeted to its lowest point (49%) since coming to Matignon but rebounded significantly (55%) the following month.[1] On the first anniversary of the Jospin government, its leader presented a modest understated aura of satisfaction and self-assurance. His cautious jubilance over the accomplishments thus far realized was due perhaps to the cognizance of the role that luck had played in the successes of the first year and the need to be constantly vigilant of pitfalls on the road to be traveled in the remaining four years. Nevertheless Jospin had reason to celebrate. The public opinion polls indicated overwhelming appreciation for his performance as *Premier Ministre* as well as for the current shared executive. At the first anniversary mark, according to a *BVA-Paris Match* poll, Jospin received favorable reactions from 63% of respondents, his best score since his investiture. Moreover, 59% gave favorable marks to the current cohabitation.[12]

The French have come to see cohabitation as an acceptable way of balancing power, of reining in a one-sided executive, forcing it to respond to the will of the people. It is not, perhaps, an efficacious mode of government. While the Constitution of the Fifth Republic created a hybrid executive, combining aspects of the parliamentary executive of the Third and Fourth Republic with elements of a presidential executive such as exists in the USA, it assumed that President and Prime Minister sharing the executive powers would come from the same party or coalition. But the Constitution of 1958 allowed for less direct democracy than the amended Constitution of today. The biggest change came in 1962 with the provision to elect the President by direct universal suffrage. This modification opened the door to an eventual cohabitation. Now the likelihood was greatly increased that the majority which elected the political majority in the National Assembly, who in turn selected the *Premier Ministre*, would be different from the majority which elected the President. This was particularly true because of the different lengths of term for the President (seven years) and deputies of the National Assembly (five years). Since the elections would not normally coincide, it was probable that the majority would have evolved in the interim.

Plans to reduce the presidential *septennat* to a five year term seem to have lost support due to the favorable reaction to the current cohabitation. Such a reduction would not necessarily prevent future cohabitations, for a cohabitation can arise when the President dissolves the National Assembly as we saw in 1997. Moreover, voting patterns and party politics going back at least as far as 1974 indicate a tendency toward alternation of political power.

Alternation of power and cohabitation offer the electorate a sense of having a measure of control over those elected to public office. Growing cynicism of politics and politicians reflected in increased rates of abstention from voting, scepticism about the ability of a single party's ability to solve the complex problems of modern society, combined with a traditional tendency to vote *against* rather than *for* issues leave many voters with a feeling of impotence to effect change by casting a ballot. Cohabitation and alternation of power restore an impression of overseeing the government's performance and forcing a change of direction when the government seems to be ineffective or insensitive to the will of the nation. It is unlikely that the third cohabitation will be the last.

Notes

[1] France Deux, 26 octobre 1995.

[2] *Libération*, 14 novembre 1995.

[3] Sondage réalisé par l'IFOP pour *Le Journal du dimanche* du 12 au 20 septembre 1996. IFOP <http://www.ifop.fr/archive/barojdd/cote9609.htm>, September 1996.

[4] "M. Jospin envisage une cohabitation en 1998" *Le Monde*, 26 juin 1996, 1.

[5] "Notre responsabilité est d'être prêts à gouverner" *Le Monde*, 2 juillet 1996, 8.

[6] "Une droite dure et molle à la fois" *Le Monde*, 3 septembre 1996, 6.

[7] "Le *PS*, pour quoi faire?" *Le Monde*, 3 septembre 1996, 14.

[8] Sondage réalisé par l'IFOP pour *Le Journal du dimanche* , du 13 au 20 décembre 1996. IFOP <http://www.ifop.fr/archive/barojdd/chir9612.htm>; <http://www.ifop.fr/archive/barojdd/jupp9612.htm>, décembre 1996.

[9] *Changeons d'avenir: nos engagements pour la France*, Parti socialiste (10, rue de Solférino, 75007 Paris) avril-mai 1998, 6.

[10] "Martine Aubry est la principale bénéficiaire des arbitrages budgétaires de Lionel Jospin" *Le Monde*, 14 août 1997, 1.

[11] Sondage *BVA-Paris Match*, réalisé du 19 au 21 février 1998. BVA <http://www.bva.fr/popularite.html>.

[12] Sondage *BVA-Paris Match*, réalisé du 25 au 27 juin 1998. BVA
<http://www.bva.fr/popularite.html>.

References

Aeschimann, Eric and Vanessa Schneider. "A Paris, le débat sur les 35 heures réveille
    l'opposition." *Libération* 15 octobre 1997.
Bezat, Jean-Michel. "L'ancienne majorité laisse le chômage à un niveau sans précédent
    malgré une légère baisse en avril." *Le Monde* 3 juin 1997, 28.
Changeons d'avenir: nos engagements pour la France. Paris: Parti Socialiste, 1998.
Chemin, Ariane and Jean-Claude Marre. "La majorité des Verts acceptent de s'associer
    avec les socialistes." *Le Monde* 25 mars 1998, 7.
Chemin, Ariane and Caroline Monnot. "Lionel Jospin n'apaise pas la colère des mouve-
    ments de chômeurs." *Le Monde* 23 janvier 1998, 6.
Jarreau, Patrick. "Le 'champ de ruines' de la droite." *Le Monde* 3 juin 1997, 1.
Jarreau, Patrick. "La majorité de Jacques Chirac reste à inventer." *Le Monde* 9 mai 1995
    in *L'Histoire au jour le jour 1939-1996* (CD-ROM 1997).
Mano, Jean-Luc and Guy Birenbaum. *La défaite impossible, enquête sur les secrets
    d'une élection*. Paris: Ramsay, 1997.
Noblecourt, Michel. "Les trois pannes de Lionel Jospin." *Le Monde* 6 mars 1997, 1+.

2

The French Communist Party in the Late 1990s: Decline, Renewal, and the Socialists

Christopher P. Pinet
Montana State University-Bozeman

The decline of the French Communist Party *(PCF)* over the past twenty years, especially since 1981, has been well chronicled. The reasons include the melting away of the French working class stemming from the loss of heavy industry and the rise of service and high tech jobs, the marginality of the Party wrought by François Mitterrand through the *Programme Commun* (Union of the Left), the rapid growth of the National Front, the Stalinist history of the Party itself and its close association with Moscow, the fall of the Berlin Wall and the former Soviet Union, the ultimate lack of credibility of Georges Marchais, and the abandonment of Marxism as a mode of critical discourse in France.

Recently, however, the French Communists have experienced an unexpected though qualified resurgence. As the result of the 1997 legislative elections, the Party saw an increase of over 50% in seats in the National Assembly from the previous parliament to 38. This makes them the only Communist Party to be represented in parliament in a Western democracy. Since the Socialists do not have an absolute majority, they must now often turn to the Communists and the Greens when they need one.[1] This dramatic electoral upturn and the appointment of three cabinet-level Communist Ministers (Jean-Claude Gayssot at Transport, Marie-George Buffet at Youth and Sports, and Michelle Demessine as a Secrétaire d'Etat at Transport and Tourism) can be explained, in part, by Lionel Jospin's understanding, early in the 1997 campaign, much as Mitterrand had in 1981 and before, of the imperative of a coalition of *rose, rouge,* and *vert* in order to win a majority in the National Assembly. Equally important were the long-term survival of alliances between Socialists and Communists at the local level (they had been long since abandoned at the national level) and the machinations of the National Front during the second round of the elections, when it refused to support the other parties on the right, thus allowing the Communists to win more seats.

In order to understand what the new Communist presence (a "new" *PCF?)* may mean for the future, its history and several theories and hypotheses about Communist attitudes towards participation and non-participation in government at the national level, as well as some of the specifics of Communist decline will be considered. An internal memorandum addressed to the local Communist Party of Villejuif, a red belt suburb of Paris (pop. 47,000) south of Paris on the National Highway #7 that has known unbroken Communist governance since 1927, will then be examined. The memorandum shows the two-sided nature of the Party and its members, who presented arguments for and against the eventual participation of the Party in the Jospin government just before that decision was finalized. The debate outlined in the memorandum is representative in microcosm of the national debate that took place over participation and points to the past, present, and future of the Party. Finally, this essay will show how, since the resignation in 1994 of Georges Marchais (Marchais died on November 16, 1997) after twenty-three years as Secretary-General, Robert Hue, the new leader, managed to reinvigorate the Party, help it to regain some of its lost credibility with the voters, and enabled it once again to play a significant role in French politics and in day-to-day government at the national level.

In *Parties and Voters in France,* John Frears furnishes considerable insight into the vicissitudes of the *PCF* over the past fifty years: "The history of the Party ... can be seen [as] a series of alternating phases, hard-line and uncompromising phases followed by conciliatory phases" (88). Frears shows that the sudden, sometimes inexplicable changes in position contributed to increased skepticism among voters who could not see the relevance of a revolutionary party in a country where revolution was no longer relevant, even on the Communist agenda. He summarizes the history and decline of the Party as follows: "... the Communist Party, having won 26-28% of the vote after the Liberation in 1945-46, stuck at around 20% for the first twenty years of the Fifth Republic, then dropped in the

1980s to 15% in 1981, plunging below 7% in the Presidential election of 1988 — the lowest share of the popular vote in the entire history of the Party since its foundation in 1920" (87).

The decline of the Communist Party also affected the Socialists because "from the 1930s the left only ever had electoral success when it went into battle stressing what united it and not what divided it. This in turn depended very often on whether world events authorized the *PCF* to coexist amicably with non-Communist parties. These conditions were fulfilled in 1973, and the elections of that year at last saw a reversal of the long decline of the left" (62).

The mid-1970s were the high point, at least until 1997, of the Union of the Left *(Programme Commun)*. It was also a time of profound change within the *PCF*. In 1976 the twenty-second Congress declared "that Lenin's notion of the Dictatorship of the Proletariat had become outdated and repressive measures against people for their opinions were for the first time acknowledged and denounced" (Frears 62-63). Then, in 1976, the left had its most successful electoral performance in municipal elections ever (always a source of strength for the Communist Party) when it won 156 out of the 221 large towns and cities. However, the Communists, who had not made the gains in the mid-70s that they had made in previous alliances and had been displaced by the Socialist Party as the leading party of the left, pulled out of the alliance and took a much harder line on issues such as nationalization. Then the Socialists swept to power in 1981, and the Communists were relegated to a marginal status in spite of being given four ministries in the first Mitterrand government, after signing an agreement supporting Soviet withdrawal from Afghanistan. After the Socialists gave up their program of nationalization in 1983 to adopt a privatization scheme more compatible with the laissez-faire capitalism of a Milton Friedman, the *PCF* withdrew its ministers in 1984.

After that the only pacts in the second round were tactical ones, although it is important to note that the Union of the Left Councils and candidate lists were maintained in the 1989 municipal elections in many cities. This cooperation at the local level continued into the 1990s and helps to explain why the PCF decided ultimately in 1997 to join the Jospin government. Though hard to prove and even debatable among Party members, the kind of meetings and votes taken at the local level in 1997 may suggest that the *PCF* has begun to reverse the "top down" management of democratic centralism (considered undemocratic by most outside observers) to embrace something closer to a model where ideas "bubble up" from the bottom. In fact, democratic centralism was formally abandoned quite late at the Party's twenty-eighth Congress in January 1994. Georges Marchais, on the other hand, remained opposed to "tendencies" or factions within the Party, believing them to be a threat to internal democracy (Jennings 57). Jennings concludes that there is little evidence that "the culture of obedience has come to an end or that ... a communist party of a new type has come into existence" (57).

Jennings's view of an intransigent Party is consistent with that of many scholars, including Frears, who in 1991 stated that the "*PCF* is a Marxist party in the sense that it accepts the Marxist analysis of the class struggle as the fundamental social reality and the basic element of historical change" (103). For him it was a party "that does not compromise with the bourgeoisie" (102). However, as recently as 1997 (before the elections), Christopher Flood wrote, in his Introduction to *Political Ideologies in Contemporary France,* that "... it does not have to be assumed that communism is doomed to fade away definitively ... even if room for manoeuvre is limited by unwillingness to sacrifice core beliefs, or to risk losing distinctiveness in relation to the *PS,* by espousing what the *PCF* regards as social democracy" (11). For Laurence Bell "the originality of social democracy is not only to have introduced Keynesian economics, the welfare state and the redistribution of income, but to have substituted these for the collective appropriation of the means of production" ("Democratic Socialism" 39).

There is, however, evidence that the Party has accommodated change, and even Jennings quotes Robert Hue's 1996 statement about "the importance of 'the spirit rather than the letter of Marx'" (59). From 1976 on French Communism argued for what it defined as "a programme of economic, social and political democracy, which it has characterized as 'the French style of democratic socialism and worker's self-management'" (Jennings quoting Marchais, 60).

If we look at Nick Hewlitt's definition of social democracy in *Modern French Politics,* we can see that the *PCF* of 1998 is far more pragmatic than Frears, Bell, or Jennings thought it could be:

> When I use the term "social democracy" I mean, very generally, a compromise between the interests of a party which emerged out of the labour movement on the one hand with the interests of the ruling class on the other hand. This has been described as "the attempt to reconcile socialism with liberal politics and capitalist society." (Hewlitt quoting Padgett and Paterson [1991], 98)

By examining the internal memorandum of the local *PCF* in Villejuif and how Party members reached the decision to join the Jospin government, it appears that, though the Party remains divided, it is in the process of accommodating itself, with some rhetorical flourishes, to the politics of compromise and to the essentially capitalist society governed by Lionel Jospin and the Socialists at the end of the 1990s. While usually supporting Jospin's version of a mixed economy in a capitalist society, the *PCF* works hard to force Jospin to retain the essential elements of a social democracy.

The internal communication,[2] addressed to all Party members in Villejuif (there were about 2,000 in 1988-89 — undoubtedly fewer now) detailed arguments made in cell meetings of 2-3 June 1997 against participation, as well as those for participation in the yet-to-be-formed Jospin government. There was, of course, a preexisting agreement between the two parties dating from April that had enabled them to maintain a united front during the legislative elections, and, in fact, the cell meetings were held to approve or disapprove a resolution from the Central Committee to join the government. Thus it is not surprising that some Party members claimed that the decision to join had already been made and were opposed a priori to participation. Others said that the Socialists would not commit on where the money would come from to bring about change — more jobs, the 35-hour work week, and the protection of Social Security, that is, retirement and health benefits — long an issue in France's largest hospital community, Villejuif. The guiding principle set forth for all Party members who participated in the cell meetings was that the Party should break with the approaches of the previous Balladur government, about as open-ended a statement as possible — one designed to encourage support for participation.

As one might have expected, there were those who were afraid that the Party would have to compromise itself too much in a coalition government with the Socialists (the other partner was the Greens — Dominique Voynet got the Ministry of Environment) as had been the case in

1981. Even though the Socialists were in a much stronger position then than in 1997, many Party members still felt that the *PCF* had been seen as complicit in the policies of the Mitterrand government of 1983 that shifted the tax burden to the working classes and that the Party should never have accepted ministerial positions in that government in the first place. In their view it would be a terrible mistake to join the new Jospin cabinet in light of the past error that had done so much to hasten the Party's decline.

Others felt that if a situation similar to the 1983 Socialist reversal were to develop, and with only 10% of the vote, the Party would not have a strong enough voice and therefore it should wait for further gains; otherwise failure would be inevitable in the long run. Specifically, one critic asked what would happen if a Communist Minister were forced to privatize *EDF*, the nationalized French electricity company, or close hospitals such as Paul Brousse.[3] A related comment had to do with what would happen to Communist credibility if it were to accept participation in the government and then withdraw two or three months later. There were also those who felt — and this represents a very strong historical tendency — that the Party would be more effective in opposition than in power because it would not have to compromise its principles by participating in a social democratic society. Variations on this theme were that one could not trust the Socialists though the Communists and Socialists have often cooperated in municipal elections in Villejuif, that the Party should not negotiate with them at all (the old hard-line stance of the *"purs et durs"),* and that the Socialists' program was too ambiguous.

Another of the main sticking points for those opposed to participation was the whole question of Europe and the euro. In recent years the *PCF* has been very nationalistic — bringing it closer, ironically, to the National Front, and it has always opposed the euro much as it did the Maastricht Treaty. Indeed, one of its planks was to call for a referendum on the euro.

One can see then, that there were a significant number who felt that participation in the Jospin government would undermine the Party's professed opposition to many of his policies and that any initiatives that the Communists might have brought forth would be watered down or taken over by the Socialists just as they had drained members from the Party in the 1980s. Most of these concerns are not surprising in Villejuif, traditionally a conservative, Stalinist Communist municipality. In essence, this negative view of the national Socialist Party has dominated the municipality even longer than the national Party.

On the other side were the guardedly optimistic, or the *oui, mais* element. Their view — and the one that eventually won out — was that the Communists would do better on the inside than on the outside; that, after gaining 10% of the popular vote in the elections and increasing their electoral representation by more than half in the National Assembly to 38, they would lose any new-found credibility if they did not participate. One interesting variation on this theme was "The non-communists who voted for us did it so that we would join the government; they are telling us to meet our responsibilities. We have to take those wishes into account even if it is we who must decide on joining or not" (author's translation).

This new view is revealing in that it reflects the new Secretary-General, Robert Hue's wish and practice of gaining greater credibility with the general public in order to attract new followers and to rid the Party of its long-time Stalinist image. This kind of *transparence* certainly goes against the past and points to the desire for change among the rank and file. It also shows the need within the Party to react to conservative factions such as Jean Poperen's *reconstructeurs,* Pierre Juquin's *rénovateurs,* Charles Fiterman's *refondateurs,* the latter a former Communist Minister in the 1981 Mitterrand government. For this new element, the Party would never be in a better position than the present one to regain momentum.

Another individual reminded one of the long-time militant approach to problem solving by the Party in and out of government in terms reminiscent of Khruschev: "Au gouvernment, un communiste ce n'est pas la même chose qu'un socialiste. Les ministres communistes doivent taper sur la table" ("In government, a Communist is not the same thing as a Socialist. The communist ministers have to pound on the table" [*Memorandum,* author's translation]).

A related view and one that proved to be true in the two years that followed the coalition government's rise to power, implied that whatever else the Party did, it would have to mobilize people in the streets: "The permanent and daily pressure exercised by the French people, is the only guarantee that the accords [between Socialists and Communists] will be respected. Texts do not make things happen. Struggles are paramount. Communists into the streets ... with the people" (*Memorandum,* author's translation). This exhortation to action, is, of course, traditional Communist rhetoric, but in this case it points to the two-pronged strategy carried out by the Communists: Communist ministers and deputies in the National Assembly eventually go along and vote to support the Socialists but only after criticizing them. Then there is the Communist-controlled labor union, the *Confédération générale du travail (CGT),* on the outside protesting Jospin's policies through strikes in the street like those of the truckers in early 1998, and the *SNCF (Société nationale des chemins de fer français),* transit workers, and high school students, all of whom struck during the fall of 1998.

Another comment that foreshadowed but also highlighted a new spirit of compromise among the rank and file, was the suggestion that the Party needed to remain open to those who had voted for the Gaullist *RPR (Rassemblement pour la République)* and Giscard d'Estaing's *UDF (Union pour la démocratie française),* and even, yes, the National Front — as long as those voters were interested in change. In the early 1990s, one would never have heard this kind of statement from a Communist in Villejuif where there are no *FN (Front national)* members on the municipal council — much less at the national level.

When the vote was taken in the cells, of the 299 ballots cast, 60.5% voted to participate in the government and 33.8% not to; 5.7% abstained. Although this was an overwhelming and surprising majority for a formerly Stalinist municipality, there were those who insisted that the cell meetings to vote *oui* or *non* came with too short notice. Others protested that the decision to participate had already been made at the highest level and that the vote was merely an exercise of form. This may help to explain the relatively low number of Party members who took part in the cell meetings. One member even suggested cynically that the Party's sole strategy since 1993 had been to help the Socialists get back in the majority in the National Assembly.

Most did feel that the Party was in a better position to participate than in 1981 when the Socialists had a much larger margin of victory, and that the Party could play a more important role than before. The memorandum closes with a list of Communist demands that would have to be made as a coalition member of the new government:

1) The Minimum Wage *(SMIC)* would have to be raised considerably (It was raised slightly in 1997-98 as it is every year).

2) The move to a thirty-five hour work week without a decrease in salaries must occur (This measure was still being debated well after the Jospin regime took power.)

3) Rents should be frozen.

4) The value-added tax *(TVA)* should be reduced.

5) Employment should be a priority (After Jospin took over, the unemployment rate went down from 12.6% to about 11.8% and was stuck on that figure for a long time).

6) Jobs for youth should be emphasized (The *SNCF* was to take on 400 new workers as the result of the 1998 strikes, but these were short-term jobs).

7) Privatization should be stopped (This has not and will not happen, though initially the Socialists took a middle path of carrying out partial privatization — affecting the Crédit Lyonnais and Aérospatiale).

8) Social Security should be adequately funded.

9) The immigrant question should be addressed (Although many legal immigrants were granted citizenship under the new government [it has moved away from the *loi Pasqua*] and more again after demonstrations in 1998, the question of illegal immigrants and citizenship was still being debated at the time of this book's publication).

The internal debate in Villejuif reveals attitudes that point to both the rigid past of the Party and the more recent need to find compromise in order to restart a moribund remnant of a much-divided Party. It also makes clear that the *PCF* subscribes to democratic socialism and has been more than willing to bend principles in order to remain a player.[4]

Yet the debate with the Party goes on, as was pointed out in a front-page article in *Le Monde* in June 1998. The article opens with the comment that for one of the few times in history, the Secretary of the Party is more popular outside his party than inside. Indeed, all the polls between 1996 and 1998 showed Robert Hue to be extremely popular with the French public. In fact, a poll published in September 1998 ("Tableau de bord politique") showed that 31% of the French public had a good opinion of Monsieur Hue. 70% had a good opinion of Marie-George Buffet at Youth and Sports, and 54% approved of Gayssot at Transportation. Both of these percentages were up from July 1998. Even Craig R. Whitney, writing in the June 3, 1997 *International Herald Tribune* portrayed Hue positively as "a bearded man with a physique and sense of humor of a

Friar Tuck, [who] is no loyal follower of the likes of Stalin" (8). In an article of 20 January 1998, John Vinocur referred to Hue as a "jovial TV-weatherman type" and described Hue's contentment with the Party's new role as a partner in the Jospin government and its new popularity with the public: "Mr. Hue points gleefully to the bourgeois origin and assumed objectivity of an end-of-the-year poll in the conservative daily newspaper *Le Figaro* that shows the Communists getting a more favorable judgment [37 percent] and a less negative opinion [51 percent] than either of the major components of the rightist opposition, the Gaullists and the *UDF"* (2).

The article in *Le Monde* also suggests that Hue is more popular with the Socialists than with his own party, some of whom have called for the creation of a "vrai parti communiste" (1). In spite of open opposition to Hue in some quarters — including, at times, the Communist deputies in the National Assembly — in the spring of 1998 the often rebellious Paris Communist Federation voted 41-10 to denounce the methods and practices of the opposition to Hue. Ironically, Hue could now (because he has outside support) characterize the opposition as a Stalinist plot, thus turning on its head the party line under Georges Marchais. Hue's strategy has been ingenious and, for the most part, successful. On the one hand, Communist Transport minister, Jean-Claude Gayssot, went out of his way to appease the truckers during their strike in early 1998. Then, in October 1998, Gayssot claimed solidarity with the subway, commuter train, and bus drivers who went on strike paralyzing Paris. On the other hand, the strikers, with *CGT* and other union support could make their demands known through the strike itself, and Gayssot could use that leverage with Jospin. Since 1997 Hue has met with Italian Communists, appeared on French television, and attended the Cannes film festival to broaden his base and declare a new post-Stalinist age for the Party. Still, many of the old-timers bemoan the lack of a "party line." As though to confirm their fears, Hue softened demands on the tax on fortunes *(ISF)* and has spoken of his European leanings, thus showing a very pragmatic sense of timing. The *Le Monde* article states that the real test for Hue will come with the European elections and their regionalization. In fact, a poll published in October 1998 showed that only 8 percent would support a Communist candidate in these elections ("Questions d'actualité"). Though the Party opposes regionalization of the elections, this change would most likely help it to win additional seats.

In conclusion, it can be said that, first, it seems clear that at both the local and national levels the winds of change were very pronounced within the *PCF*. The poll of September 1998 showed that 77 percent of its members would support a vote of confidence for Jospin if one were held ("Tableau de bord politique"), up 20 percent from July 1998; on the other hand it was split fifty-fifty over satisfaction with the current government. In the late 1990s, Robert Hue was carrying on a successful strategy of rapprochement through the media with diverse elements of French society and other French and European political parties (he almost scheduled a meeting with British Prime Minister, Tony Blair, in 1998). He hoped that this strategy would gain a broader base for the Party. It is also clear that Hue had little choice: the *PCF* had reached rock-bottom; but with the demise of the former Soviet Union and the death of Georges Marchais, Hue understood that this was his one chance to free the Party from the strait-jacket of its past. By supporting the Socialists through public statements and Communist votes in the National Assembly, Hue demonstrated good will and openness to change. At the same time Communist ministers sympathized with strikes organized by the *CGT* and the other labor unions, as well as with popular movements such as those of the homeless during the winter of 1997-98 and the French high school students in the fall of 1998. This kept Jospin and the Socialists sensitive to their social obligations. For the moment, the French Communist Party occupies a place once held by the Socialists themselves — the self-same Socialists who moved more and more to the center of French and even European politics. In reality, this may have made the Communists the only true party of the left remaining in France, one that seems to be supporting the very tradition of social democracy (with all its ambiguities) that it still claims to eschew in public statements. In that sense, the French Communist Party, now much more clearly a French party, has become the conscience of the busily privatizing Socialists.[5]

Notes

[1] See my article, "The 1997 French Socialist Surprise Legislative Victory and the American Press," in *The Journal for International Business* 9.2 (1998): 38-48, for a

discussion of why the Socialists won in 1997 and what their program was during their first year in power.

    [2] I will refer to this communication as *Memorandum*. It was transmitted to me in a personal correspondence and is seven pages long.

    [3] Villejuif has three hospitals: Paul Brousse does liver transplant research; Gustave Roussy is a world-renowned cancer institute; and Paul Guiraud is a mental hospital.

    [4] Consult Janine Mossuz-Lavau's *Que veut la gauche plurielle*, ch. 2, "La gauche communisante," for detailed views of what Communists wanted in a new government of the left.

    [5] Parts of this article were presented as a paper, "Internal Communications of the French Communist Party in the Parisian Red Belt," at the European Studies Conference held in Omaha, Nebraska in October 1998.

References

Bell, Laurence. "Democratic Socialism." *Political Ideologies in Contemporary France*. Ed. Christopher Flood and Laurence Bell. Washington: Pinter, 1997. 16-52.

Chemin, Ariane. "Quand 'Robert et Lionel' lassent les communistes." *Le Monde* 27 juin 1998: 1, 16.

Flood, Christopher. "Introduction." *Political Ideologies in Contemporary France*. Ed. Christopher Flood and Laurence Bell. Washington: Pinter 1997. 1-16.

Frears, John. *Parties and Voters in France*. London: Hurst & Company, 1991.

Hewlitt, Nick. *Modern French Politics: Analysing Conflict and Consensus since 1945*. Malden, MA: Polity Press, 1998.

Jennings, Jeremy. "Communism." *Political Ideologies in Contemporary France*. Ed. Christopher Flood and Laurence Bell. Washington: Pinter 1997. 52-73.

Memorandum (my title). French title: "Résumé des réunions de cellules des 2 et 3 juin 1997 à propos de la participation, ou non, de ministres communistes au gouvernement? Un résumé de ce qui s'est dit dans les cellules de Villejuif pendant la consultation." Juin 1997: 1-7 (my numbering).

Mossu-Lavau, Janine. *Que veut la gauche plurielle?* Paris: Odile Jacob, 1998.

Pinet, Christopher P. "The 1997 French Socialist Surprise Victory and the American Press." *The Journal of Language for International Business* 9.2 (1998): 38-48.

"Questions d'actualité. Sondage BVA réalisé pour *Paris Match*." <www.yahoo.fr/ promotions/sondages/quesactu>, 15-17 octobre 1998, pp. 1-2.

"Tableau de bord politique. Sondage BVA réalisé pour *Paris Match*." <www.yahoo.fr/ promotions/sondage/politique>, 17-19 septembre 1998, pp. 1-4.

Vinocur, John. "Clear Skies for the Communist Weatherman." *International Herald Tribune* 20 January 1998: 2.

Whitney, Craig. "Communists Sniff Heady Scent of Power." *International Herald Tribune* 3 June 1997: 1, 8.

3

French Environmental Policy: Better Late than Never

Michel Gueldry
Monterey Institute of International Studies

For a long time, both environmental politics and environmental studies in France were characterized by historical backwardness. Environmental awareness and policy became significant societal forces only at the very end of the 1980s. In 1993, Laurent Ménière wrote that, "In the early 1980s, that is to say yesterday, who, in France, really took an interest in the environment? Very few people indeed. But, twelve years later, environmental policy is a concern for more than 50% of French citizens, and, for one voter out of seven, it is a critical policy." Environmental policy went from being a political sideshow in the 1960s to "a new priority" in the 1990s (Ménière 347). Thus, this chapter describes French environmental policy from the 1960s to the late 1990s, stressing three closely interconnected aspects: citizens' awareness of environmental issues, green parties' dynamics, and governmental involvement.

1960s and 1970s: Political Infancy

French environmentalism began in the 1970s as a diffuse and culturally radical movement. But, gradually, its ideas led to the creation of several political parties, two of which participated in several cabinets in the 1980s and 1990s. Like other "new social movements" of the 1960s and 1970s, such as feminism and regionalism, French environmentalism was at first a dissenting voice, and was considered marginal and "exotic" by mainstream political parties. In many respects, it was viewed in this way because it aimed at breaking away from the old socio-political order and creating a new one. René Dumont, an agronomist and specialist in international food supply issues, and the unsuccessful *écologiste* candidate in the 1974 presidential elections, epitomizes this self-consciously utopian aspiration with his provocative 1973 book *L'Utopie ou la mort.* In international relations, *écologie* was then resolutely in favor of the developing world and often anti-capitalistic. René Dumont also wrote numerous books about the economic woes of Africa (1983), which he attributed largely to the colonial legacy and the indigenous bourgeoisie's post-colonial choice in favor of a Western-type of economic development. In domestic policy, *écologie* embraced regionalism, anti-centralization, anti-authoritarian values, local activism, and social experimentation, including communal living.

In political terms, the *écologistes'* greatest battle was against the nuclear program of civilian energy. Initiated in the late 1950s, this technocratic (non democratic) program was conducted with great vigor by the French government, animated by nationalistic concerns for technological and energy self-sufficiency, and by the oil crisis of the early 1970s. In March 1974 conservative Prime Minister Pierre Messmer embarked on an ambitious policy of *"tout électrique, tout nucléaire"* which was determined to build no fewer than 170 *centrales nucléaires* within 25 years! In fact, between 1980 and 1988, France would build on average four such plants each year, then slowed down somewhat, reaching a total of 58 plants by 1998, which is still a world record.

Anti-nuclear demonstrations targeted *le plan Messmer.* Anti-nuclear activism inspired by far-Left tactics of violent confrontation against the "military-industrial complex" culminated with the violent Creys-Malville (in the Isère) demonstration of July 31, 1977, which left one dead and many wounded. As Dorothy Nelkin, Michael Pollack and James Jasper argue, Creys-Malville clearly showed the limits of radical action against the technocratic establishment and forced a redefinition of environmental political strategies. Bernard Prendiville attributes the ineffectiveness of anti-nuclear forces in the 1970s to the virtual exclusion of minority opinion from the political process, the weakness of "intermediaries" between the state apparatus and the citizenry, which left "little form of protest other than direct confrontation with the state," the inability of the courts to curb administrative power, the close-knit character of the military-civilian nuclear complex, and the general apathy and uncritical nationalism of the electorate (Prendiville 16-18).

The *ministère de l'Environnement*, created in 1971 under the conservative government of Georges Pompidou, had fewer than 500 civil servants at its disposal, only a symbolic budget, and no regional representatives to implement its decisions or report local violations of environmental laws. Also, it was not a full-fledged ministry, but only a *ministère délégué* with little prestige, no political muscle in the parliament and no constituency either in public opinion, the media, or the business community. In addition, its personnel was often *en détachement*, i.e., they came from other governmental agencies and ministries, and worked for the new ministry of the environment on a temporary basis. Worse still, many of them originated from "technical ministries" (usually transportation or industry), and came with preconceived notions of what a business-friendly environmental agency should be. It is little wonder that Robert Poujade, the first official to head the new agency, voiced his frustrations about his experience by entitling his 1975 book of political recollections *Le ministère de l'impossible*.

The 1978 *Amoco Cadiz* catastrophe, in which a supertanker crashed off the coast of Brittany, causing an enormously destructive oil spill, did not spur Valéry Giscard d'Estaing's conservative government to question the rules of the game. After all, France and the world were in the throes of an economic crisis. This is why in the late 1970s and very early 1980s, many on the Left charged that conservatives only paid lip service to the environmental cause, and merely sought to capture votes without challenging the economic and social status quo. This discontent slowly started to spill over to middle-of-the-road and moderate Right citizens. Disgruntled with the status quo, a widening and diverse group began to cast their vote in favor of François Mitterrand, the candidate of the "unified Left," an alliance among Communists, Socialists and various environmentalist groups. This coalition was perceived as more responsive to environmental concerns. In this respect, it may be argued that the "spirit of May 1968" — questioning the rules of the socio-economic game — won something of a posthumous victory with Mitterrand's election in May 1981. Significantly, Huguette Bouchardeau, who managed the *ministère* only twelve years after Poujade, but this time under the socialist government of François Mitterrand, also related her experience in a 1986 book with a resoundingly optimistic title: *Le ministère du possible*.

Since the Late 1980s: A Slow Process of Legitimization

Mitterrand's May 1981 election raised hopes among environmentalists, but his support of both military and civilian nuclear programs demonstrated the glaring absence of a global alternative in this particular domain. However, January 1984 marks an important political shift for environmentalists, as the first Green party, *les Verts*, was then created in order to better prepare for the elections to the European Parliament, which still yielded disappointing results. But the July 1985 sinking of the *Rainbow Warrior* in the Auckland (New Zealand) harbor, was met with a mixture of apathy and cynicism by the French people. The *Verts* proved unable to use this act of state terrorism against the Greenpeace flagship to further question France's technocratic commitment in favor of nuclear energy and nuclear armaments.

Nonetheless, because of international concern about the rain forest, global warming, the depletion of the ozone layer (witness the Montreal summit in 1987), and because of the growing awareness of the impact of Chernobyl on the French public in 1986 (despite the French officials' stonewalling), the late 1980s were a turning point in environmental conscience-raising. Presidential elections, with their costly electoral machinery and majority voting system, have never been kind to environmentalists. This is why, in May 1988, Antoine Waechter, then the *Verts*' leader, obtained a disappointing 3.3 percent of the votes in the first round of presidential elections. On the contrary, regional and European elections, with their proportional representation voting system, have proved more rewarding. This is why the *Verts*, keeping an independent stance from both traditional Right and Left, scored an impressive 10.67 percent of total votes at the 1989 European elections.

Brice Lalonde, another environmental leader, was appointed Minister of the Environment in 1988, and may be considered the first such official with real political muscle. In 1990, he created a rival environmental party, *Génération Ecologie* (GE), seen as more moderate than *les Verts* (then led by Antoine Waechter and Dominique Voynet) and more sympathetic to François Mitterrand's views. Lalonde even accepted the nuclear industry, trying only to limit its development and to strengthen legislation on nuclear waste. In addition, environmentalists rode an electoral high wave until 1992, when the subsequent recession and the division of *les Verts* (from which Antoine Waechter's *Mouvement Ecologique International* branched off in 1994) further weakened their political impact. With his 1990 *Plan national pour l'environnement*, Lalonde reorganized and strengthened environmental administrative structures. The international catastrophes of Bhopal in India (where a chemical leak in a Union Carbide plant killed thousands in 1984) and Sandoz in Europe (the 1986 pollution of the Rhine by the Swiss chemical company) rendered his task easier. With Brice Lalonde's leadership as Minister of the Environment, *écologie* matured into a socially legitimate and politically savvy movement. At the same time, the *ministère* widened its scope of action. In the 1970s, it had spent most of its meager budget on water policy and industrial waste management without directly affecting wider industrial orientations. Since the early 1990s, the budget and personnel of the *ministère* have greatly expanded while its scope of action has widened significantly to include research and development (R&D), recycling policy, air and noise pollution control, public education, nuclear waste disposal, and increased international cooperation (conferences of Montreal, Rio de Janeiro, Kyoto and Buenos-Aires).

The French public's approval of Mitterrand's unilateral moratorium on nuclear testings in 1992, and its subsequent massive disapproval of Chirac's unilateral decision to resume these testings in late 1995 both testify to a growing sensitivity toward environmental issues. The belated signing of the Treaty of Roratonga (definitively banning all nuclear testings) in 1996 by "Hiro-Chirac" himself also constitutes a late victory for the visionaries of the 1970s.

Ideology and Sociology of Environmentalists

The intellectual sources of today's environmentalism in France are many: Romanticism, the "personalism" of Emmanuel Mounier, modernism, post-industrial philosophies, neo-Marxism, utopian-*proudhonisme*, and millenarianism. This mixed bag is disconcerting by its very heterogeneity, and Prendiville is correct in pointing out that "environmental ideology is difficult to pin down" (Prendiville, 163). Because of these millenarian, apocalyptic, anti-technological and anti-productivist associations, some French observers consider all of environmentalism as anti-humanist and potentially totalitarian, while others denounce its aspirations as *pétainisme* or *poujadisme vert* — i.e., a far-Right rural and anti-modernist ideology. But this clearly constitutes an exaggeration.

From the early 1970s to the early 1980s, French environmentalists were split between a reformist, non-violent strand, and various Marxist, anarchist, and radical splinter groups. Today, these original divisions remain, although the political leverage of truly radical *écologie*, such as *Alternative Rouge et Verte*, is extremely limited. The progressive institutionalization of the *Verts* provides an indication of how mainstreamed yesterday's Green radicals have become. The *Verts* originally assembled in loosely organized local groups, repudiated "vertical" and central political organization and rejected anthropocentrism as an organizational social principle. In 1984 they abandoned some of their founding principles, formed a structured political party and embraced environmental reformism. Indeed, since 1997, Dominique Voynet has participated in Lionel Jospin's *majorité plurielle* as *Madame la Ministre de l'Environnement*.

According to Prendiville, the core group of environmentalists today are well-off, educated professionals, with less religious conviction than the national average, but highly committed to unionism, and especially active in the *Confédération Française Démocratique du Travail (CFDT)*. They tend to be individual home owners living mainly in towns of fewer than 10,000 people. They also see themselves as a part of a diverse and wide social group, that of the "enlightened middle-class" (Prendiville 159). Beyond this core group, environmental awareness has penetrated large segments, if not the vast majority, of the French citizenry. Highly visible incidents such as the current BSE (bovine spongiform encephalopathy or "mad cow") scandal, the recurring air pollution in major cities (notably Paris and Strasbourg), the contamination of Breton aquifers and rivers by the waste from hog and poultry farms, the strong opposition to the extension of expressways (when extension of railways would provide better, less polluting transportation to greater numbers of people) have all shown the public the urgency of a historical conciliation between the economy and the natural world.

Green Political Culture and French Political Culture

For many years, the political culture of the *Verts*, with their insistence on democracy within their own organizations, rotating mandates, internal primaries, and attempts at strict gender equality stymied their political action. Since the 1980s, environmentalists have indeed adapted to the times, but their influence is still significantly curtailed by structural features of the French polity. Jean-Luc Mathieu offers a left-wing critique of current French attitudes towards environmentalism by stressing that major parties from both the Right and the Left share a narrow pro-business attitude (Mathieu 17). He lambastes France's restrictive conception of environmental issues, the weakness, both financial and legal, of government agencies in charge of implementing protective laws, a general laxity towards law-breakers (very evident with hog farmers in Brittany), and governmental disinterest vis-à-vis the international dimension of any effective Green policy. In his critique of national political features, Mathieu singles out the scarcity of checks and balances in French public life.

French environmentalists' electoral ups and downs are thus largely explainable by the relative weakness of grassroots democracy, the discreet collusion of the main parties of the Right and the Left regarding nuclear and industrial issues, the central role of governmental bureaucracy, and the financial dependence of most associations on the government. In addition, the preeminence of presidential elections in French political life since 1962 has imposed a "vertical strategy," while majority representation (as opposed to proportional majority representation) favors big parties in Parliament, and breeds "*unempowerment* on the part of the citizen." (Prendiville 89) In addition, the current fragmentation of environmentalists into three parties (Dominique Voynet's *Verts*, Antoine Waechter's minuscule *Mouvement Ecologique International, MEI,* and Brice Lalonde's *Génération Ecologie*, largely regarded as a vehicle for his own ambitions) does little to improve their electoral strength.

Environmental Issues in the 1990s: Causes for Concern

In the late 1990s, environmentalists seem to be on a roll again. Dominique Voynet, a founding member of *les Verts* and herself a presidential candidate in May 1995, went to the Ministry of the Environment in June 1997 with a substantive agenda and strong popular backing. Her party, a small but critical component of Lionel Jospin's *majorité plurielle* has boasted three Members of Parliament and numerous *conseillers régionaux* since the March 1998 regional elections. She faces hundreds of sensitive cases and difficult budgetary choices. Among the most pressing issues are the following:

- France has long committed itself to becoming a world leader in nuclear waste reprocessing. The *Compagnie Générale des Matériaux Nucléaires (COGEMA)*, an official company of nuclear waste reprocessing with strong links to both the military-industrial complex and the *nucléocratie*, has grown into one of the world leaders in this highly technical and politically sensitive domain. *COGEMA's* main facility in La Hague in the Cotentin region has been shown by Greenpeace to dispose unlawfully of toxic wastes in the English Channel. Tackling the issue of nuclear wastes means taking on powerful industrial, financial, and politically entrenched interests — a daunting task in a period of *cohabitation* of a Socialist Prime Minister with a conservative President. Germany's decision (January 1999) to abandon its nuclear program and stop exporting its nuclear waste to La Hague has ignited a controversy between the two countries, because the *COGEMA* stands to lose considerable amounts of money.

- *Superphénix*, the *surgénérateur* (fast breeder reactor) of Creys-Malville, has been at the center of a heated political battle ever since its official opening twelve years ago. In February 1998, the *Verts* won their final battle against this symbol of nuclear hubris. The nuclear complex will cease operations in ten to fifteen years (the slowness of this process is due to technical imperatives and local economic conversion). This *cause célèbre* has finally been won. But there are still fifty-seven more *centrales nucléaires* to deal with.

- Opinionated resistance on the part of *Chasse-Pêche-Tradition* against European Union directives regarding bird hunting. Their electoral gains in the 1998 regional elections only emboldened them to claim special hunting rights for the Southwest region of France (Aquitaine) in the name of subsidiarity and local rights.

- Air pollution in Paris (and many other cities): Some progress has been made with *circulation alternée*, the *pastille verte*, the introduction of electric and *Gaz de Pétrole Liquéfié* vehicles, electric buses for public transportation companies, etc. The combination of CO_2, NO_2, O_3, sulfur and lead in the Parisian skies has already contributed to the deaths of thousands of residents, a fact that has made *Le Monde*'s front page many times. Often heralded as a significant step in the right direction by a lethargic or complacent press, *circulation alternée* is not a fix. It is not based on any scientific process (since it does not eliminate older, more polluting vehicles), may be circumvented (by buying a second, more polluting car), and constitutes only a short-term remedy. Long-term structural issues regarding city planning must still be addressed, among them the need to levy hefty taxes on highly polluting diesel engines and oversized recreational vehicles, and the paradigmatic reorientation of the *Plan d'Occupation des Sols* (zoning laws) in order to create integrated communities within cities, or *quartiers* with a residential area together with schools, businesses, a shopping center, sport facilities and parks.

- Asbestos in public buildings: The university at Jussieu, built in the 1970s before asbestos was found to be a health risk, is currently being rehabilitated, and its thousands of students relocated to other Parisian universities. However, when it comes to asbestos contamination, Jussieu, though the most notorious case of asbestos-related pollution, is only the tip of a much larger iceberg. In addition, legal actions are currently being hindered by the very long-term nature of asbestos-related ailments.

- The level of dioxide released by domestic waste incinerators is abnormally high. Once released in the atmosphere, this chemical finds its way into cows' milk and the food chain. The 1998 closure of three such plants near Lille may constitute the beginning of a trend.

The Future of French Environmental Policy: Cautious Optimism

Because of unemployment and electoral promises, Lionel Jospin's cabinet is under intense pressure to give priority to the economy. But even Alain Juppé's conservative cabinet (May 1995-May 1997) offered a number of *arbitrages* in favor of environment minister Corinne Lepage — for instance against *Electricité de France (EDF)* in the Val-Louron *(Pyrénées). (Arbitrages* are arbitrations by the Prime Minister when two ministers with colliding sectoral interests differ on a particular policy choice.) A Left-wing cabinet with significant Green backing should be able to do at least as much as the conservatives did. Dominique Voynet is now in charge of both the environment and the *aménagement du territoire*. In other words, environmental protection is no longer approached as a reactive, piecemeal policy, but as part of the "structural development" of the national territory. In general, the Left remains more committed to environmental protection than the Right, but the level of public awareness is such that no government can afford to fully ignore it.

Green politics has evolved from a series of expedient initiatives that carefully avoided core political issues such as nuclear energy and municipal planning to a more legitimate and profitable endeavor. The best cause for optimism is the creation of jobs for environmental protection, management and public education, as well as the emergence of dozens of eco-companies. Giant international corporations such as Lyonnaise des Eaux-Dumez and Vivendi (the recently renamed CGE conglomerate), among the top five in the world for water services, have been guilty of political corruption in the past. But their internationally recognized technical expertise, combined with sound regulation and political oversight, should facilitate environmentally-sound water policy and job creation in France in this area.

French cultural rigidities regarding the environment are sometimes formidable — and baffling. For instance, the perils of *tabagisme*, or second-hand smoking, although recognized by the November 1992 *Loi Evin* are still routinely dismissed as an "American obsession." Still, in the long run, environmental policy in France will very probably be strengthened because of the European Union. Nordic democracies as well as Germany and Austria promote a political agenda emphasizing environmental issues, democratic accountability, and transparency. Depending on which issues are considered, between 50 and 75 percent of current French environmental laws have their source in EU legislation despite subsidiarity. For instance, catalytic converters imposed by EU directives on certain types of cars are now standard features, despite French automakers' resistance to Brussels in the 1980s (especially Peugeot, which enjoys a lion's share of the diesel market in France). Both the February 1992 Maastricht treaty (Title XVI, Articles 130R to 130T) and the October 1997 Amsterdam treaty (Title XIX, Articles 174 to 176) have significantly extended the EU's authority in the domain of environmental policy.

At one time, not so long ago, the environment was virtually absent from the French political and legal landscape. It was also construed as a single issue (read "narrow") policy that distracted policy makers from serious (read "economy and employment") issues. But, the environment has proved to be a trans-party policy dealing with interconnected issues of public health, industrial reorientation, agricultural policies and urban development. It has also gained considerable recognition in the legal profession, so much so that concerned citizens and groups can now initiate legal action (*se constituer partie civile*) against violators of environmental laws, corporations *and* the government alike. Since March 1994, the new *Code Pénal* allows private citizens and Green organizations to sue all parties responsible for environmental abuses and provides for stiffer financial penalties. This parallels well the new but steady development of "policing through green taxes."

Core environmentalists remain committed to social reformism, and what some consider an unrealistic worldview (Furet 1, 15). They consider Lionel Jospin's *35 heures* plan a litmus test of his commitment to social reform, they supported the *chômeurs* (unemployed) protests in December 1997, and remain ambivalent, if not downright negative, about liberalism and global capitalism. René Dumont (1988, 1995) and Antoine Wachter (1991) continue the old struggle against capitalistic excesses. But ultimately their success as environmentalists depends upon the public's realization that economic development can no longer work against the environment, and vice versa. Slowly but surely, French citizens have come to realize the necessary compatibility between economy and environmental protection — and its urgency. As Michel Barnier, former Minister of the Environment (1993-95), puts it in his 1990 book, the current "environmental challenge" may be summed up by a beautiful paradox: *Chacun pour tous*.

References

Barnier, Michel. *Chacun pour tous: le défi écologique*. Paris: Stock, 1990.
Bouchardeau, Huguette. *Le Ministère du possible*. Paris: Alain Moreau, 1986.
Bourdeau, Philippe, and David Stanners, eds. *Europe's Environment. The Dobris Assessment*. Copenhagen: European Environmental Agency, 1995.
Collier, Ute, Jonathan Golub, and Alexander Kreher. *Subsidiarity and Shared Responsibility. New Challenges for EU Environmental Policy*. Baden-Baden: Nomos Verlag, 1997.
Dumont, René. *L'Utopie ou la mort*. Paris: Le Seuil, 1973.
---. *Seule une écologie socialiste*. Paris: Robert Laffont, 1977.

---. *Stranglehold on Africa.* London: A. Dutsch, 1983.

---. *Un monde intolérable. Le libéralisme en question.* Paris: Le Seuil, 1988.

---. *Le XXI* siècle est mal parti.* Paris: Arléa/Le Seuil, 1995.

Ferry, Luc. *Le nouvel ordre écologique. L'arbre, l'animal et l'homme.* Paris: Grasset, 1994.

Furet, François. "L'énigme française." *Le Monde,* 23 Sept. 1997: 1, 15.

Guyomard, Jacques. *L'intégration de l'environnement dans les politiques intra-communautaires.* Rennes: Apogées, 1995.

Institut Français de l'Environnement (IFEN). *L'environnement en France. Rapports sur l'état de l'environnement en France, 1994-1995.* Paris: Dunod/IFEN, 1994.

Jasper, James M. *Nuclear Politics: Energy and the State in the United States, Sweden and France.* Princeton: Princeton UP, 1990.

Lepage, Corinne. *"On ne peut rien faire, Madame le ministre...".* Paris: Plon, 1998.

Mathieu, Jean-Luc. *La défense de l'environnement en France.* Paris: PUF, 1994.

Ménière, Laurent. *Bilan de la France, 1981-1993.* Paris: Hachette, 1993.

Ministry of the Environment. *Environnement et développement. L'expérience et l'approche françaises.* Paris: La Documentation Française, 1991.

---. *Pour que l'eau vive.* Paris: La Documentation Française, 1992.

Nelkin, Dorothy, and Michael Pollack. *The Atom Besieged: Extraparliamentary Dissent in France and Germany.* Cambridge: MIT Press, 1981.

OCDE. *Examens des performances environnementales. France.* Paris: OCDE, 1997.

Poujade, Robert. *Le ministère de l'impossible.* Paris: Calmann-Lévy, 1975.

Prendiville, Bernard. *Environmental Politics in France.* Boulder: Westview, 1994.

Prieur, Michel. *Droit de l'environnement.* Paris: Dalloz, 1991.

Serres, Michel. *Le contrat naturel.* Paris: François Bourin, 1990.

Waechter, André. *Dessine-moi une planète. L'écologie, maintenant ou jamais.* Paris: Albin Michel, 1991.

4

The Crisis of the French Social Protection System

Alan J. Singerman
Davidson College

Thirty years ago the "Events" of May '68 shook France to its very foundations. What began as a small demonstration of student dissatisfaction in Paris became a series of violent confrontations between students and the police throughout France, and, subsequently, a national strike by over 10 million workers paralyzing the whole country for several weeks. This is a rare occurrence indeed, yet those of us who happened to be residing in France in the final few months of 1995 were witness to a public uprising with haunting similarities to the famous *Evénements*. Beginning with a student strike in the middle of October, joined by massive groups of civil servants the following month, by the end of November the country was virtually paralyzed. The national train system and the Paris *métro* and bus system were on strike, as well as many employees of the Post Office throughout the country. Strike days were declared by the national gas, electrical power and telephone companies, along with Renault, Air France, and Air Inter, the state-owned banks, the Parisian taxi drivers, the miners in Lorraine, and even the Social Security and Internal Revenue offices, all of whom participated, with students, teachers, and doctors, in massive demonstrations throughout the end of November and the middle of December before trailing off at the approach of the Christmas holidays. In Tours, massive demonstrations blocked traffic in the city for hours on end — with marchers beating drums, sounding air horns, and blowing smoke. The local railroad employees diligently laid down iron tracks in the middle of the main boulevard in front of the *Hôtel de Ville* to express their displeasure with government policy. The purpose of this study is to discuss what happened, and why, in the "events" of fall 1995 and to put them in their broader economic and social context.

Let us begin with the university problem. France has the dubious distinction, among the European countries, of having the largest number of college students and, with the exception of Spain, spending the least per student. This has created severe overcrowding of classes and general deterioration of living and learning conditions at the university. In the middle of October, at the beginning of the 1995-96 school year, the students at the University of Rouen decided to take a stand and went on strike, demanding funds for additional teaching positions, administrative and maintenance personnel, classrooms and dorms. Three weeks later, after obtaining 9 million francs from François Bayrou, the Minister of Education, the Rouen students terminated their strike and went to class. The lesson was not lost, however, on the dozens of other financially strapped universities in France, many of whom immediately went on strike also, forming a national coordinating committee, and demanding a budgetary commitment to thousands of new teaching and service positions. As the student strikes became more and more widespread, with violent confrontations in several cities, the minister gradually sweetened the pot, eventually offering to budget 2,000 new teaching positions and the same number of new service positions.

In the midst of these tense negotiations, and with about a third of the 75 French universities closed down, Alain Juppé, the neo-Gaullist Prime Minister, decided that this was a propitious moment to announce to the French people an ambitious plan to effect sweeping changes in the French system of social payments, including national health insurance, family allocations, and retirement benefits.[1] It was no secret that the system was in deep financial trouble, with a 124 billion franc deficit for the *régime général* over the previous two years (1994-1995) and another 60 billion franc deficit projected for 1996 if no action were taken by the government [2] — which had been in a crisis mode since the deficit shot up from 15.6 billion in 1992 to 56.4 billion the following year. The total deficit had reached 250 billion francs. The *Plan Juppé*, as the set of projected corrective measures came to be known, was a comprehensive in-depth overhaul of the system designed to solve the growing deficit problem by requiring financial sacrifices from virtually all of the social partners. While the fight to keep the French social protection system solvent was hardly a novelty — there had been, on the average, a new bailout plan every eighteen months since 1973 (Bouffechoux, 187) — the *Plan Juppé* was the most ambitious reform ever attempted, affecting the most fundamental structures of the system.

The government's proposal, applauded by a broad majority of the *députés*, including part of the opposition, called for both an increase in revenues and a decrease in expenditures. On the one hand, it announced the creation of a new tax of 0.5%, called the *Remboursement de la Dette Sociale* (RDS), applying to an extremely wide variety of revenues and lasting 13 years. In addition, social security premiums were to be increased, as well as the health insurance premiums of retirees and the unemployed. Monthly family payments (*allocations familiales*), benefiting all families with at least two children, were to be taxed for the first time, beginning in 1997. Doctors and pharmacists would contribute a lump sum of 5 billion francs, businesses another 2.5 billion. And everyone's income taxes would rise due to the elimination of the normal 20% deduction on income before it becomes taxable in France. On the other hand, to bring under control the explosion of medical costs, it was decided that the *carnet médical*, a portable medical record already in use for septuagenarians since 1994,[3] would be put into general use in order to reduce the number of visits to different doctors for the same problem (the *"nomadisme médical"*). More significantly, the government planned to change the Constitution and pass the necessary laws to give the National Assembly the authority to determine each year how much money would be budgeted for health insurance payments to doctors. Finally, the retirement plans of civil servants in the various government services would be modified to require them, like workers in the private sector (see below), to pay an additional 2 1/2 years of premiums to retire with full benefits. The special retirement plans of certain categories of government employees, like railroad, subway, postal, electricity and gas workers, would be subject to even greater modification, adding, for many, three or more years of activity before retirement. It is true that retirement benefits in France represent alone over 40% of the social budget each year, by far the largest burden on the system.

In any case, this is bitter medicine for a population which has already swallowed a special "solidarity tax" called the *Contribution Sociale Généralisée (CSG),* established by the Rocard government in 1991 at 1.1% and increased to 2.4% in 1993, as well as two increases in the copayment for hospital stays during the same period, a 2% increase in the Value-Added Tax (to 20.6%) in August 1995, and regular decreases in the reimbursement of doctors' fees and pharmaceutical expenses — from 75% in 1971 to under 60%, on the average, in 1994 (Catala 140). In addition, as mentioned above, the retirement plans of all private sector employees had already been modified, in July 1993, increasing the average retirement age, while the formula for calculating pensions was also changed to reduce benefits overall.[4] All this in a country which is enduring an unemployment rate above 12%.

While this was the general social climate in which the *Plan* was presented, one element in particular set off the explosion of resentment. Despite the seriousness of the deficit in the health insurance branch, well over half the total deficit in both 1994 and 1995,[5] it was in fact the proposal to modify the government retirement plans which, in little more than a week, closed down the public transportation system and the post office and propelled the employees out into the streets with the students, soon to be joined by teachers and many other categories of civil servants. It should be remembered that fully 20% of the French work force is employed by the government; it is by far the biggest employer in the country. It is also important to know that about half of these employees earned less than 8,500 FF a month at the time, and that their salaries had just been frozen at the beginning of September, precipitating a broad strike on October 10, barely a month before the announcement of the *Plan.* The only truly bright spot in their career, other than job security, is their right to retire early, depending on the onerousness of their job. While the normal retirement age in France, since the Auroux laws in 1982 under the Mauroy government — and before the reform of 1993 — was 60, an employee of the *SNCF,* for instance, who spends his/her working life on trains moving around France, or a subway train driver who spends twenty-five years rolling from station to station beneath the Paris streets, can retire as early as 50. Other categories of workers, such as sailors and miners, drivers of postal trucks, electrical linemen, or subway maintenance workers, can take retirement as early as 55 (not to mention opera singers, who may retire at 40...). In addition to the revision of the retirement plans of the *fonctionnaires*, moreover, the Juppé government had chosen this moment to announce a plan to abandon a certain number of unprofitable railroad lines to private enterprise, which would service them with smaller, more profitable trains. There is no better way to antagonize French government workers than to speak of privatizing what is considered to be a fundamental public service. All of the above should help to explain the initial anger generated by the *Plan Juppé*, which brought over a million angry people into the streets on December 12, the largest national day of demonstration, touching virtually every large city in France.

As the opposition stiffened and the public outcry rose, Juppé beat a hasty retreat on a certain number of proposed measures. He quickly dropped the plan to tax family subsidies. The government's proposal to eliminate the 20% deduction before taxable income, announced by the *Ministre de l'Economie et des Finances* a few days after the presentation of Juppé's reform to the National Assembly, was immediately repudiated by the Prime Minister. And, above all, the public service retirement plans were left intact and the proposal to sell elements of the national railroad system to private investors shelved. With these concessions in hand, the trains began to move again, just in time for the Christmas holidays. Many key elements of the *Plan,* however, remained in effect, and Juppé himself, whose resignation was loudly sought by the labor unions who organized most of the demonstrations, had weathered the storm — for the moment at least.

Reflecting over the events of November-December 1995, most commentators agree with the former socialist Prime Minister, Michel Rocard, who did not take issue with the need to reduce the deficit, but rather with the approach adopted by Juppé. Rocard suggested (*Le Monde,* 9 Dec. 1995: 8) that Juppé committed three fundamental errors: first, he attempted to effect several controversial reforms simultaneously, provoking the animosity of a large majority of the French public at the same time; second, he attempted to impose his plan virtually without any serious concertation with the people concerned, declaring that he would rule essentially by decree (by *ordonnance*) until the appropriate laws were passed; and third, he both increased the solidarity tax *(CSG)* and created a new tax, the *RDS,* without compensating these measures by a reduction in social charges (as Rocard had done when he created the *CSG* in 1991) to avoid overwhelming people with modest incomes. The mixture of tactical errors proved to be unduly provocative.[6]

The "aftermath" of the social upheaval is scarcely less interesting than the events themselves. Having lost the battle over retirement plans, the Juppé government would immediately begin a long struggle, with the nation's private doctors, the *médecins libéraux,* who vigorously oppose reforms which appear to endanger both their traditional prerogatives and their earning potential. The government's hand was considerably strengthened, however, by the revision of the Constitution (February 19, 1996) establishing a new category of laws, the *lois de financement de la Sécurité sociale,* giving the Assemblée Nationale the power to set health care spending limits each year, as foreseen in the *Plan* (Bigaut 8-10), as well as by the *ordonnance* of April 24, 1996, which established the new managed health care measures and the sanctions for infractions. While the social crisis has passed, the financial dilemma of the social protection system remains, and medical expenses are responsible, as mentioned above, for well over half the annual deficit. The government announced that it would limit the increase in medical spending for 1996 to 2.1% and threatened serious sanctions against doctors who exceeded the limit. The doctors' unions stiffened their resistance to the announced goals, stressing the fact that they cannot refuse to treat their patients, and it is unfair to expect doctors to treat them for free when they have reached their prescribed cost limit. An approach currently used in Germany, in which the set medical fees for each treatment can be raised or lowered so that the yearly total does not exceed the budgeted amount, has met a frosty reception in France, where doctors have attempted to mobilize public opinion against reforms by raising the specter of health care rationing. The standoff continued, despite a four-year agreement finally signed in February 1996, between two doctors' unions and the three principal health insurance offices, stipulating a maximum 1.5% increase in national expenditures for general practitioners the following year — a 2.4% increase in fees, 1.3% for prescriptions (Bouffechoux 158-160).[7]

Juppé also maintained his plan to generalize the *carnet médical* or *carnet de santé*, as it is variously called, but here again the initiative was, and still is, being resisted by both the doctors and the public. By the end of 1996, only about half of the population, at best, was using the portable medical record, and, in the absence of sanctions of any kind, many doctors were apparently encouraging their patients not to bother with it (Bouffechoux 90; Bui17).[8]   A debate has begun about the problem of *le secret médical*, doctor-patient confidentiality, in the use of the *carnet*, and about patients' rights, which had formerly included the right to control what was recorded in their medical files.[9] Moreover, a *carte à puce*, an individual electronic card referred to as *Vitale 1*, is scheduled to replace the traditional paper *carte d'assuré* before the end of 1999, and was, in fact, distributed to parts of Brittany as early as May 1998. A second generation of electronic cards will contain the complete medical records of the holder. By the end of 1998, all doctor's offices were to be equipped with computers and the current submission of treatment forms (*feuilles de soins*) gradually replaced by electronic transmission of health care data. Needless to say, the prospect of computerized personal health care records, with the attendant questions of access and privacy rights, has considerably enlivened debate in this area (Pellet 853-879).

On yet another front, doctors are chaffing about the accelerated development of the *Références Médicales Opposables (RMO)*, which are national guidelines making certain prescriptions and practices, considered to be of dubious therapeutic value, ineligible for reimbursement. The *RMO*, along with the *carnet de santé* and the coding of medical treatments (to enable stricter controls) are, in fact, one of the principal means of reducing health care costs through what is referred to as the *maîtrise médicalisée*, the curbing of unnecessary office visits and prescriptions, as opposed to the *maîtrise comptable*, the reduction of expenses by budgetary means — both of which are expanded in the *Plan Juppé*. Private doctors protest, in particular, what they see as a growing restriction of their "freedom to prescribe," one of the fundamental tenets of private medical practice, as the number of RMO rises rapidly (from 24 in 1993 to 65 in 1994 to 147 in 1995) and the system of sanctions for violations stiffens under the new legislation.[10]

One might ask, why now? Why did the Juppé government try to do so much so fast? A partial answer lies, not too surprisingly, in the European Union, and, particularly, in the creation of the new European currency, the euro. As is well known, the eligibility of each country to participate in the use of the new European currency was to be determined (and was determined) at the beginning of May, 1998, according to each country's ability to meet a certain number of economic criteria. The most difficult criterion for most countries to meet, including France, stated that the annual deficit must not exceed 3% of the Gross Domestic Product. The Prime Minister thus felt compelled to take governmental measures to beat the deficit down to the required level. Since France and Germany have taken a leading role in the development of the European Union, it was unthinkable that France would not be able to use the euro.

As an epilogue to this social saga, Juppé and the then ruling right-wing coalition in France paid a severe price for the Prime Minister's undisputed political courage in launching reform. Recognizing that additional austerity would be necessary to master the deficit, Jacques Chirac decided in April 1997, to dissolve the National Assembly and schedule legislative elections a month later, instead of the regularly scheduled elections in May 1998. Chirac calculated that, with an overwhelming majority in the Assembly (471 seats of 577), his coalition would easily win the elections and then be safe for another five years, allowing them to put into place the necessary austerity measures without having to incur the wrath of the voting public the following year. The strategy backfired. The public had apparently not forgotten the *Plan* of a year and a half before and was fearful, justifiably, of the other shoe being dropped. In June 1997, the left-wing coalition, dominated by Lionel Jospin's Socialists, won control of the National Assembly.

This remarkable upset did not prevent the social protection saga from continuing, with surprising twists and turns. No sooner was Jospin's government in place than he announced his intention to establish means testing for family benefits which had formerly been universal, setting the ceiling for eligibility at 25,000 francs a month for a family with two children — a move which even the conservatives under Juppé had not dared attempt![11] Under intense pressure from the pro-family lobbies and the labor unions, however, Jospin abandoned the means testing plan ten months later (July 1998) in favor of a change in the rules governing the deduction for dependents in the calculation of income taxes (lowering the ceiling of the *quotient familial*).[12] In an effort to tackle the problem of unemployment, which has contributed heavily to the woes of the welfare finances, the Jospin government proposed, and passed into law (May 1998), a reduction of the work week from 39 to 35 hours, to take effect in the year 2,000. Although opponents denied that this strategy would be effective, supporters estimated that it would produce 20,000 to 40,000 new jobs (Mital 18), a prediction which seems justified by encouraging results tabulated by the administration at the end of 1998: 20,000 to 30,000 jobs already saved or created by the move to the 35-hour week in certain industries.

When we step back and look at the fray in a broader context, it is apparent that France is in the throes of a struggle to redefine its social welfare philosophy in the context of current economic realities. While the principle of national solidarity enshrined in the first article of the French code of the *Sécurité sociale* (1945) remains intact, as does the duty of the nation, affirmed in the Constitutions of 1946 and 1958, to provide assistance to individuals and families, it is clear that the current system of benefits, even assuming healthy economic growth, is simply beyond France's means. In the search for alternatives, the traditional debates between public and private financing (for example, national vs. private pension plans, *répartition* vs. *capitalisation*) have been revived,[13] as have those concerning the fundamental principles underlying the social protection system. While the attempt to reform the medical insurance system is severely complicated by the multiplicity of health plans (nineteen in all),[14] both the Juppé and the Jospin governments have promoted the idea of a *régime universel* of health insurance in which premiums and benefits would be equalized throughout the system, making it easier to control financially, and in which eligibility for benefits would be based simply on residency rather than employment.[15] In essence, the Juppé governement planned to nudge France away from its long-held "Bismarckian" tradition of basing rights to benefits on professional activity (leaving relatively unprotected a certain segment of the population) toward the "Beveridgian" philosophy of providing benefits to all needy citizens.[16] At the same time, this modification would tend to justify a move toward tax-based financing of the system (*fiscalisation*), as opposed to employee contributions (*cotisations*), a logic which is already present in the government's practice of absorbing annual deficits, as well as in both the *RDS* and the *CSG* (the latter increased to 3.4% in 1997 and scheduled to rise to 7.5% in 1998, with a corresponding drop in the salaried employees' health insurance premiums, the *cotisations maladie*).[17] The French model has become, more and more, a clear compromise between Bismarck and Beveridge (Palier and Bonoli 30), which is, in fact, not atypical of most Western European countries today, which tend to combine features of both systems.

The problems plaguing the French social protection system are far from being solved. The French government must find a way to mollify the nation's doctors and garner their support if any meaningful reform is to be made in the area of health insurance. To this end, the Socialists abrogated, at the beginning of July, 1998, the prior agreements negotiated with two doctors' unions by the Juppé government (March 1997), and began to seek a new compromise.[18] At the end of 1998, the conflict had not yet been resolved, and the Jospin government was itself threatening to control health costs by adopting the German approach of floating rates of insurance reimbursement (*les lettres clés flottantes*), calculating rates according to the volume of medical activity by each specialty — a measure which had already been applied to the radiologists the previous July, reducing their reimbursement by 13% per treatment. Although optimism prevails, with a brightening economic picture for France, and there is even talk of balancing the budget of the *Sécu* in 1999 (Gilson, 24 Sept., 28), the majority of the doctors' unions are still offering stiff resistance to restrictions on medical spending and, especially, to continuing provisions for financial sanctions (in the *loi de financement de la Sécurité sociale* for 1999) in the case of budget overruns. On another front, to encourage use of the *carte de santé* and to reduce the number of office visits, Jospin quickly borrowed Juppé's proposed *contrats de santé* (modeled on the American Preferred

Provider system), renaming them *contrats de confiance*. In this system (referred to as a *filière de soins*), all patients are encouraged to choose a general practitioner whom they must consult first (and none other) before going, if authorized by their doctor, to a specialist.[19] The problem of the retirement plans of civil servants and other special plans (e.g., *EDF, SNCF, RATP)* also remains of major concern, especially with the prospect of massive retirements of baby-boomers beginning in the year 2000 and deficits projected in nearly all the retirement plans by 2005 (Philippon and Tatu 20). The 1993 reform of the private sector retirement plans, similar to what was proposed in the *Plan Juppé* for public service employees, produced a striking reduction in the deficit in that area, from 39.5 billion francs in 1993 to 13.5 in 1994 and 5.8 in 1996 (after a 10.1 billion surplus in 1995). The current five-year plan (February 1999) recommends, in fact, that the Socialist government go beyond what Juppé proposed (raising the minimum number of years of premiums from 37.5 to 40) by increasing the minimum number for all workers to 42.5 — very gradually, however, the new minimum not being fully implemented in both the private and public sectors until the year 2019. Can the French system afford, indeed, to preserve the privileges, no matter how well justified, of a broad segment of the population? This question, as well as many others, will have to be addressed firmly if the current social protection system in France is to survive.

Notes

[1] Plan presented to the National Assembly on November 15, 1995 (see *Le Monde*, 16 Nov. 1995: 1; 17 Nov. 1995: 8). For a detailed study of the provisions of the "Plan Juppé," see Stasse, 17-23.

[2] The actual deficit of the *régime général* (salaried workers in the private sector) in 1996 was 51.6 billion, down from 67.4 billion in 1995 (Viossat 65).

[3] The *carnet de santé* was instituted in January 1994, for all persons over 70 suffering from at least two illnesses (Harichaux 848).

[4] Beginning in 1993, and over a ten-year period, pensions will gradually be based on average salary during the best 25 years rather than the best 10 years — while pensions of civil servants are still based on the last *six months* of their career . . . (Maquart 88). Moreover, private sector old age pensions are now indexed, since 1993, on inflation rather than on salaries, which tends to reduce benefits further.

[5] 32.2% of 56.6 billion francs in 1994, 39.7 of 67.4 billion in 1995, and 33.6 of 51.6 billion in 1996 (Viossat 65).

[6] For an in-depth discussion of this question, see Borgetto, 686-709.

[7] The Convention was signed by the *Union collégiale des chirurgiens et spécialistes français (UCCSF)* and by *Médecins-Généralistes de France (MG-France),* the

latter being only one of the four general practitioner unions concerned; the other doctors' unions violently opposed the agreement. As Bouffechoux remarks, appropriately, this brings the legitimacy of the *convention* into question — a fact which will escape neither the new Socialist government (see below) as it searches for a compromise with the doctors, nor the *Conseil d'Etat* (see note 17, below).

[8] Anne-Marie Casteret (64) reports, in the middle of 1997: "Deux fois sur trois, le carnet de santé ne sert pas. Dans la moitié des cas, le malade oublie de le présenter. Quand il le sort de sa poche, un tiers des praticiens le négligent."

[9] In the *carnet* itself, it is explicitly stated that "aucune mention médicale ne peut toutefois être portée sur ce carnet sans votre accord" (p. 4).

[10] The guidelines are referred to as *opposables* precisely because penalties are forseen for physicians who do not respect them. For a succinct discussion of the RMO, see Dubois, 748-749.

[11] The Juppé government did manage, however, to lower family benefits, reducing the deficit from 38.9 billion in 1995 (nearly as large as the health spending deficit) to 12.8 billion in 1996. Overall, according to Viossat (65, 66), the Plan Juppé saved nearly 31.5 billion francs in 1996.

[12] In this approach, only families with incomes greater than 36,000 francs a month will be affected, and the philosophy behind the *allocations familiales* is respected.

[13] *Répartition* refers to a system in which retirement pensions are financed by revenues from those still working; *capitalisation* refers to private pension funds based on personal savings, with or without employer contributions.

[14] There are, in comparison, no fewer than 538 different national retirement plans in France, making global reform in this area a Gargantuan task (Bezat 5).

[15] A bill has been recently approved by the *Conseil des ministres* (March 99), calling for universal health coverage (*la couverture maladie universelle* or *CMU*) by January 1, 2000, which will provide coverage to an additional 150,000 inhabitants and free medical care for everyone earning less than 3,500 francs a month — about six million people.

[16] A "Bismarckian" system, named for the 19th-century Prussian chancellor who originated the first program of modern social insurance, covers primarily employees, is financed by their premiums, and is managed by organizations representing both employers and workers; a "Beveridgian" system, named for William Beveridge, the founder of Britain's National Health System (1942), covers all citizens, including those who are not working, is financed largely by taxes, and is administered by the government. For a brief discussion of the two systems, see Palier and Bonoli, 30-33.

[17] For a detailed discussion of the possible impact on taxpayers of this proposed shift, which would, principally, transfer a greater part of the tax burden to earnings on capital investments, see Lhaïk 32-33.

[18] The *Conseil d'Etat* ruled on July 3, 1998, that a) the single specialists' union that signed the March 1997 Convention did not legitimately represent the profession and b) the monetary penalties (see Articles 32-33 of the Convention), to be imposed on the general practitioners if medical costs arising from their services exceeded the budget, were inequitable (Gilson, 15 July, 27).

[19] As an enticement, the patients would not have to pay the whole bill for the visit at time of treatment, as is current practice; the doctor's fee, above the 30% copayment (*ticket modérateur*) would be paid directly by the national health insurance (*tiers payant*), as is now done for pharmaceutical expenses. Cooperating doctors would receive 150 francs for every client they signed up, plus 30 francs per client to be used to comput-

erize their offices. To help reduce pharmaceutical costs, doctors would agree to include at least one generic drug in each prescription (or 10% of the total prescription).

References

Alfandarie, Elie and Françoise Monéger, ed. *La Protection sociale en cause.* Paris: Dalloz, 1997.

Barbier, Christophe. "Social: Juppé cherche la 3e voie." *L'Express* 23 Jan. 1997: 18-19.

Bezat, Mean-Michel. "L'inévitable réforme du système de santé." *Le Monde. Dossiers & Documents* (Feb. 1996): 1-8.

Bigaut, Christian. "La Sécurité sociale devient l'affaire du Parlement." *Regards sur l'actualité* 220 (April 1996): 3-11.

Borgetto, Michel. "Une réforme 'au forceps' ou le discours de la méthode." *La Protection sociale en cause.* Ed. Alfandarie (see reference) 686-709.

Bouffechoux, Thierry. *La Santé en France. Le Médecin, le malade et l'Etat.* Paris: Le Monde-Editions, 1997.

Bui, Doan. "Santé: Mais où est donc passé le carnet?" *Le Nouvel Observateur* 16 Jan. 1997: 17.

Catala, Christophe. "L'offre et la demande dans le domaine de la santé." *La Protection sociale en France* (see reference). 135-142.

Casteret, Anne-Marie. "Le carnet de santé mort-né." *L'Express* 5 June 1997: 64.

Chatagner, François. *La Protection sociale.* Paris: Le Monde-Editions, 1993.

Dubois, Louis. "La réforme de la médecine libérale: le statut des médecins." *La Protection sociale en cause.* Ed. Alfandarie (see reference). 743-755.

Gilson, Martine. "Budget: les recettes de Super-Jospin." *Le Nouvel Observateur* 23 July 1998: 26-27.

---. "Martine Aubry: les médecins avec moi!" *Le Nouvel Observateur* 15 July 1998: 26-28.

---. "Sécu: Martine prend des risques." *Le Nouvel Observateur* 24 Sept. 1998: 28.

Harichaux, Michèle. "Réformes de l'assurance maladie et protection des assurés." *La Protection sociale en cause.* Ed. Alfandarie (see reference). 842-852.

Lhaïk, Corinne. "CSG Opération danger." *L'Express* 18 Sept. 1997: 32-33.

---. "Retraites: le débat occulté." *L'Express* 15 May 1997: 74-75.

MacFarlan, Maitland and Howard Oxley. "La Réforme du secteur santé." *Tertiaire* 71 (March-April 1996): 35-40.

Maquart, Bruno. "Les régimes de retraite." *La Protection sociale en France* (see reference). 85-90.

Mital, Christine. "Ouf, la croissance revient!" *Le Nouvel Observateur* 19 Feb. 1998: 18.

Palier, Bruno and Giuliano Bonoli. "Le Modèle français." *Problèmes économiques. La Protection sociale. Handicap ou atout économique?* 2,493-2,494 (6-13 Nov. 1996): 30-33.

Pellet, Remi. "La protection des personnes à l'égard des traitements informatisés des données à caractère médical depuis les ordonnances du 24 avril 1966." *La Protection sociale en cause.* Ed. Alfandarie (see reference). 853-879.

Phillipon, Thierry and Natacha Tatu. "Français. Comment vos retraites ont été amputées." *Le Nouvel Observateur* 5 Nov. 1998: 18-20.

"Le Plan Juppé pour financer la Sécurité sociale." *Le Monde* 16 Nov. 1995, SA Le Monde-CEDROM-SNi Inc., 1987-1997.

Protection sociale en France (La). Paris: La Documentation Française, 1997.

"Réforme de la Sécurité sociale (La)." *Le Monde* 17 novembre 1995, SA Le Monde-CEDROM-SNi inc., 1987-1997.

Remy, Jacqueline. "Politique familiale: le changement de cap," *L'Express* 25 Sept. 1997: 34-35.

Stasse, François. "'Plan Juppé': les ordonnances sur la santé et la Sécurité sociale." *Regards sur l'actualité* 223 (July-August 1996): 17-23.

Viossat, Louis-Charles. "La Sécurité sociale." *La Protection sociale en France* (see reference). 59-68.

Von Maydell, Bernd. "L'Avenir de la Sécurité sociale au plan international." *Tertiaire* 66 (May-June 1995): 43-48.

5

La France dans l'Europe de l'an 2002, ou comment une France peut en cacher une autre

Claud DuVerlie
University of Maryland Baltimore County

En 1999, l'Europe aura connu son heure de vérité avec l'union économique et monétaire. L'introduction de la monnaie unique s'est faite sans accroc au 1er janvier 1999 et sa mise en circulation sous forme de coupures se fera au 1er janvier 2002[1]. L'avènement de l'euro, salué comme le grand événement historique de la fin de ce siècle, signifie que l'intégration européenne se poursuit.

Dans cet article, nous nous proposons de faire le point sur la construction de l'Union européenne (UE), d'en tracer les grandes perspectives et d'en analyser les effets sur la société française sous forme de changements, de résistances et de défis. Au rythme des transformations actuelles, il est clair que la France de l'an 2002 accusera de très profonds changements et présentera un tout nouveau visage, qui ressemblera très peu à la France (traditionnelle) de nos manuels scolaires. Pour mieux comprendre la métamorphose à laquelle nous sommes en train d'assister, retraçons brièvement la marche vers l'Union européenne et ses principaux objectifs tout en les replaçant dans leur contexte actuel.

Objectifs et perspectives de l'Union

Depuis sa création en 1957, l'Union européenne s'est extraordinairement développée tant sur le plan géographique — elle compte actuellement quinze Etats membres — que sur le plan politique et institutionnel. Ses traités fondateurs de 1957 ont été révisés trois fois:

l'Acte unique en 1987, le Traité sur l'Union européenne ou Traité de Maastricht en 1992 et le Traité d'Amstersdam en 1997. Et en dépit d'une histoire bien souvent tortueuse, l'Union européenne démarre d'un seul grand principe, d'une « idée simple » disait Jean Monnet selon laquelle « il n'y a d'avenir pour l'Europe que dans l'union » (Fontaine 65). Cette idée, élaborée en profession de foi européenne, vise:

> [...] une union sans cesse plus étroite entre les peuples de l'Europe, dans laquelle les décisions sont prises le plus près possible des citoyens. Telle est la *finalité* essentielle de l'Union européenne, fondée sur la notion d'un progrès économique et social équilibré et durable, sur l'affirmation de l'identité européenne dans le monde et sur l'instauration d'une citoyenneté européenne pour les ressortissants de ses pays membres *(Agenda 2000)*.

Pratiquement jusqu'à aujourd'hui, la France et l'Allemagne ont été les deux gros moteurs de cette construction qui s'est faite en grande partie au niveau des gouvernements et avec un minimun de consultation populaire. Le gros choc et grand réveil populaire en France ont eu lieu en 1992 lors du fameux traité de Maastricht et lorsqu'il est devenu clair à tous que l'avènement de la monnaie unique et la construction d'une politique étrangère européenne empiétaient aussi sur la « souveraineté nationale ». De l'Europe, conçue initialement comme un grand marché économique, on faisait un pas décisif vers une conception beaucoup plus fédéraliste. Malgré des résistances et une opposition toujours considérables, l'Union est une idée qui suit son chemin. Le Président de la République, Jacques Chirac, saisit toute occasion pour affirmer devant ses auditoires que, pour lui, l'Europe doit être un tout.

L'unification est un lent processus ponctué de quelques coups d'accélérateur comme celui du traité de Maastricht, ce formidable programme de relance de la construction européenne.

Traité de Maastricht (1992)

Ce traité, signé en 1992, comporte plusieurs volets dont les principaux sont: la mise en place d'une politique étrangère et de sécurité commune (PESC) susceptible de conduire le moment venu à une défense commune; l'établissement d'une citoyenneté européenne; le renforcement de la « cohésion », c'est-à-dire, de l'effort consenti pour moderniser, mettre à niveau les pays les moins riches de la Communauté économique européenne (CEE); et la coopération accrue en matière judiciaire et policière.

Le volet le plus remarqué par les citoyens français s'avèra être la mise en place progressive d'une Union économique et monétaire (UEM) qui permettrait à terme la réalisation du « marché unique ». Les principaux rouages de ce marché unique étaient la Banque centrale européenne (BCE) et la Banque européenne d'investissement (BEI); l'Institut monétaire européen (IME), créé le 1er janvier 1994, et la Monnaie unique au 1er janvier 1999 *(Nouvel Observateur:* 1-16).

Le choc et grand débat national qui s'ensuivit est dû au fait que François Mitterrand, alors Président, décida que l'adhésion des Français au Traité de Maastricht se ferait par référendum. On se souviendra de la campagne tumultueuse qui eut lieu autour de Maastricht. Le « oui » français à Maastricht, en septembre 1992, fut un « oui » bien modeste mais tout de même un « oui » — 51% de oui contre 49% de « non ». Ce résultat favorable à l'Union indique une grande coupure sociologique qui a fait dire à Philippe Séguin et Charles Pasqua que plus rien ne serait comme avant.

Rappelons encore que ce traité de Maastricht incorpore les dispositions de l'Accord de Schengen. En 1985, la Belgique, la France, le Luxembourg, les Pays-Bas, et la République Fédérale d'Allemagne (RFA) ont signé à Schengen un accord dans lequel ils s'engageaient à supprimer progressivement les contrôles à leurs frontières communes et à instaurer un régime de libre circulation pour toutes les personnes, ressortissants des Etats signataires, des autres Etats de la Communauté ou de pays tiers.

Les Douze s'engageaient à réaliser un « espace sans frontières », dans lequel la libre circulation des marchandises, des personnes, des services et des capitaux serait assurée. C'est un traité qui repose sur la distinction entre « frontières extérieures » et « frontières intérieures ». L'implémentation, prévue initialement pour le 1er janvier 1993, ne sera probablement pas terminée avant l'an 2000.

Le traité de Maastricht, signé le 7 février 1992, prévoyait dans l'Article N la convocation d'une nouvelle conférence intergouvernementale en 1996. Elle eut lieu en 1997. Entre temps, au 1er janvier 1995, l'Europe des Douze est devenue l'Europe des Quinze (avec l'inclusion de l'Autriche, de la Finlande et de la Suède) au terme du premier élargissement en dix ans. Ce sont donc quinze pays européens qui se réunirent à Amsterdam en juin 1997 pour délibérer sur un nouveau traité européen.

Le Traité d'Amsterdam (juin-octobre 1997)

Le Sommet d'Amsterdam de juin 1997 a réuni quinze chefs d'Etat et de gouvernement pour mettre au point le pacte de stabilité qui devait surveiller la mise en place de la monnaie unique. Le Traité d'Amsterdam visait quatre grands objectifs: placer l'emploi et le droit des citoyens au cœur de l'Union; supprimer les dernières entraves à la libre circulation des personnes et renforcer la sécurité; permettre à l'Europe de mieux faire entendre sa voix dans les affaires du monde; rendre plus efficace l'architecture institutionnelle de l'Union en vue du prochain élargissement (*Questions-réponses*: 1).

Son résultat concret est un texte politique de quelques feuillets, sous le titre de « Résolutions du Conseil sur la stabilité, la croissance et l'emploi », qui comporte deux volets: le premier porte sur le pacte de stabilité et de croissance, c'est-à-dire, le mécanisme de surveillance de l'euro. Ce pacte est accompagné d'une structure de coordination renforcée; on ne parle pas de gouvernement économique, les Allemands n'en voulaient pas, mais de pôle de coordination sur l'ensemble des politiques, et pas seulement budgétaires. Le deuxième volet porte sur les actions à mener avec la Banque Européenne d'Investissement (BEI). La BEI est bénéficiaire à hauteur de cinq milliards de francs; elle pourrait prêter dix fois plus dans de nouveaux domaines tels que la technologie, l'environnement, la santé, le logement, c'est-à-dire tous les secteurs où l'on peut créer des emplois. Elle pourrait aussi aider au financement de grands travaux toujours en attente.

Lors d'une seconde réunion à Amsterdam, le 20 octobre 1997, les quinze ministres des Affaires étrangères signèrent le traité conclu les 16 et 17 juin dans la même ville par les chefs d'Etat et de gouvernement de l'Union européenne. Il n'entrerait en vigueur qu'à l'issue des procédures de ratification qui allaient se dérouler dans les quinze pays, alors que la monnaie unique serait déjà lancée.

Sur un plan important, ce sommet d'Amsterdam aura été un échec car, à l'origine, il devait prévoir le fonctionnement d'une Union européenne comprenant plus de vingt membres. Mais la réforme institutionnelle qui s'imposait a été repoussée à plus tard.

Réforme institutionnelle

Si l'UE met tant de temps à se construire c'est qu'un grand nombre de décisions d'ordre communautaire doivent se faire à l'unanimité. La réforme fondamentale, attendue à Amsterdam, était de remplacer le vote à l'unanimité par une généralisation du vote à « majorité qualifiée » (71% des voix) au sein du Conseil des ministres, afin d'empêcher un seul pays de bloquer les décisions. Sans cette réforme institutionnelle, repoussée à plus tard, toutes les questions qui resteront soumises à l'unanimité dans une union à vingt-cinq seront bloquées. D'autres réformes attendues sont secondaires comme, par exemple, la réduction de la taille de la Commission européenne car elle peut être temporairement compensée en renforçant l'autorité de son président.

Parmi les éléments positifs de ce traité, on peut citer le chapitre sur l'emploi, la sécurité intérieure ou encore la politique étrangère. On a donné plus de pouvoir au Parlement européen et à la Cour de justice — ce qui devrait assurer une meilleure protection des libertés individuelles.

Le Traité d'Amsterdam en bref

Le Traité d'Amsterdam, qui remplace le traité de Maastricht de 1992, comporte un certain nombre de modifications ainsi que quelques dispositions nouvelles. En ce qui concerne les institutions, la repondération des voix entre petits et grands pays et la réduction du nombre de commissaires sont reportées au prochain élargissement. Le nombre des députés européens ne devra pas dépasser 700 (contre 626 auparavant), quel que soit le nombre d'Etats membres. Le vote à majorité qualifiée (71%) est un peu étendu. Le Parlement européen (PE) voit augmenter ses pouvoirs. Les décisions en matière de contrôles frontaliers, d'asile, d'immigration, restent à l'unanimité, au moins pour cinq ans. Mais la Cour de justice et le PE ont un droit de regard sur ces matières. Une dimension sociale est rajoutée à l'Union, avec un nouveau chapitre « Emploi » et l'intégration du protocole social de Maastricht. Des « coopérations renforcées » sont prévues entre les Etats membres, quand une majorité d'entre eux y sont prêts. En politique étrangère et en matière de sécurité, des stratégies communes seront définies à l'unanimité, avec le droit de veto national. Leur mise en œuvre sera votée à la majorité qualifiée. Le secrétaire général du Conseil des ministres représentera l'UE sur la scène mondiale *(Libération* 3 octobre 1997). Finalement, le sommet d'Amsterdam a prévu un Sommet extraordinaire pour traiter de l'emploi qui s'est tenu à Luxembourg en novembre 1997.

Elargissement

L'élargissement de l'Europe est à la fois une nécessité politique et une occasion unique selon une déclaration du Sommet de Madrid (décembre 1995). *L'Agenda 2000* de l'UE réaffirme l'objectif d'une Europe plus forte et plus large. Il y est dit, en particulier: « L'élargissement est un dessein historique pour l'Europe. C'est aussi une chance pour l'Europe: pour sa sécurité, pour son économie, pour sa culture, pour sa place dans le monde » *(Agenda 2000).* Cependant, en l'absence de réforme institutionnelle, tout élargissement paraît plus que problématique.

Jean-Claude Juncker, Président du Conseil européen, déclarait peu après Amsterdam:

> Avant tout nouvel élargissement de l'UE, j'aurais préféré un approfondissement plus important de l'UE, parce que je crois que l'union politique est nécessaire. Cela dit: je ne pense pas que le Traité d'Amsterdam sera le dernier: très vite, lorsque quatre ou cinq pays auront rejoint l'Union, on s'apercevra qu'il n'est pas possible de continuer comme cela et qu'il faut changer les règles du jeu institutionnel (Dauvergne 57)[2].

De l'Europe monétaire à l'Europe politique

Le grief principal de certains politiques (Philippe Séguin et Charles Pasqua, par exemple) à l'encontre de l'union monétaire est qu'elle entraîne une perte de souveraineté nationale pour la France. Mais de nombreux autres politiques avancent que, dans un contexte de forte interdépendance des économies et de liberté de mouvement des capitaux, la mise en oeuvre d'une politique monétaire autonome est devenue une illusion. De fait, avec le processus de l'union monétaire, la majorité des Etats-membres perdra une prérogative qu'elle ne pouvait plus exercer depuis longtemps. En gérant collectivement la politique monétaire de l'UEM, les banques partageront au contraire une souveraineté effective sur la gestion de l'une des plus fortes monnaies du monde. Et l'union monétaire ouvre la voie à l'union politique, à vocation fédérative, de l'Europe.

Il semblerait que les Quinze misent maintenant sur la monnaie unique pour faire progresser l'Europe. Mais est-il réaliste de reporter sur l'euro tous les espoirs de l'Europe car l'union monétaire ne saurait se substituer à l'union politique. Selon Jean-Claude Juncker:

> Dans un raisonnement idéal, on aurait dû réaliser l'union politique avant de se lancer dans la construction de l'Europe monétaire, parce que l'union monétaire ne va pas exister sans union politique. Mais nous savions que nous ne pourrions pas réussir cette union politique avant la fin du siècle, aussi avons-nous décidé de faire d'abord l'Union économique et monétaire. Faire le choix inverse, c'eût été renoncer à l'UEM — la dernière ambition de l'Europe d'ici la fin du siècle (Dauvergne 58).

Certains leaders européens comme Jean-Claude Juncker parient sur la monnaie unique pour donner un coup de fouet à l'Europe politique. Pour Juncker « c'est une sorte de loi de la nature: mettez en commun ce segment important de la souveraineté nationale qu'est la monnaie et vous n'échapperez pas aux conséquences qui en découlent ». En cas de choc économique, par exemple:

> [...] s'il existe une union monétaire, un gouvernement ne peut plus réagir par un ajustement monétaire (une dévaluation). Il sera donc très tenté de se lancer dans le dumping social, voire fiscal. Mais tout le monde réalisera alors rapidement qu'il n'est pas possible d'évacuer le problème de cette manière, et l'idée qu'il faut doter l'Union de tout un cortège de règles sociales minimales s'imposera (Dauvergne 57).

A la croisée des chemins

Toute la vie française autant celle des institutions que celle des particuliers est entrée dans une dynamique qui, tour à tour, peut prendre soit une dominante française soit une dominante européenne. La réglementation européenne se fait sentir dans de nombreux secteurs d'activité: agriculture, pêche, chasse, industries, banques, consommation, etc. Alors que l'influence de Bruxelles devient omniprésente, celle de l'Etat français se trouve progressivement restreinte par les réglements, les lois communautaires et les actions des institutions européennes.

D'autre part, le gouvernement français n'est plus l'interlocuteur privilégié des intérêts français à Bruxelles. De plus en plus de groupes d'intérêts sociaux français, y compris les autorités régionales, les compagnies et même les syndicats sont enclins à aller directement à Bruxelles plutôt que de s'appuyer sur l'Etat pour représenter leurs intérêts (conflits des routiers, Air France, Renault-Vilvorde). Les particuliers eux-mêmes commencent à utiliser les cours européennes de justice pour leurs différends avec les institutions françaises. Dans un nombre croissant de domaines la jurisprudence européenne prend le pas sur la justice française. Ainsi, en 1999, « La Cour européenne juge la France pour tortures » *(Libération* 19 mars 1999) en examinant la plainte d'un homme pour violences policières. Pour la première fois, l'Etat français risquait d'être condamné pour actes de « tortures », une accusation rarissime en droit européen, souligne *Libération*. De tels phénomènes montrent indubitablement combien l'autonomie de l'Etat a été réduite.

Le passage à l'euro vient de s'effectuer dans les meilleures conditions. Bien qu'il soit encore prématuré pour parler du succès de la monnaie unique, il est déjà clair que ses conséquences et son impact sur la vie quotidienne des Français est énorme et que l'euro sera un formidable catalyseur de changement. Rien que dans le domaine de la consommation, avec l'avènement de l'euro, les trois cents millions de consommateurs de la zone euro peuvent dès à présent comparer les prix sans se livrer à une difficile gymnastique de conversion, ce qui devrait pousser les entreprises à ajuster les prix vers le bas. Le consommateur n'hésitera pas à faire mille kilomètres pour faire un gros achat comme une automobile ou du matériel hi-fi *(France-Amérique* 7 janvier 1999).

La nouveauté est de fait une transparence économique totale qui s'applique aussi bien aux salaires, à l'imposition et aux régimes de taxation, au coût de la vie qu'aux bénéfices sociaux et aux coûts de la productivité. Pour les Français, c'est tout leur système de références qui vient de basculer et qui leur donne désormais une perspective « européenne » sur toutes leurs activités. Personne ne sait aujourd'hui les incidences réelles que va susciter cet « élargissement » de la perspective. A court terme, il va sans nul doute inciter les Français à plus de voyages dans l' « Euroland » pour des achats avantageux. Mais ira-t-il jusqu'à les convaincre de s'établir dans un pays de l'Union pour y poursuivre des études ou parce que les salaires y sont plus élevés? Ou encore, combien d'artisans et commerçants français iront s'établir dans un pays de la Communauté pour échapper à la trop lourde fiscalité française et venir accélérer le fameux mouvement de délocalisation? Il faudra attendre plusieurs années pour savoir comment les Français tireront exactement avantage des nouvelles possibilités de l'Europe et voir, dans quelle mesure, par exemple, ils seront prêts à accepter une offre d'emploi dans l'un des pays de l'Union.

Le lancement de l'euro vient relancer la construction européenne. Mais peut-on déjà entrevoir l'avènenenent d'une Europe politique? Il est encore trop tôt pour se prononcer. Malgré les dernières avancées, nous sommes seulement parvenus à une autre croisée des chemins et le choix de la direction à prendre se dégagera de la cacophonie politique de 1999 tant les opposants à l'Europe restent en force. Avant sa démission, Philippe Séguin, européen combien réticent, déclarait dans sa campagne pour les élections européennes que le Rassemblement pour la République (RPR) recherchait « non pas les Etats-Unis d'Europe mais l'Europe unie des Etats » *(Journal Télévisé,* France 2, 12 février 1999) sans élaborer pourtant sur ce que serait cette « Europe unie des Etats ». Un tel slogan indique sans doute que le projet européen reste indécis, voire volontairement ou stratégiquement diffus. Sa longue histoire reste profondément marquée par une progression saccadée qui conjugue les avancées avec les replis. C'est seulement dans la durée longue que la progression devient claire.

Ce mouvement de balancier rend les prévisions d'évolution particulièrement difficiles tant les perceptions diffèrent sur les transformations actuelles. D'un côté, des politiques de premier plan tels que Philippe de Villiers, Charles Pasqua, ou Jean-Pierre Chevènement s'effraient de l'abandon de souveraineté de la France et se voient déjà dans un Etat européen qui ne veut pas dire son nom. Pasqua ne perd aucune occasion pour sonner l'alarme: « Qu'on cesse de nous mentir. Dès que [le Traité d'Amsterdam] sera ratifié, nous aurons créé de toutes pièces un Etat en soi, qui bat monnaie à Francfort, fait la loi à Bruxelles, rend la justice à Luxembourg, laissant aux Etats subsidiaires la seule prérogative de lever l'impôt » (Bresson). Tout à l'opposé, Daniel Cohn-Bendit, député européen, tête de liste des Verts aux élections européennes, s'en prend à l'inertie française et demande à poursuivre l'unification européenne sans autre délai:

Et si, en attendant l'euro de 2002, nous nous lancions dans l'unification européenne par quelques chantiers volontaristes et ambitieux qui changeraient notre vie? [...] enfin, l'unification territoriale de l'Europe, celle-ci passant par l'adhésion des pays de l'autre côté du mur qui, comme les anciennes dictatures (Espagne, Portugal, Grèce) n'ont d'avenir démocratique, et nous avec, que dans l'Europe unie *(Le Monde* 4 février 1999).

Mais aussitôt Cohn-Bendit de s'inquiéter: « La nouvelle Europe serait-elle une illusion? L'Europe unie, unifiée par sa monnaie, une plaisanterie? Pas de grand dessein pour les Européens? Bref, retour à la case départ » *(Le Monde* 4 février 1999). C'est montrer à quel point nous nous trouvons à la croisée des chemins et que, même dans cet après-euro, la direction future est loin d'être assurée. Un éditorial du *Monde* (16 janvier 1999) discerne quatre scénarios possibles de l'après-euro: 1) « le modèle de la séparation » selon lequel l'économique serait disjoint de l'Europe; 2) « le modèle libéral pris au mot » qui verrait la France suivre le modèle effréné du libéralisme américain;   3) « le retour de la souveraineté nationale » grâce aux marges de manœuvre aménagées par l'euro; et 4) « le modèle fédéraliste » que laisse entrevoir l'entrée de la monnaie unique. Un éventail de possibilités aussi ouvert montre que rien n'est définitivement joué, même à ce stade. Autrement dit, « la marche obligée vers le fédéralisme, que certains dénoncent en raison de son caractère subreptice, n'a donc rien d'inéluctable » *(Le Monde* 16 janvier 1999).

Ni le repli frileux du « retour à la souveraineté » ni « une Europe fédérale » ne sont à exclure pour l'instant. Les facteurs qui influeront sur la marche future de la construction européenne sont aussi multiples que complexes et seront sans aucun doute moins l'émanation de la volonté des partis politiques que de la nécessité économique et du sentiment populaire. Autrement dit, le destin de l'Union sera désormais beaucoup plus fonction de l'évolution des mentalités, surtout dans la classe politique. Or s'il existe toujours en France des îlots de résistance assez farouches à l'Union tels que les chasseurs, les pêcheurs ou les agriculteurs, d'autres secteurs en nombre toujours croissant se rallient à l'Union sous l'effet de puissants avantages fiscaux ou économiques.

La grande question reste: « jusqu'où l'intégration? Et à quelle vitesse? » La formule de Philippe Séguin « une Europe unie des Etats » est un oxymoron qui caractérise assez l'indécision du projet politique. Si l'on rappelle que Philippe Séguin, antieuropéen qui vota « non » à Maastricht en 1992, était avant sa démission en 1999 chef de liste du RPR aux élections européennes, on ne prendra que mieux conscience de la marche à reculons vers l'Union et de la distance entre le discours et le pragmatisme politique. Jean Monnet ne cessait de répéter ce qui était pour lui une vérité: « Nous n'avons pas le choix: ce sera ça ou l'effacement » (Fontaine 65). Peu étonnant alors que la volonté politique de construction de l'Union se trouve aussi obscurcie par la dénégation des politiques. Les politiques français qui participent à la construction de l'Europe sont amenés bien souvent à le masquer, sans doute à des fins électorales.

Entre temps, ce qui est objectif, c'est que les institutions européennes pèsent de plus en plus dans la vie des Français. A l'euro qui constitue la plus grande part de souveraineté cédée à ce jour à l'Europe viennent s'ajouter une multitude d'autres parcelles de souveraineté désormais transférées à Bruxelles. En plus des secteurs économiques classiques — agriculture, pêche, industries, énergie, transports, c'est l'individu lui-même qui peut aujourd'hui chercher recours contre les institutions françaises directement devant les diverses juridictions européennes. Le droit communautaire vient modifier directement, sans ratification législative nationale, l'ordre juridique interne de l'Etat; les citoyens peuvent invoquer des recours juridictionnels externes contre les lois de leur pays; des institutions nationales tirent certaines de leurs compétences d'un pouvoir qui leur est extérieur. Maintenant, l'intégration monétaire à plusieurs vitesses et la politique européenne de sécurité multiplieront ces traits pluralistes, irréconciliables avec le modèle de l'Etat-nation de la tradition classique.

La construction européenne se double d'un démantèlement lent et pragmatique de l'architecture nationale-étatiste. C'est la signification du mot « nation » qui est en train de changer. A l'opposé du modèle uniforme, centralisé et hiérarchisé de l'Etat-nation, émerge un nouveau modèle de la France fondé sur un réseau multiple, diversifié et de plus en plus décentré de pouvoirs et de droits qui, par la même occasion, construisent graduellement une nouvelle définition de l'identité française. Ne pouvant plus fermer les yeux sur ce qui est devenu une évidence, les politiques se trouvent désormais obligés d'aborder ouvertement la question pour tenter d' « articuler Europe et nation ». Le Parti socialiste (PS) au pouvoir à la fin du XXe siècle estime qu'il doit « politiser l'Europe » et, dans un document préparatoire à sa convention « nation-Europe » de mars 1999, veut faire du « besoin de plus d'Europe » une réponse à la « crise de l'appartenance » à la nation en prônant une « Fédération d'Etats-Nations ». Le texte désavoue « une vision nostalgique de la souveraineté nationale » et voit dans la reprise de la notion de fédération d'Etats-nations, déjà adoptée en avril 1996, une synthèse entre le « fédéralisme nécessaire » et le respect des « compétences essentielles de la nation ». Cette notion lui paraît ouvrir la voie, pour le XXIᵉ siècle, au renforcement d'un « vouloir-vivre ensemble » (Noblecourt 3 février 1999). Le document politique du PS innove en ce qu'il reconnaît on ne peut plus clairement le nouveau modèle de souveraineté française désormais partagée entre des instances fédérales et nationales et accompagnée d'un résultant décentrement des pouvoirs et des droits. La mission essentielle pour les politiques se trouve maintenant déplacée vers la préservation d'un équilibre entre ces deux polarités. Dans cette nouvelle configuration, il reviendra surtout à l'Etat-nation le rôle d'encourager et de coordonner plutôt que de diriger et de contrôler (Kassim 176) et un rôle fondamental d'intégration dans le cadre de la citoyenneté et de la solidarité, entre les générations, entre les territoires. Au dire des dirigeants du PS, « Nous avons besoin de plus d'Europe pour préserver la fonction d'intégration que remplissent les Etats nationaux » *(Le Monde* 3 février 1999).

La campagne et les élections européennes de juin 1999 furent un succès pour le PS et les partis du gouvernement. Les résultats — en dépit du taux record d'abstention des Français — s'avèrent favorables à la construction européenne. D'une part, les eurosceptiques, nationaux républicains passionément opposés à la construction européenne, ont perdu et sont en train de devenir minoritaires dans le pays. D'autre part, on note aussi un important changement d'attitude de la classe politique française: les leaders nationaux qui, dans le passé, répugnaient à siéger à Strasbourg, ont cette fois promis d'occuper leur siège car le Parlement européen est désormais investi, par les traités de Maastricht et surtout d'Amsterdam, de pouvoirs réels. Serge July écrit dans *Le Monde:* « L'Europe accélère: il importe de se précipiter à Strasbourg, d'investir les commissions, d'influer sur les groupes. L'Europe se fait non seulement au Conseil européen mais aussi à Strasbourg » (July).

Conclusion

L'avenir de l'Europe se dessinera dans les réponses à toute une série de questions prenant en compte l'élargissement annoncé de l'Union: quelles seront les finalités d'une Europe de trente Etats-membres? Comment marchera une Europe à trente? Les institutions et les mécanismes actuels pourront-ils être adaptés à ce changement? A combien de pays l'euro est-il extensible...? Ces questions se trouvent au cœur d'un rapport que Jacques Attali a remis à Hubert Védrine, ministre des Affaires étrangères, en juillet 1999. Attali se place non pas dans la perspective d'une Union à trente, généralement retenue dans les réflexions actuelles, mais dans celle d'une Europe qui, à l'échéance 2020, compterait trente-cinq, voire quarante membres. Cette extension aux confins du continent est, selon lui, inéluctable car de l'intérêt de tous. Le pire, souligne Attali, serait de ne rien faire et de subir:

> La France, recommande-t-il, devrait donc annoncer prochainement, dans un vaste élan de générosité continentale et de cohérence stratégique, son intention d'assumer l'inévitable élargissement de l'Union européenne à 35 ou même 40, de promouvoir chaleureusement ce qu'elle ne peut plus éviter, tout en proposant aux Quinze de réformer leurs institutions pour s'y préparer (Attali).

Les recommandations de Jacques Attali, sans doute encore trop hardies pour les politiques, confirment toutefois « l'accélération de l'Europe ».

Notes

[1] L'ancêtre de l'euro, l'ECU (European Currency Unit) est devenu l'unité de compte européenne, le 13 mars 1979. L'euro a remplacé l'écu en 1996: les Allemands ont avancé le fait que l'écu s'était affaibli face au dollar et au yen et qu'il fallait redorer le blason de la monnaie unique européenne.

[2] Il y a au moins onze pays de l'Europe de l'Est, plus l'Ile de Chypre au large de la Turquie dont on considère la candidature à l'UE. Ces pays candidats ont été divisés en deux groupes. Le premier comprend la Pologne, la Hongrie, la République Tchèque, l'Estonie, la Slovénie et Chypre. Mais ces sept pays ne seraient pas admis dans l'UE avant l'an 2003 au plus tôt. Dans un deuxième groupe, on trouve la Roumanie, la Bulgarie, la Slovaquie, la Lettonie et la Lituanie; ces cinq pays sont moins bien préparés

économiquement et politiquement pour faire partie de l'UE. Mais, en attendant, ils sont invités à des stratégies de pré-adhésion, notamment à former des partenariats avec l'UE.

Références

[Les articles des quotidiens *Le Monde, Libération,* et *France-Amérique* proviennent de leurs sites Internet respectifs et ne comportent donc pas de pagination: *Le Monde* <http://www.lemonde.fr/>, *Libération* <http://www.liberation.fr/> et *France-Amérique* <http://www.franceamerique.com>]

Agenda 2000: pour une Union plus forte et plus large. Strasbourg/Bruxelles 16 juillet 1997. <http://europa.eu.int/comm/agenda2000/overview/fr/>.

Attali, Jacques. *Rapport au ministre des Affaires étrangères. Europe 2020: Pour une Union plurielle,* <http://attali.com.Rapports%20sur%20l'UE.html>, juillet 1999.

Barnier, Michel. « Il faut parler de la France et de l'Europe en même temps ». *Le Monde* 19 janvier 1999.

Beuve-Méry, Hubert. « Joschka Fisher vient en aide à Daniel Cohn-Bendit ». *Le Monde* 2 mars 1999.

Bresson, Gilles. « Le MDC fait un triomphe à Pasqua l'antieuropéen ». *Libération* 19 novembre 1999.

Chirac, Jacques. « Chirac: n'ayez pas peur de l'Europe » (conférence de presse). *Libération* 17 avril 1998.

Cohn-Bendit, Daniel. « Changer la France pour construire l'Europe » (Point de vue). *Le Monde* 3 février 1999.

Bresson, Henri (de). "Les Quinze trouvent un compromis sur le financement de l'Union." *Le Monde* 27 mars 1999.

Dauvergne, Alain. « L'Euro, aiguillon de l'Europe politique ». *Le Point* 6 septembre 1997: 56-58.

Duhamel, Alain. « La Querelle des « souverainistes ». *Le Point* 15 avril 1998: 58.

« Davantage d'Europe « pour préserver la fonction d'intégration » des Etats ». Editorial. *Le Monde* 3 février 1999.

Flynn, Gregory, ed. *Remaking the Hexagon: the New France in the New Europe.* Boulder: Westview Press, 1995.

Fontaine, François. « Jean Monnet: l'Europe, cette idée simple ». *L'Express* 2 décembre 1988: 65-71.

Guigou, Elizabeth. « L'Europe à la croisée des chemins ». *The French Review* 65 (1992): 869-873.

Hartmann, Peter. « L'Agenda 2000, épreuve de vérité pour l'Union Européenne ». *Le Monde* 24 mars 1999.

July, Serge. « L'accélération de l'Europe » (Editorial). *Le Monde* 12-13 juin 1999.

Kassim, Hussein. « French Autonomy and the European Union ». *Modern & Contemporary France* vol. 5 no. 2 (May 1997): 167-180.

Krause, Joseph. « La France face à la construction européenne ». *Contemporary French Civilization* vol. XVII, no. 1 (Winter/ Spring 1993): 1-17.

Lemaître, Philippe. « Le Débat sur la construction européenne peut être relancé ». *Le Monde* 27 mars 1999.

« Les Consommateurs européens peuvent désormais comparer les prix ». *France-Amérique* 7 janvier 1999.

« Les quatre scénarios de l'après-euro ». Editorial. *Le Monde* 16 janvier 1999.

« Les Quinze ont failli à leur devoir. Le Contenu du traité ». *Libération* 3 octobre 1997.

Noblecourt, Michel. « Le Parti socialiste veut « faire l'Europe » sans « défaire la France ». *Le Monde* 17 janvier 1999.

---. « Le PS à la recherche d'une position équilibrée sur la construction européenne ». *Le Monde* 3 février 1999.

Newhouse, John. *Europe Adrift*. New York: Pantheon Books, 1997.

Pasqua, Charles. « Non à l'euroland, oui à l'Europe ». (Point de vue). *Le Monde* 19 janvier 1999.

Questions-réponses sur le traité d'Amsterdam. Commission Européenne. Direction générale X.

« Archives prioritaires d'information ». Bruxelles, 1997.

« Le Traité de Maastricht. Principaux extraits ». *Le Nouvel Observateur* 17 juin 1992: 1-16.

Union Européenne (L'). *Les Traités de Rome et de Maastricht*. Paris: La Documentation Française, 1992.

Vital-Duvand, Brigitte. « La Cour Européenne juge la France pour torture ». *Libération* 19 mars 1999.

II. Social issues - La vie sociale

6

Les mutations de la famille

Alain Kimmel
Centre international d'études pédagogiques

Depuis environ vingt-cinq ans, l'institution familiale a subi de profondes transformations. Le mariage et la natalité sont en déclin, le divorce et le concubinage sont en progression constante, la famille traditionnelle (« nucléaire ») éclate, phénomènes qui entraînent l'émergence de nouvelles formes de familles, « monoparentales » ou « recomposées ». Pour faire face à ces mutations, les pouvoirs publics prévoient d'adapter la politique familiale aux nouveaux modes de vie, en envisageant diverses mesures dont l'octroi d'un cadre juridique plus particulièrement destiné aux couples homosexuels.

Au lendemain de la Seconde Guerre mondiale, les mariages et les naissances « explosent »: en 1947, on enregistre 423 000 unions, contre moins de 300 000 en 1939. 90% de la population se marient, 10% divorcent et il naît 2,5 enfants par femme. Le modèle dominant — la famille type — qui s'établit alors est celui d'un couple tôt marié et ayant donné rapidement naissance à au moins deux enfants. Cette « famille nucléaire » va, dans l'ensemble, demeurer stable jusqu'au début des années 70.

Régression du mariage et progression du divorce

Pour le mariage, la rupture peut être datée de 1972, mais elle ne fait que suivre un mouvement amorcé dès 1965 aux Etats-Unis et en Scandinavie. Cette année-là, on dénombre encore 416 000 unions mais, à partir de ce moment, c'est un long déclin qui commence pour atteindre, en 1994, le plancher de 254 000 (chiffre le plus faible du siècle en temps de paix). Depuis, on a enregistré une stabilisation, voire même une certaine remontée

(284 000 mariages en 1997), mais le taux de nuptialité (c'est-à-dire le rapport entre le nombre annuel de mariages et le nombre d'habitants) qui, à partir du XVIIIe siècle, s'était stabilisé entre 7 et 8 mariages pour 1 000 habitants, est tombé à moins de 5 en cette fin de siècle (compte tenu des remariages d'hommes ou de femmes divorcés). D'où la notion de « démariage » forgée par la sociologue Irène Théry. Dans le même temps (mais peut-être est-ce une des causes premières de ce phénomène?), on assiste à l'effondrement des mariages religieux catholiques. De 1973 à 1989, leur nombre a diminué de plus de la moitié, passant de 300 000 à 145 000. En termes de comportements sexuels, on constate que les croyants obéissent de moins en moins aux prescriptions de l'Eglise: 75% des couples ont recours aux moyens contraceptifs chimiques et 21% sont divorcés.

L'âge moyen du mariage a également connu d'importantes variations: en 1972, il était de 24,5 ans pour les hommes et de 22,4 ans pour les femmes; en 1980, il passe respectivement à 26,1 et 23; en 1990 à 27 et 25; à la fin des années 90, il se situe à près de 30 ans pour les hommes et plus de 28 ans pour les femmes. Désormais, seulement 7% des jeunes mariés ont moins de 21 ans (36% en 1972) et, au total, un couple sur huit n'est pas marié contre un sur trente-cinq en 1970.

Le divorce a été institué en 1792 (on dénombrait, l'année suivante, un divorce pour trois mariages), aboli en 1816 à la suite de la proclamation du catholicisme comme religion d'Etat (mais la séparation de corps reste admise), puis rétabli en 1884. Jusqu'en 1974, il demeure un « divorce-sanction »: le mariage ne peut être « cassé » que s'il est avéré que l'un des conjoints a commis une faute grave. Ce sont alors les tribunaux qui doivent déterminer la culpabilité de l'un ou de l'autre, décider, par exemple, de confier le ou les enfants à celui qui a obtenu le divorce « à son bénéfice » et fixer le montant de la « pension alimentaire » que le mari devra verser à son épouse.

Avec la loi du 11 juillet 1975, le divorce devient plus facile. L'arbitrage est rendu par un « juge des affaires matrimoniales ». Le divorce pour faute est maintenu et représente actuellement environ 43% des cas, mais on admet désormais deux autres types de divorce. Le divorce par consentement mutuel ou « requête conjointe » se fait soit à la demande des deux époux qui n'ont pas alors à justifier de leur décision (42% des cas), soit à la demande de l'un des époux et avec l'accord de l'autre (13%.). On reconnaît également le divorce résultant d'une rupture de la vie commune de plus de six ans (1,5%). Dans ce cas, la séparation peut être prononcée à la demande de l'un des conjoints contre la volonté de l'autre.

Désormais, l'enfant n'étant plus *de jure* attribué à celui qui a obtenu le divorce à son bénéfice, il est presque systématiquement confié à la mère (85 à 90% des cas); ce qui est de plus en plus critiqué, car en contradiction avec une législation qui pose le principe de l'égalité de l'homme et de la femme.

Au début du siècle, on comptait 10 000 divorces et ce nombre ne va cesser d'augmenter, passant de 30 000 en 1950 à 60 000 en 1975, 107 000 en 1985 et environ 120 000 en 1997. En d'autres termes, cela représente aujourd'hui plus d'un divorce pour trois mariages et un sur deux à Paris. Sensiblement plus fréquent, le divorce se produit également de plus en plus tôt, généralement après deux à cinq ans de vie commune contre sept à huit en 1972 et trois à cinq en 1981. Contrairement à ce qui se passait naguère, la présence d'enfants n'est plus un obstacle au divorce: la probabilité de divorcer n'est plus liée à la composition de la famille. Très répandu à Paris, le divorce l'est également dans les grandes villes, parmi les classes moyennes, chez les jeunes couples ou ceux qui ont eu leur premier enfant avant le mariage. Mais, de fait, il progresse dans tous les milieux sociaux, parmi toutes les classes d'âge et à l'issue de mariages de durée très variable. L'accroissement des divorces a bien entendu pour conséquence l'augmentation du nombre d'enfants de divorcés: ils sont estimés actuellement à environ 1,5 million, ce qui correspond à deux classes d'âge. Un million d'entre eux vivent chez un beau-parent et environ 500 000 avec des demi-frères ou demi-soeurs.

Essor du concubinage et affaiblissement du couple

En 1962, on estimait à environ 300 000 le nombre de couples vivant en concubinage, ils seraient aujourd'hui 4,2 millions, soit environ 14% des couples. Dans la génération des 20-49 ans, environ un homme et une femme sur deux vivent désormais en union libre; ils n'étaient encore qu'un sur trois en 1986. Ces chiffres constituent la proportion la plus forte en Europe après le Danemark. Ce phénomène, qu'on a également appelé « cohabitation hors mariage » ou « mariage à l'essai », n'est certes pas nouveau, mais il est désormais durable et loin d'être seulement une anticipation ou une préparation au mariage, il constitue un autre choix de vie. Précédée,

au début des années 70, par la « cohabitation juvénile » qui n'était qu'une
« étape transitoire », la « cohabitation adulte » est devenue « le principal
mode d'entrée dans la vie du couple »[1]. Certes, bon nombre de couples
d'abord « cohabitants » se marient souvent au bout de quelques années,
mais entre 1970 et 1998 on est passé de 20% à 87% pour la cohabitation
avant mariage. Le mariage ne signifie donc plus alors constitution d'un
couple, mais « institutionnalisation », légalisation d'un état de fait. Si pendant un certain nombre d'années, compte tenu de la diminution des mariages et de l'accroissement du concubinage, le nombre de couples est resté à
peu près stable, leur proportion n'a cessé de baisser depuis 1982, qu'ils
soient mariés ou non. Pour les hommes de 25 ans, elle est passée de 55% à
39% et, pour les femmes, de 71% à 58%. Dorénavant, après une rupture
(divorce ou séparation), seulement 23% des hommes et 17% des femmes
de 35-39 ans se remarient ou s'engagent dans un nouveau couple. Comme
l'avait souligné, il y a déjà dix ans, le démographe Gérard-François
Dumont: « Il n'y a pas de vase communicant entre la montée de l'union
libre et la baisse des mariages. Il y a diminution de la vie du couple,
globalement »[2].

Il faut également mentionner l'existence d'un troisième type de
couple: celui que les sociologues appellent « semi-cohabitants » ou
« couples à distance ». Il s'agit de couples dûment constitués, mais qui ont
choisi de vivre séparément. Ils ont été recensés à partir de 1988 et représentent aujourd'hui officiellement 5,8 millions de « célibataires » et 5%
des couples.

Déclin de la natalité

A l'instar des mariages, les naissances ont sensiblement diminué
depuis une vingtaine d'années. Jusqu'à la fin des années 60, environ
850 000 enfants naissaient chaque année, soit un indice de fécondité de 2,1,
c'est-à-dire le seuil indispensable pour assurer le remplacement des générations. De 2,9% en 1964, il est tombé à 1,8 au cours des années 70, puis
s'est stabilisé à ce niveau dans les années 80, avant de rechuter à partir des
années 90 pour atteindre 1,6 en 1994 (708 000 naissances). Ces chiffres
correspondent à un taux de natalité d'environ 12 naissances pour 1 000
habitants. Cette situation a conduit certains à proclamer la démographie
française « en danger ». Ainsi, en 1993, une députée RPR du Nord,

Colette Codaccioni, dans un rapport remis au Premier ministre, Edouard Balladur, écrivait : « La France n'a plus d'enfants. La France se meurt. La France n'a plus d'avenir ». Dans le même sens, un certain nombre de personnalités d'horizons idéologiques divers lançaient un « SOS jeunesse, appel pour sauver l'avenir ». Ce texte, qui agite le spectre d'une France suicidaire par dénatalité, affirme que « négliger la politique familiale ne fera qu'aggraver une crise économique et sociale qui risque de devenir mortelle ».

Que l'on partage ou non ce pessimisme, force est de constater que l'indice actuel de fécondité est le plus bas que la France ait connu depuis la Première Guerre mondiale, même s'il est, en 1997, remonté à 1,7, ce qui place la France au troisième rang en Europe, après l'Irlande et la Suède. On observe par ailleurs que les femmes deviennent mères de plus en plus tardivement: en 1980, les femmes de moins de 25 ans donnaient naissance à 37% des enfants et celles de 30 ans ou plus à 26%; actuellement, la proportion est inverse: les premières mettent au monde environ 20% des enfants et les secondes 40%. Désormais, l'âge moyen de la maternité est de 28,7 ans contre 26,8 ans en 1980.

Si le nombre global des naissances a régulièrement régressé depuis vingt-cinq ans, celui des naissances « hors mariage » (on disait naguère « illégitimes ») est en hausse constante, en raison de l'accroissement du concubinage. En 1998, elles représentaient environ 40% de l'ensemble des naissances, contre 11% en 1980 et 22% en 1986. Avec ce chiffre, la France est sur le même plan que les pays scandinaves et l'Angleterre, mais dépasse largement l'Allemagne (10,5%), l'Espagne (9,7%) ou l'Italie (6,7%). Il faut signaler que ces naissances hors mariage ne sont pas des naissances « hors couple ». Le taux de naissances non reconnues par le père demeure stable entre 3% et 4%.

Ce déclin de la natalité a pour corollaire le vieillissement de la population: sur environ 60 millions d'habitants, la part des jeunes de moins de 20 ans n'est plus actuellement que de 26 % contre plus de 28% en 1988, alors que, dans la même période, celle des personnes de 65 ans et plus est passée de 13,5% à 15%. Pour la première fois de son histoire, la France comprend davantage de personnes âgées d'au moins 60 ans que d'enfants de moins de 15 ans.

Familles monoparentales, « recomposées » et autres

Outre le vieillissement, les différents changements qui viennent d'être évoqués ont également eu pour conséquences la formation de nouveaux types de famille définies comme « monoparentales » et « recomposées ». On compte actuellement environ 1,8 millions de familles monoparentales, soit une famille sur huit, contre 700 000 en 1970. En ce qui concerne les enfants, cela revient à dire que 15% des moins de 19 ans (2 millions) vivent avec un seul de leurs parents. Dans 85% des cas, le chef de famille est une femme (on parle alors de famille « matrifocale »), âgée de moins de 40 ans pour 44% d'entre elles (68,5% ont entre 30 et 49 ans). La majorité de ces femmes sont divorcées (environ 43%), séparées (17%), célibataires (25%) ou veuves (15%). 82% sont actives (contre 68% de celles qui vivent en couple) et 80% perçoivent des prestations familiales et des allocations de logement. Parmi les pères de familles monoparentales, 43% ont entre 40 et 49 ans. Dans deux tiers des cas, la monoparentalité survient après une période de mariage interrompue par un divorce, une séparation ou un décès. C'est dans les villes, notamment à Paris, que l'on trouve la majorité de ces familles.

La multiplication des divorces, des séparations, des remariages ou des reconstitutions de couples a entraîné la formation de familles dites « recomposées ». Ce nouveau type de famille, dans laquelle « un couple élève un ou plusieurs enfants qui ne sont pas de lui »[3] a été identifié par une équipe de sociologues et de démographes qui ont publié les résultats de leurs travaux dans un ouvrage intitulé *Les recompositions familiales aujourd'hui*. Les auteurs dénombrent alors 660 000 de ces familles, dont 332 000 comprennent des enfants du couple observé et des enfants d'une précédente union et 329 000 qui ne comportent aucun enfant du couple témoin. Au sein de cette nouvelle structure cohabitent en une « tribu composite » 1,5 million de demi-frères et de demi-soeurs de moins de 25 ans, des pères et des belles-mères, des mères et des beaux-pères. Selon certains spécialistes, il existerait ainsi quelque vingt-six « compositions » familiales, selon les causes de rupture du couple d'origine (divorce, séparation, décès), les formes de « recomposition » (mariage, remariage, concubinage), les modes de garde des enfants, l'attitude du « nouveau » parent, etc. Aujourd'hui, on estime à environ un million le nombre de ces familles et à plus de deux millions le nombre d'enfants de moins de 25 ans qu'elles abritent. Autrement dit, les familles recomposées comprennent en moyenne plus d'enfants (2,2) que les familles « classiques ». Qu'on les appelle « nucléaires » ou « conjugales », celles-ci ne représentent plus dorénavant qu'un tiers des foyers fiscaux.

Vers de nouvelles formes d'union?

C'est à l'occasion de la conférence annuelle sur la famille qui s'est tenue à Paris en juin 1998, sous la présidence du Premier ministre, Lionel Jospin, que plusieurs experts ont remis les rapports qui leur avaient été commandés sur l'ensemble des problèmes juridiques, économiques et sociaux qui intéressent ce domaine. Il s'agissait notamment de tenter d'apporter des réponses à un certain nombre de questions concernant le statut de l'union libre par rapport à celui du mariage, la possibilité de divorcer sans avoir recours au juge, la protection légale à accorder aux couples homosexuels, la préservation de l'enfant et de sa relation avec ses deux parents séparés.

Préalablement à cette manifestation, plusieurs propositions de loi ou projets concernant les modalités de vie commune et le statut juridique des couples non mariés (frères et sœurs, concubins hétérosexuels et homosexuels...) avaient été déposés à l'Assemblée nationale ou présentés dans des rapports au cours des années et des mois précédents. Il y eut d'abord, en novembre 1992, une proposition de loi émanant de huit députés socialistes et visant à créer un contrat d'union civile (CUC) pour deux personnes non mariées, passé devant un officier d'état civil, le co-contractant étant assimilé au conjoint pour les successions et le droit du travail. Cette proposition de loi n'a pas été discutée. Au printemps 1995, c'est l'association AIDES de lutte contre le Sida qui prépare un nouveau projet, le Contrat de vie sociale (CVS), analogue au précédent mais comportant notamment de nouveaux droits sociaux. En octobre de la même année, la fédération nationale AIDES et un Collectif pour le CUS proposent, sur le même modèle, un Contrat d'union sociale (CUS), que ne pourraient cependant souscrire ni les ascendants-descendants, ni les frères et sœurs. Cette nouvelle formule sera soutenue, quelques mois plus tard, à l'occasion de la *Lesbian and Gay Pride* du 22 juin, par quinze personnalités politiques. Parmi elles, Martine Aubry, Elizabeth Guigou, Bernard Kouchner et

Catherine Trautmann, futurs ministres du gouvernement Jospin, un an plus tard, signent dans *Le Monde* un appel en faveur du CUS.

En janvier 1997, les députés socialistes déposent une proposition de loi relative au CUS. Il ne pourrait notamment être accordé aux fratries et aux couples mariés et devrait faire l'objet d'une déclaration conjointe devant un officier d'état civil. En juillet de la même année, d'autres députés, appartenant à « la gauche plurielle », déposent une nouvelle proposition de loi instituant un Contrat d'union civile et sociale (CUCS). Elle reprend les dispositions du CUS mais en l'ouvrant aux frères et sœurs. En avril 1998, un projet de Pacte civil de solidarité (PACS) est remis à la commission des lois de l'Assemblée nationale. Au même moment, le ministère de la Justice rend public le rapport rédigé par le professeur de droit, Jean Hauser, qui propose la création d'un Pacte d'intérêt commun (PIC) concernant deux personnes — frères et sœurs, personnes déjà mariées, couples hétérosexuels ou homosexuels — décidant d'organiser tout ou partie de leurs relations pécuniaires et patrimoniales en vue d'assurer leur vie commune. Outre des dispositions générales (les contractants ne sont pas obligés de passer devant un notaire ou un maire, ils peuvent rompre par décision conjointe ou à l'initiative de l'un d'eux...), le PIC entraîne un certain nombre de conséquences.   Fiscales d'abord: par exemple, les signataires constituent un foyer fiscal soumis à une imposition commune, avec un nombre de parts équivalent à celui d'un couple marié dans la même situation.   Sociales ensuite: un des deux contractants à la charge de l'autre assuré-social pourrait devenir son ayant-droit pour les prestations en nature des asssurances maladie, maternité et invalidité, sans condition de durée du pacte...   Enfin, l'adoption serait rendue possible pour les concubins hétérosexuels et non plus pour les seuls couples mariés depuis plus de deux ans.

Lors de sa présentation à l'Assemblée nationale, en octobre 1998, le projet de loi sur le PACS a d'abord été rejeté, avant d'être réexaminé puis repoussé à juin 1999, à l'issue de débats souvent houleux.   La probable officialisation de ce que d'aucuns ont appelé un « mariage gay » et d'autres un « mariage du troisième type » a également suscité de vives polémiques chez certains intellectuels et parmi les responsables des principales religions, tous plus ou moins violemment opposés à ce projet, considéré comme une véritable « révolution sociale ». Le PACS a finalement été adopté en octobre 1999.

Au cours de l'année 1998, quatre rapports sur les questions familiales ont donc été remis au gouvernement. Le premier, intitulé *Couple, filiation, et parenté aujourd'hui. Le droit face aux mutations de la famille et de la vie privée* et rédigé par Irène Théry, sociologue et juriste, directrice d'études à l'Ecole des hautes études en sciences sociales, formule 135 propositions. Elles impliquent notamment une profonde réforme du Code civil qui, selon l'auteur, n'est plus adapté à l'état actuel des mentalités et des mœurs. Elle envisage donc de le modifier dans trois directions: le couple, la filiation, les successions. En premier lieu, elle estime qu'il faut d'abord reconnaître la diversité des couples et la valeur croissante accordée à la liberté individuelle dans le mariage comme dans le concubinage. Elle préconise ainsi d'ajouter une cinquième procédure de divorce aux quatre déjà existantes, un divorce sur simple déclaration commune sans intervention d'un juge ou d'un avocat. Elle suggère ensuite d'aligner le régime des concubins avec enfants sur celui des couples mariés avec enfants et d'accorder aux couples homosexuels des droits sociaux et fiscaux. En ce qui concerne la filiation, elle propose de mettre fin à la différence de traitement entre enfants légitimes et enfants naturels, d'élargir les posssibilités d'adoption aux concubins homosexuels, de favoriser le principe de « coparentalité » dans les familles recomposées et de supprimer l'accouchement sous X[3]. Enfin, pour les successions, elle se prononce en faveur d'une réforme « de fond en comble » du droit en la matière, celui-ci n'ayant pratiquement pas changé depuis 1804. Elle dénonce en particulier les difficultés que rencontrent beaucoup de couples pour connaître les moyens de protéger le conjoint survivant, l'imposition qui frappe les concubins en cas de décès et l'inégalité des droits des enfants du fait de la naissance. Les « mutations anthropologiques » de la famille ainsi constatées sont, selon I. Théry, la conséquence de trois phénomènes profonds: la dynamique de l'égalité des sexes, l'investissement croissant dans la personne de l'enfant et l'allongement de la durée de vie.

Les trois autres rapports ont été celui de la députée socialiste Dominique Gillot, « Pour une politique de la famille rénovée », celui de Michèle André, ancienne secrétaire d'Etat aux droits des femmes, sur « La vie quotidienne des familles » et, enfin, celui de Claude Thélot, inspecteur général de l'INSEE (Institut national de la statistique et des études économiques), sur le thème « Bilan et perpectives » de la politique familiale.

De l'ensemble de ces textes, deux idées forces semblent ressortir. La première est que « c'est l'enfant qui fait la famille ». Dans cettte optique, un couple marié ou vivant en concubinage ne constitue pas une famille s'il n'a pas d'enfants. *A contrario*, une personne seule, femme ou homme, avec un ou plusieurs enfants représente une famille. La seconde idée est que la vie de famille n'est pas délimitée une fois pour toutes. On peut être célibataire un temps et vivre en couple ou former une famille, monoparentale ou recomposée, durant une autre période de la vie. Dans cette conception, la famille serait quelque chose de « dynamique », d'évolutif, et donc aussi d'aléatoire. Ces nouvelles visions de la famille n'empêchent pas D. Gillot de conclure son rapport sur une note plus traditionnelle, puisqu'elle souligne que « la famille reste la cellule de base de l'éducation et de la cohésion sociale ».

Il est intéressant à cet égard de se reporter à quelques enquêtes d'opinion sur la famille réalisées durant les années 90. En 1993, par exemple, une enquête de l'INSERM (Institut national de la santé et de la recherche médicale) auprès de jeunes de 11 à 19 ans montrait que pour 75% d'entre eux, la vie familiale était « agréable et détendue ». En 1994, les résultats de la consultation nationale lancée par le Premier ministre d'alors, Edouard Balladur, auprès des 15-25 ans, ont fait apparaître que, pour les 1 500 000 jeunes qui ont répondu à ce questionnaire, la famille est un « îlot de bonheur » dans lequel 90% d'entre eux se sentent à l'aise. L'ensemble de cette classe d'âge place la famille en tête de toutes les valeurs. Ils la considèrent, selon Philippe Broussard du *Monde*, comme :

> [...] le plus sûr refuge contre les bourrasques de l'époque. Par gros temps, elle demeure le seul point d'ancrage qui vaille, un îlot d'affection et de sécurité. Oubliés la rebellion de 1968, les envies d'indépendance et le rejet des structures traditionnelles... Retour au classique. Papa, maman, les frères et sœurs, pour le meilleur et pour le pire. Pourquoi? Par amour sans doute. Par nécessité aussi[4].

En juin 1995, un sondage IFOP-*Le Monde* révélait que 48% des Français acceptaient l'idée de donner le droit de se marier aux couples homosexuels et que 56% approuvaient les maires qui avaient alors décidé d'accorder à ces couples un certificat de concubinage.

Si les Français paraissent unanimes dans leur appréciation de la famille, il n'en est pas de même parmi les experts. Dans sa *Sociologie de la famille contemporaine*, François de Singly n'hésite pas à écrire, non sans paradoxe: « Si la famille est à ce point prisée, c'est parce qu'elle ne veut plus rien dire — c'est une enveloppe vide ». Ce que conteste totalement une autre sociologue, Agnès Pitrou, pour qui la famille est une « réalité concrète », notamment parce qu'elle est « le premier distributeur, le plus immédiat, de biens et de services ». De fait, 80% des Français ont été aidés par leur famille pour se loger ou trouver un emploi; 30% des enfants sont gardés par leur grand-mère pendant que les parents travaillent et 27% passent au moins cinq semaines de vacances par an chez leurs grands-parents. Cette « solidarité familiale » est favorisée par la proximité: 60% ont un enfant qui habite dans leur département, 30% dans le même quartier et 12,5% dans la même rue.

Une chose est sûre désormais: la famille, à l'image de la société actuelle, est diverse, plurielle, hétérogène. Mais, quels que soient sa configuration, sa dénomination, son statut, elle constitue une réalité incontestable dont « la présence, comme le rappelait le Premier ministre, Lionel Jospin, lors de la Conférence de juin 1998, n'a jamais été aussi essentielle ». « Nucléaire » ou « élargie », la famille est un refuge. Refuge contre la dureté des temps, la crise économique, le chômage, l'exclusion, la dissolution du lien social. Plus la société est impitoyable, plus les individus se replient sur la sphère familiale ou sur un « noyau » de substitution qui en assure la fonction s'il n'en porte pas le nom. L'avenir, on le sait, n'est écrit nulle part; il serait par conséquent vain de prétendre annoncer ce que sera la famille en France à l'horizon du troisième millénaire. Peut-être la famille « traditionnelle », qui reste encore le modèle largement dominant, sera-t-elle devenue minoritaire; peut-être au contraire aura-t-elle effectué son « grand retour », comme certains signes — (légère) progression des mariages et des naissances — le laissent actuellement paraître? Dans tous les cas, et quelle que soit la forme qu'elle revêtira, elle devrait rester, selon la belle formule d'une association familiale, « le lieu de vie où s'apprennent en premier la fraternité, le partage, la responsabilité, la conscience d'appartenir à un groupe, la communauté de destin ».

Notes

1 *Pour la liberté familiale*, PUF, 1986.
2 *Population & Sociétés*, n°293, septembre 1994.
3 Lorsqu'une mère ne désire pas que le lien de filiation soit établi entre elle et

son enfant, la déclaration de naissance est faite non pas par elle, mais par une personne qui a assisté à l'accouchement. Dans ce cas, l'enfant est généralemet adopté mais, s'il essaie de retrouver sa mère par la suite, cela lui sera impossible car il n'y aura aucune trace du nom de cette dernière.
    [4] *Le Monde*, 24 septembre 1994.

Références

« La famille dans tous ses états », *Actes de la recherche en sciences sociales,* n° 113, Paris: juin 1996.

Bloss, Thierry. *Les Liens de famille. Sociologie des rapports entre générations.* Paris: PUF, 1997.

Cordero, Christiane. *La Famille.* Paris: Le Monde Poche, 1995.

« La famille malgré tout », *Panoramiques,* n° 25, Paris: Arléa-Corlet, 2ᵉ trimestre 1996.

Meulders-Klein, Marie-Thérèse et Irène Thery (sous la direction de). *Les Recompositions familiales aujourd'hui.* Paris: Nathan, 1993.

Roussel, Louis. *La Famille incertaine.* Paris: Le Seuil-Points/Odile Jacob, 1992.

Segalen, Martine. *Sociologie de la famille.* Paris: Armand Colin, 1996.

Singly, François (de). *Le Soi, le couple et la famille.* Paris: Nathan, 1996.

---. *La Politique familiale.* Paris, La Documentation Française, 1996.

--- (sous la direction de). *La Famille en question.* Paris: Syros, 1996.

---. *Sociologie de la famille contemporaine.* Paris: Nathan, 1993.

Sullerot, Evelyne. *Quels Pères, quels fils ?* Paris: LGF, 1995.

---. *Le Grand Remue-ménage.* Paris: Fayard, 1997.

Thery, Irène. *Recomposer une famille.* Paris: Textuel, 1995.

---. *Le Démariage.* Paris: Odile Jacob, 1996.

---. *Couple, filiation et parenté aujourd'hui. Le droit face aux mutations de la vie privée.* Paris: Odile Jacob/La Documentation Française, 1998.

7

France's Aging Population

Alice J. Strange
Southeast Missouri State University

Old age is a subject increasingly on the minds of the French. They witnessed François Mitterrand complete his second term as president at the age of seventy-eight in 1995. When Jeanne Calment died in 1997 at the age of 122, the event was front-page news and generated a host of related articles about the aging of the French population. In 1998 the thirtieth anniversary of the events of May 1968 was a reminder to the activists of '68 of their own aging and their coming retirement, less than a decade away. In demographic terms, France begins the twenty-first century with the prospect of a revolution among the generations, due to a dramatic increase in the number of elderly persons. Public leaders and individuals alike are beginning to grasp the new realities which this demographic shift will bring. It is helpful for us to look at the magnitude of the problem and some of the forces which produced it, as well as the range of public and personal issues which must be addressed. Many aspects of French life will be affected by the nation's response to the aging question.

The case of Jeanne Calment offers a startling example of what an increasing lifespan may mean. Thanks to her well-documented birth on February 21, 1875, she was reliably acclaimed as the world's oldest person at the time of her death on August 4, 1997. Madame Calment was fortunate in never having suffered a serious medical problem. She became a source of pride and a symbol for the good life in France, the country which nourished her to a healthy old age. A woman who was born before Marcel Proust and who was already ten years old when Victor Hugo died became a media celebrity in her last years. She outlived her only child by 63 years and her husband by 35; she died with no close relatives. Although she had enjoyed a long independent life, she had lived in an old-age home the last twelve years of her life, completely under the care of the state.

Jeanne Calment is an appropriate standard-bearer for the growing cohort which is following in her footsteps. The number of centenarians is frequently cited in the popular French press as an illustration of the rapid increase in the elderly population. The number grew from approximately two hundred in 1950 to six thousand in 1997. In the next half century, the number of French citizens who reach the age of 100 may increase as much as 25-fold to 150,000 by 2050. This situation was unforeseen by most officials, including authorities of the social security system. It was recently necessary to create a "centenary" designation for social security numbers, since the practice of using the last two digits of the year of birth would not accommodate someone who lived over one hundred years. Such longevity had not been envisaged by the creators of the system.

The number of younger elderly, retired but not dependent, will increase dramatically as well. By one projection, as many as two-thirds of the French population could be over the age of 60 by the middle of the twenty-first century (Remy 63). The good news of a longer life is offset by worries about physical and financial problems. Jeanne Calment's example demonstrates that it is possible to live a healthy life into advanced years, but also that a period of dependency may require resources beyond the individual's means.

Demographers have long been aware of the trends towards an aging population in all of the world's industrialized countries, and France stands near the top of this list. Until the end of the eighteenth century, demographic behavior was characterized by both high birth rates and high mortality rates. A large family was important in a society where children could contribute economically to family wealth by working on family farms or in other productive capacities. A high birth rate also offset the effects of high infant mortality, since not every child would survive to adulthood. With the coming of industrialization and urbanization, a second demographic pattern took over. Children contributed less and required more in terms of support and education. In the early decades of the twentieth century, parents began to limit the size of their families. They could give children a better chance at life if they had fewer children.

In recent years a change in societal attitudes has come about which contributes to an even lower birth rate. No longer is it assumed that children are part of an individual's future. A high value is placed on personal self-fulfillment and development of one's talents. The decision to have children is a conscious one based on the belief that children bring emotional satisfaction and enrich one's life. Society today is tolerant of behavior which leads to a lower birth rate, including cohabitation, birth control, and abortion. A few observers who hold to traditional beliefs wonder why young French couples are so hesitant to produce offspring. It seems that for many people children are welcomed to the extent that they do not overly disrupt personal and career goals. The child-friendly measures which France has taken, including family subsidies or *allocations familiales,* maternity benefits, and child care provisions, have not succeeded in producing more births.

By the early nineteenth century throughout Europe, death rates began to fall and by the end of the century (and somewhat earlier in France), birth rates also saw a decline. In the mid-eighteenth century, the average birth rate in France was around five children per woman, but at that time between 26 percent and 29 percent of infants died before their first birthday. By 1830 the birth rate had declined to four children per woman, by 1890 to three children, and it has been fewer than two children for the past twenty years.

There is no indication that France's declining birth rate is likely to reverse its course. It currently stands at 1.7 children per woman, compared to the baby-boom high point of 2.9 in 1964. For an even replacement of the generations, with a balance in the number of births and deaths, a birth rate of 2.1 is necessary. The declining birth rate means that the twentieth century has seen major adjustments in the population pyramid. Young people constitute a smaller and smaller portion of the total population. In 1900, about one third of the French population was under 20 years of age, whereas at century's end the under-twenty age group has declined to about 26 percent. At the other end of the life span, the number of those over 65 (considered the demographic beginning of old age) was eight percent in 1900. In 1995 it stood at over 15 percent , and it is expected to reach 17 percent by 2015 (Aulagnon, "Etre vieux"; Mamou, "Le vieillissement"). France has become one of the world's oldest countries in terms of average age.

Until the Second World War, the statistical increase in the older population was due to the decline in the birth rate rather than an actual increase in the number of elderly. For a time this decreasing birth rate was somewhat hidden by the fact that an increasing number of infants were surviving. Now that the infant mortality rate has stabilized, the effects of a declining birth rate are more evident. A decline in infant mortality and improved medical care for all ages have resulted in an increased life expectancy. The life expectancy in France is among the highest in the world, 74 years for men and 82 years for women, compared to a United States life expectancy of 73 for men and 79 for women (Mermet 114). At the turn of the twentieth century, the average life expectancy in France was about 45 years. The increase in longevity is expected to increase France's overall population by 2005 to the point that France will overtake the United Kingdom as the second most populous country in the European Union, after Germany.

For both the individual and for French society, the question of old age goes hand in hand with retirement from working life and the financial consequences of this transition. Old age pensions constitute one of the four major programs of the French social security system, along with health, unemployment, and the family. During working years, employee contributions are deducted from a worker's salary; the employer contributes a greater amount. Retirement benefits for an individual are based on the average of the worker's top earnings over a period of twenty-five years (increased from ten years in 1993). Employees may retire at the age of 60 but they receive the maximum benefit only if they have contributed to the system for a period of 40 years (37.5 years prior to 1993). Benefits vary, of course, with years of contributions and salary earned. The minimum annual pension in 1998 was 41,651 francs (about $7,000 according to the exchange rate at the time) for an individual or 74,720 francs (about $12,500) for a couple. Old-age benefits consume approximately half of the social security system's expenditures, a 10 percent increase since the 1960s (Lormeau, "Vers la guerre économique"). In 1994 social security benefits collectively claimed 30.5 percent of France's gross domestic product, placing it in fourth place at that time among the countries of the European Union and well above the EU average of 28.6 percent ("Convergence européenne").

Since the French system is based on the principle of redistribution, by which the contributions of the working population finance the pensions of the retired, the population shift is a worrisome development. The ratio of workers to retirees is projected to decline from the current two workers for each retiree to 1.3 per retiree by 2020. The watershed year for the old-age pension system is often cited as 2005, the year when the oldest group of baby-boomers will retire. At that point the number of persons who retire each year is expected to rise to 750,000 annually, up from the approximately 520,000 persons who currently retire each year (La Rocque 44).

Today France is a country whose citizens retire relatively early. Some workers nearing retirement are offered financial incentives to leave, allowing a younger person to take the job. By the age of 58, half the working population has retired. Only five percent of men over 65 are still in the work force (compared to 15 percent in the United States), the lowest among the world's leading industrialized nations.

As these figures indicate, the issue of mandatory retirement has not been a major concern; most workers are eager to retire. One exception has been in the domain of politics, where there have been calls to establish an upper age limit. The example of François Mitterrand, in ill health when he left office at the age of seventy-eight, supports this call, but there is no real likelihood that it will be heeded. French politicians in high office have often spent many years rising through the ranks until they reach the top, and they are not likely to institute an age ceiling. President Jacques Chirac began a seven-year term at the age of sixty-three.

In the long view, sociologists have pointed out that the concept of aging has changed, and that French society should reconsider what it means to be old. Those who retire at 60, today's commonly accepted target, are likely to be much healthier and more vigorous than previous generations and can look forward to a longer life span. Statistically, a man who was 59 years old in 1900 could count on living another 10 years; in 1985, the same was true for a man of 67. For women the lifespan differences were even more striking. A woman who was 62 years old in 1900 could expect to live another ten years; in 1985, the same was true for a woman of 74.

Since many people who retire are still physically able to work, it would seem logical to consider raising the retirement age, thereby placing less strain on the retirement system. There is also a counter-movement urging a lowering of the retirement age to 55 for all, as a way of making more jobs available to young people. There is disagreement about the issue on many fronts. Some argue against manipulating retirement rules as a tool to reduce unemployment. There are those who believe that the next thirty years will see a shortage of young people to fill existing jobs, creating a manpower shortage, and that the economy will need older workers. At this point, a substantial increase in the retirement age is probably not politically possible, and a lowering of the age would add to the problems of the social security deficits.

The deficit in the old-age pension fund stood at between seven and eight billion francs in 1997 (Bezat, "Lionel Jospin demande au Commissariat"), and future strains are evident. As we have noted, the ratio of workers to retirees is decreasing. In the future it will be necessary to increase contributions or reduce benefits. The system's problems were marginally addressed in 1993, when measures were put into place to assure its short-term financial viability. The number of years of contribution required was increased and the future benefits of retirees were slightly reduced. Other recent reforms have consolidated the branches of the old-age bureaucracy in an attempt to reduce administrative costs. Experts generally agree that an eventual increase in the retirement age is likely, in view of the long-term problems of the system. Also being discussed is the possibility of submitting old-age recipients to a means test, providing fewer benefits for affluent senior citizens, just as the government intends to subject the family allocations benefits to certain financial conditions.

The geographical distribution of the aging population is uneven throughout the regions of France. Forty-seven departments have a population whose average age surpasses the national average. These aging departments, located for the most part in the south, cover 52 percent of the territory of France but are home to only 37 percent of the population. A combination of factors contributes to this situation. Some of these departments are in attractive retirement locations; other departments have experienced a migration of young people away from the area, with a subsequent decline in the birth rate. At the other end of the scale, some 30 departments have a higher birth rate than the French average (although still less than the 2.1 replacement rate), and count 45 percent of the population in 29 percent of the area (Parent 220: 25). This distribution of population, with both densely- and sparsely-populated regions, will have implications for the allocation of the country's resources for the elderly.

The population situation is resulting in a modification of the relationship of the individual to the state in the matter of old-age benefits. The French have traditionally tended to look to the government to oversee the well-being of society. Only recently have they been encouraged to take personal initiative to assure a comfortable retirement. As a first step, individuals are urged to ask for a projection of their personal retirement benefits. In a turn-around of attitudes unimaginable even a decade ago, the bureaucracy has begun to encourage this request for information by providing outreach workers at various public events, such as the 1998 *Foire de Paris,* in order to answer the publicís questions. The hope is that individuals will then take responsibility for supplementing these benefits by a program of personal savings and investment. They could take advantage of a system of tax-advantaged individual retirement accounts *(plans d'épargne retraite,* or *PER)* which was put into place in 1996, fulfilling a campaign promise made by Jacques Chirac.

Because of retirement benefits and accumulated assets, the over-50 age group constitute a powerful economic force in French society. Contrary to the image sometimes evoked in the public mind, old age in France does not mean poverty; quite the reverse is true. In 1996, those over 50 represented about 30 percent of the French population and held fully half of the wealth of all households. Two out of three own their home, and one in three owns additional real estate. At the end of the 1990s the buying power of the elderly is 30 percent above that of those under 50 years old, and is increasing at a faster rate. This is especially understandable when one considers the high rates of unemployment among the youngest members of the work force. At present trends point to an increasingly higher standard of living among the old and a wider gap between their living standard and that of households composed of those under 30. This group of over-50s is destined to become the richest over-80 age group in French history.

There is, however, a growing gap between the richest and the poorest of the elderly. An estimated eleven percent of those over the age of 80 live in financial insecurity and emotional isolation, often in an urban area. Some have lived in the same apartment for half a century and have seen the passing of their circle of friends and relatives. A domestic animal may be their only companionship. Their lives are restricted to routine habits; they pass their time with television or the view from their window. Often fearful of strangers, they refuse the help of home health aides. Occasionally, a media story recounts a tragic death of an elderly person in such circumstances, reinforcing a popular notion that old age is accompanied by loneliness and poverty (Dassonville, "Tranches de solitude"). Although they are the exceptions, the elderly who suffer from emotional isolation and its consequences represent a problem which needs to be addressed.

The manufacturing and advertising sectors of the economy are turning their attention to the over-50 age group. A report issued in 1997 declared that the future belongs to senior citizens, a sort of *papy-boom* market, corresponding to the economic power of the baby boom. Economists see a range of needs which will demand to be met in the coming years. Opportunities range from providing prepared foods and selling home alarm systems to offering choices in medical and social services which might be an alternative to placement in an institution.

An imaginative marketing campaign aimed at senior citizens has been undertaken by the *RATP,* the Paris metro and bus system, which itself celebrated its centennial in 1999. The *RATP* invites retirees of the Paris region (where the average retirement age is 55) to take advantage of specially-planned activities on Thursdays, such as Internet activities at the *Palais de la découverte* or a lecture on gardening at the Cité des sciences de la Villette. In calling the program *Jeudis seniors,* the *RATP* draws on the connotation of freedom associated with Thursday in the minds of senior citizens, who in their youth had a holiday from classes on Thursday afternoon. Since senior citizens are more likely than younger people to use public transportation, and they tend to buy bus or metro tickets rather than use cheaper weekly or monthly passes, the *RATP* expects to increase revenue by appealing to this growing market.

The population situation is also resulting in a modification of the relationships among family members. In economic terms, there is an inherent war between the generations. Many of today's very old people lived in difficult conditions for much of their life, while the generation behind them benefited from economic growth. That younger generation, which today is itself retiring, was willing to share the gains with their elders in generous old-age benefits to their parents, and they believe they have earned the same privileges. But the rate of economic progress they knew as adults is not true for today's young adults, who are often unwilling or unable to make the necessary contributions to maintain current old age benefits for their parents. A new balance may need to be established to distribute resources fairly among the generations. Another economic consideration, the question of inheritances, comes into play. Inheritances are delayed as the elderly live longer and property is passed on to adult children who may already be old rather than to younger family members. An increase in the rate of circulation of family assets among generations may be desirable.

On the personal level, family relationships are changing. While elderly people are living longer, young adults are postponing marriage and, for economic reasons, may be living with their parents. People in their forties and fifties may be in charge of their parents' care while providing financial aid to unemployed young adult children. One retiree out of every three still has at least one living parent, and many families have already begun to see four or even five generations living at the same time. In 1990, 26 percent of women who were 60 years old found themselves surrounded by both their parents and their grandchildren (Parent 221: 25).

If an elderly person reaches extreme old age or becomes dependent or disabled, decisions must be made about appropriate care. Elders may need nursing services, help with domestic tasks, and help with decision making. Professionals in the field distinguish between formal and informal sectors of service providers. The formal sector includes both government-provided services and privately-run services. Informal care is provided by family, friends, and neighbors. At present formal home help and home nursing services are mainly operated by the private sector. The social security system reimburses the cost of home nursing care, but usually not the cost of home help, except for those with very low incomes where need is assessed by a doctor or social worker. There is currently much public discussion about providing additional social security funds to the dependent elderly. Meals in communal settings or delivered to the home may be available, but the geographic distribution of services is uneven. As for institutional settings, France has no facility which serves precisely the same function as an American nursing home, which offers long-term skilled nursing care. There are long-stay hospitals and medical-care sections of retirement homes, which together house about two percent of the elderly population. Another four percent of the elderly, who require less nursing care, reside in retirement homes or private commercial residences. Hospice care (*soins palliatifs*) for a dependent old person, or a terminally ill person of any age, first appeared in 1987. With the growing dependent elderly population there is discussion about reforms in institutional care. In France as in almost all of the EU countries, the surge in dependent elderly has taken officials by surprise, and the current services are saturated. There is general agreement that there is insufficient availability of appropriate professional care, both public and private, and of financial benefits to support it.

The family plays a major role in providing informal care for the elderly. Over three-fourths of dependent elderly live at home, either with relatives or with substantial support from them. Often it is a daughter or another female relative who provides the largest share of daily care, sometimes being drawn into the task little by little or as a temporary measure, which may last for a very long time. The family caregiver often makes great personal sacrifices; family conflict is rarely absent. There is a need for additional support for families in caring for their elderly members.

Given the dimension of the demographic trends evident today, there is naturally a growing concern about what this situation means for the future of France. Some analysts see positive results. They note that an increase in the number of retirees may alleviate the unemployment crisis among the young. A stable population puts fewer demands on the environment. It permits society to provide a better education for its children and a better quality of life for citizens of all ages. A contrary view maintains that the long-term consequences of a shrinking work force are detrimental to prosperity. France may be unable to supply the manpower needed to propel the economy forward and to support the retired cohort, which in turn may lead to a decline in the standard of living. The country will become *la France ridée,* a nation whose loss of growth and dynamism will be accompanied by a corresponding decline in national influence (Remy 62-63). Since the magnitude of the coming shift is unprecedented, there is great uncertainty about its effects.

Demographers point out that, with deaths surpassing births, the only source of new citizens is immigration, which is tightly controlled throughout most of the countries of the European Union. A return to the recruitment of foreign workers seems unlikely. The general conclusion is that the size of the French population will stabilize and then begin to decline within the first half of the twenty-first century.

For the time being, the public is undergoing a process of heightened awareness about the issue of an aging population and what it means for them as individuals. Several sectors of the French media are playing a role in this process. Publishers are issuing self-help and informational works destined to improve the quality of life of senior citizens. In 1995, the television magazine *Qui Vive* devoted four successive evenings of programming to the changing concept of old age. In May 1998, a lengthy article in *L'Express* alerted readers to the necessity of verifying their retirement benefits and of taking steps toward personal savings and investments (La Rocque 44; 48). Readers were especially urged to consider financial options beyond the traditional life insurance. In the same month, Canal Plus devoted an evening's programming to issues of interest to the sizeable group of viewers nearing retirement. Advice on finances, health, and lifestyle choices personalized the experience of aging.

The audience for such programming will continue to increase as greater numbers of French citizens approach the end of their working life. While in the coming years few people will live to Jeanne Calment's record age of 122, many elderly will reach their 90s or even the century mark. It is clear that every sector of French society will feel the effect of the country's aging population in the twenty-first century.

References

Aizicovici, Francine. "Les départs à 55 ans pèsent sur les retraites." *Le Monde* 18 Dec. 1996, sec. Initiatives: 4.
Aulagnon, Michèle. "Etre vieux aujourd'hui." *Le Monde* 18 Dec. 1995, sec. Radio-Télévision: 15.
---. "Le bonheur à cent ans." *Le Monde* 4 May 1998, sec. Radio-Télévision: 5.
---. "Le nombre de gens âgés et très âgés explose." *Le Monde* 5 Oct. 1995: 6.
---. "Le vieillissement de la population met en jeu les solidarités familiales." *Le Monde* 6 Aug. 1997: 6.
Bezat, Jean-Michel. "Financement des régimes de retraite français: attention, travaux!" *Le Monde* 3 Dec. 1996, sec. Economie: 3.
---. "Les jeunes pourraient se lasser de payer pour les pensions des plus âgés." *Le Monde* 11 Jan. 1997: 6.
---. "Lionel Jospin demande au Commissariat au plan un nouveau Livre blanc sur les retraites." *Le Monde* 24 Apr. 1998: 30.
Bobasch, Michaëla. "La RATP propose aux 'seniors' la semaine des quatre jeudis." *Le Monde* 9 Feb. 1998: 21.

Bosworth, Barry, and Gary Burtless. "Budget Crunch: Population Aging in Rich Countries." *Brookings Review* 15:3 (1997): 10-15.

"Convergence européenne de la protection sociale." *Le Monde* 2 July 1997, sec. Initiatives: 4.

Curtis, S., D. Bucquet and A. Colvez. "Sources of Instrumental Support for Dependent Elderly People in Three Parts of France." *Ageing and Society* 12 (1992): 329-354.

Dassonville, Aude. "Jeanne veut rester chez elle jusqu'à la mort." *Le Monde* 30 Nov. 1996: 8.

---. "Tranches de solitude." *Le Monde* 18 Apr. 1997: 13.

Follea, Laurence. "La consommation des 'seniors' est appelée à se développer fortement." *Le Monde* 22 Apr. 1997: 9.

"La France, qui a perdu sa doyenne, compte 6 000 centenaires." *Le Monde* 6 Aug. 1997: 1.

Grellet, Gilbert. "Pouvoir et vieillesse." *Le Monde* 14 Oct. 1996: 11.

Herzlich, Guy. "La longévité et sa rançon." *Le Monde* 24 June 1995: 1.

"Huit minima sociaux." *Le Monde* 27 Feb. 1998: 6.

Hugman, Richard. *Ageing and the Care of Older People in Europe.* New York: St. Martin's Press, 1994.

Izraelewicz, Erik. "Jeunes et vieux, l'autre fracture sociale." *Le Monde* 25 Aug. 1995: 1+.

Kaa, Dirk J. van de. "Europe's Second Demographic Transition." *Population Bulletin* 42:1 (1987): 1-57.

La Rocque, Jean-Pierre de. "Retraite: comment garantir vos revenus." *L'Express* 21 May 1998: 42-53.

Lormeau, Patricia. "Vers la guerre économique entre les générations?" *Le Monde* 2 Apr. 1997: 12.

Mamou, Yves. "Le 'big bang' des fonds de pension." *Le Monde* 4 Mar. 1997. sec. Economie: 1+.

---. "La famille est le principal pourvoyeur de soins aux personnes âgées." *Le Monde* 29 May 1997, sec. Economie: 2.

---. "Gérer la vieillesse." *Le Monde* 29 May 1997, sec. Economie: 1+.

---. "Le vieillissement source de déclin?" *Le Monde* 7 Apr. 1998, sec. Economie: 1+.

Mauduit, Laurent. "La détention du patrimoine financier reste très fortement concentrée." *Le Monde* 16 May 1998: 7.

Menanteau, Jean. "Génération sandwich." *Le Monde* 13 Sep. 1995, sec. Initiatives: 2.

Mermet, Gérard. *Francoscopie 99.* Paris: Larousse, 1998.

Parent, Alain. "Le vieillissement de la population française." *Regards sur l'actualité* 220 (1996): 21-32.

---. "Effets passés et à venir du vieillissement démographique." *Regards sur l'actualité* 221 (1996): 15-26.

Remy, Jacqueline. "Les Scénarios d'une France ridée." *L'Express* 2 Jan. 1997: 62-65.

Raffarin, Jean-Pierre. "Emploi: pour une solidarité nouvelle entre générations." *Le Monde* 14 Jan. 1998, sec. Initiatives: 4.

Ribbe, Miel W., et al. "Nursing Homes in Ten Nations: A Comparison between Countries and Settings." *Age and Ageing* 26 (1997): 3-12.

Roland-Lévy, Fabien. "Les députés de la majorité créent des plans d'épargne-retraite." *Le Monde* 23 Nov. 1996: 6.

Troyansky, David G. "The New Age of Old Age." *Ageing and Society* 14 (1994): 429-447.

8

Démocratisation de l'enseignement en France: illusion ou réalité?

Marie-Christine Weidmann Koop
University of North Texas

Si l'éducation a toujours été présente dans les préoccupations des différents gouvernements qui se sont succédé depuis la Révolution de 1789, il a fallu attendre les lois de Jules Ferry des années 1880-1882 pour que l'enseignement devienne gratuit et obligatoire pour tous, garçons et filles, de 6 à 13 ans. Cependant, ces lois n'ont pas été promulguées dans un souci de promotion sociale. En effet, le système éducatif tel qu'il était organisé se caractérisait par son dualisme: d'une part, les lycées conduisant une minorité d'enfants issus de milieux privilégiés vers des études longues et, d'autre part, les écoles primaires qui amenaient au certificat d'études primaires (CEP) les enfants les plus doués des milieux populaires (père paysan, ouvrier, employé, artisan, petit commerçant). Malgré les améliorations considérables qui ont été apportées au système éducatif, les cadres de la nation se recrutent toujours dans les milieux privilégiés. Ce sont surtout les travaux de Pierre Bourdieu et Jean-Claude Passeron qui, à partir des années 1960, ont mis au jour le fait que l'école, loin de favoriser la mobilité sociale, demeurait l'instrument privilégié de la reproduction des classes sociales *(Les Héritiers* et *La Reproduction)*. Cette même époque a vu dans l'enseignement secondaire l'arrivée massive des jeunes de la génération du *baby boom*. Ce phénomène démographique s'est produit lors d'une période de croissance économique sans précédent (1945-1975) qui s'est traduite par une forte augmentation du niveau de vie des Français et une demande accrue d'éducation. Or le système éducatif, de par ses structures, n'était pas conçu pour accueillir ces milliers de jeunes issus des classes moyennes. Le ministère de l'Education nationale s'est alors trouvé contraint de prendre des mesures pour adapter les programmes à ces nouvelles exigences et les transformations successives ont donné lieu, à long terme, à une réforme profonde de l'enseignement secondaire.

C'est en étudiant l'évolution du baccalauréat, diplôme phare du système éducatif français, que l'on peut mesurer les progrès réalisés dans ce domaine. Créé à l'origine comme premier grade universitaire, le « bac » a toujours rempli une double fonction: sanctionner la fin des études secondaires et permettre l'accès aux études supérieures. Conçu dès ses débuts comme marque d'appartenance à une élite sociale, il ne concernait que les jeunes issus des milieux privilégiés. Il s'appuyait sur un programme théorique et la sélection se faisait par l'étude du latin. Or les nouveaux besoins de la part des entreprises ont engendré la création des bacs de techniciens et des brevets de techniciens supérieurs (BTS) dont la première session eut lieu en 1969. Cependant, après quelques années, il est devenu évident que ces diplômes offraient peu de perspectives de carrière. Si le niveau d'éducation des Français augmentait, la sélection des élites se faisait à un niveau toujours plus élevé et toujours parmi les mêmes classes sociales. Les pourcentages des jeunes titulaires du bac étaient en augmentation mais demeuraient relativement bas: 12,5% d'une classe d'âge en 1960, 20% en 1970, 25,33 % en 1979, 28% en 1983. En 1985, Jean-Pierre Chevènement, alors ministre de l'Education, lançait l'objectif des « 80% d'une classe d'âge au niveau du baccalauréat ». La même année voyait la création des bacs professionnels avec une première session en 1987. Afin de réaliser l'objectif des 80%, la loi d'orientation de Lionel Jospin (juillet 1989) réformait le baccalauréat en simplifiant les structures de ce dernier et en offrant des filières variées, susceptibles d'être intégrées par un plus grand nombre d'élèves. Un autre objectif de cette réforme était de limiter la prééminence des mathématiques qui avaient peu à peu supplanté le latin comme outil de sélection. Suite à ces modifications et à la création des bacs professionnels, plus de 60% d'une classe d'âge sont titulaires du baccalauréat à l'aube du XXIᵉ siècle, soit cinq fois plus qu'en 1960. Toutefois, les chiffres sont trompeurs car ils comprennent l'ensemble des bacs généraux, technologiques et professionnels. Si près de 70% d'une classe d'âge arrive aujourd'hui au niveau du baccalauréat, il faut bien préciser que seuls 57% des lauréats obtiennent un bac général — littéraire (L), économique et social (ES) ou scientifique (S) — alors que le taux est de 28% pour le bac technologique et 15% pour le bac professionnel. Cela signifie que seuls 34,8 % d'une classe d'âge sont titulaires d'un bac général, soit une augmentation de 30% seulement par rapport à 1960 (« Le baccalauréat 1998 »). Il faut maintenant considérer les filières et non plus les niveaux d'éducation.

Face à cette situation, on est en mesure de se demander si cette croissance a entraîné une véritable démocratisation dans l'enseignement secondaire et, par conséquent, dans le recrutement de l'élite en France. Plusieurs études sont effectuées régulièrement pour essayer de mesurer l'effet de démocratisation mais aucune à ce jour ne semble apporter de jugement arrêté sur la question. Certaines méritent cependant d'être mentionnées car elles permettent d'expliquer une partie du phénomène. Le profil des bacheliers est étroitement lié à certains facteurs dont les plus importants sont l'origine sociale et le degré d'ambition de la famille, l'âge, le sexe, les pratiques d'orientation scolaire, le type d'établissement scolaire fréquenté et les interactions des élèves avec tous les agents concernés.

I. Facteurs de la réussite scolaire

A. Origine sociale

On constate en France de fortes différenciations sociales dans la carrière scolaire des élèves, à commencer par la scolarité à l'école primaire qui semble avoir un effet durable sur le déroulement ultérieur des études. En effet, 68,6% des élèves jugés « bons » au cours préparatoire (CP) parviennent en second cycle long, contre seulement 10% des redoublants; au niveau du cours élémentaire deuxième année, ce sont 78% des « bons » élèves qui auront ultérieurement accès au second cycle long[1]. On observe une constante entre les enfants d'ouvriers (qui accèdent à un second cycle long à hauteur de 31,9%) et de cadres supérieurs (pour lesquels le chiffre correspondant est de 86,8%). Ces différenciations sociales sont telles que, vues du CP, les chances des enfants de cadres supérieurs qui sont faibles restent plus élevées que celles des enfants d'ouvriers les plus brillants (51,9%). Ces écarts proviennent de deux sources: des différences sociales de progression au cours de la scolarité ultérieure et des différences sociales dans les « choix » de carrières scolaires aux divers paliers d'orientation, en fin des classes de 5e et de 3e. La carrière scolaire au niveau du collège est deux fois plus déterminante qu'au niveau de l'école primaire car c'est à ce niveau que les jeunes doivent choisir entre le second cycle long et l'enseignement professionnel. Tous facteurs confondus, il semble que les inégalités sociales déterminent davantage la réussite scolaire que les mécanismes d'orientation (Duru-Bellat et al., « Les scolarités... » 45-52).

Une étude nationale du ministère de l'Education nationale a été effectuée à partir d'un échantillon représentatif de près de 24 000 élèves entrés en classe de sixième en 1989 (Lemaire). Ces élèves ont été suivis chaque année jusqu'en 1994-1995 afin d'établir le profil exact de ceux qui sont entrés en lycée professionnel ou en apprentissage par opposition à ceux qui se sont dirigés vers une seconde générale ou technologique. Il ressort de cette étude que plus du tiers des élèves du panel ont choisi une formation professionnelle avant ou à la sortie de la classe de troisième au collège. La moitié d'entre eux sont entrés en lycée professionnel pour préparer un brevet ou un bac professionnel alors qu'un sixième ont signé un contrat d'apprentissage pour prépaper un certificat d'aptitude professionnelle (CAP). Le choix de l'apprentissage (études très courtes) par rapport au lycée professionnel (études plus longues avec possibilité d'études supérieures) est lié à plusieurs facteurs: le parcours scolaire en primaire et au collège, le milieu social, le fait d'être étranger et le sexe. Près d'un tiers des parents d'apprentis n'ont pas dépassé le niveau de l'enseignement primaire, alors que ce pourcentage n'est que de 20% pour l'ensemble des élèves du panel; 42% des pères d'apprentis ne sont titulaires que du certificat d'études contre 28% pour l'ensemble des pères; le niveau est encore plus bas pour les mères d'apprentis alors qu'on sait le rôle que jouent ces dernières dans le suivi de la scolarité des enfants (Lemaire 76). De même, les parents d'apprentis participent moins aux réunions entre parents et enseignants, mais ils sont plus nombreux à aller voir les enseignants de leur propre initiative. Les parents d'élèves en lycée professionnel sont un peu plus nombreux à avoir obtenu un diplôme supérieur au certificat d'études. A l'opposé, les chefs d'entreprise, cadres ou professions intellectuelles supérieures sont pratiquement absents et les professions intermédiaires peu représentées parmi les parents d'élèves. Il faut ajouter à cela le fait que 44% des mères d'apprentis n'ont pas d'activité professionnelle contre 37% pour l'ensemble des élèves, alors que les enfants dont la mère travaille obtiennent généralement de meilleurs résultats scolaires. Les caractéristiques de la famille entrent également en compte: 25% des apprentis sont issus d'une famille monoparentale, contre 20% pour l'ensemble des élèves du panel, et 56% sont issus d'une famille nombreuse (trois enfants et plus), contre 48% de l'ensemble des élèves. Là encore, d'autres études ont constaté que les enfants issus de familles nombreuses ont des résultats scolaires moins bons que les autres (Lemaire 76-77).

Une étude de 1993 qui a suivi des élèves entrés en 6ᵉ en 1989 (Casabianca et al.) montre que, à l'autre extrémité de l'échelle sociale, les enfants de cadres supérieurs forment les plus gros contingents de bacheliers généraux, loin devant les professions intermédiaires. Si les enfants de cadres représentent 28% des effectifs de bacheliers, cette proportion va de 15% en technologique à 34% en général, dont 45% en série scientifique (S). A l'inverse, un bachelier sur six est d'origine ouvrière, mais un sur quatre en série technologique contre moins d'un sur dix en série scientifique. On assiste donc à une représentation de ces deux catégories sociales inversement proportionnelle à leurs poids respectifs parmi les adolescents: selon le recensement de l'INSEE (Institut national de la statistique et des études économiques) de 1990, les enfants d'ouvriers (37%) sont en effet nettement plus nombreux dans la société française que les enfants de cadres supérieurs (14%). Une étude similaire avait été effectuée auprès d'élèves entrés en 6ᵉ en 1980 *(Repères et références statistiques* 89). Selon les données issues du « panel 80 », les enfants de cadres supérieurs et d'enseignants possédaient trois fois plus de chances de devenir bacheliers que les enfants d'ouvriers: 75% contre 25%. Cet écart s'est réduit régulièrement avec l'extension du baccalauréat, puisqu'à la fin des années 60, ces mêmes chances allaient de 1 à 4,5 (12% et 55% respectivement). Aujourd'hui, il est sans doute encore plus faible, notamment avec l'essor du bac professionnel. Deux facteurs principaux expliquent les disparités sociales: des acquis et résultats scolaires inégaux et des « trajectoires » éducatives différentes — demandes plus ou moins ambitieuses de la part des parents et choix « stratégiques » d'options ou d'établissements.

> Ainsi, l'orientation en fin de 5ᵉ et de 3ᵉ ne serait pas uniquement « méritocratique »: à âges et notes identiques, et surtout à proximité de la moyenne, les enfants d'ouvriers passeraient moins souvent en 4ᵉ ou en seconde générale. Les enfants de cadres cumulent les avantages: plus nombreux et plus jeunes, ils réussissent mieux (Casabianca et al. 12).

L'analyse des panels de 1980 et 1989 qui ont suivi un échantillon représentatif d'élèves entrés en 6ᵉ en 1980 et 1989 pendant six ans de leur scolarité confirme donc la prééminence de l'origine sociale dans l'accès au niveau du baccalauréat général et technologique. Parmi les élèves entrés en 6e, le pourcentage de ceux qui avaient abandonné leurs études avant la classe de seconde était de 28% à l'échelle nationale en 1986 avec 5% seulement d'enfants de cadres/enseignants contre 39% d'enfants d'ouvriers, soit huit fois plus pour ces derniers. En 1989, l'écart s'était resserré avec une moyenne nationale de 3% d'enfants de cadres et enseignants contre 16% d'enfants d'ouvriers. Depuis les années 60, les enfants d'ouvriers sont trois fois plus nombreux à accéder au niveau du bac. Mais, si l'on compare les enfants d'ouvriers et de cadres/enseignants, la proportion de réussite n'a pas diminué en conséquence avec un rapport de 1 à 8 en 1986 qui passe de 1 à 5 en 1995. Par ailleurs, le pourcentage des enfants d'ouvriers qui quittent le système éducatif sans qualification est toujours supérieur à la moyenne nationale. Si l'on considère le pourcentage des élèves du même panel qui, six ans après leur entrée en classe de 6e, se trouvaient en première ou en terminale générale et technologique, on dénombrait 86% d'enfants de cadres/enseignants contre seulement 30% d'enfants d'ouvriers en 1986; en 1995, les enfants de cadres/enseignants y étaient pour 88% contre 42% pour les enfants d'ouvriers, ce qui représentait une progression de ces derniers qui passaient ainsi d'un rapport approximatif de 1 à 3 en 1986 contre 1 à 2 en 1995 *(Repères et références* 89).

A l'opposé des thèses précédemment évoquées, Raymond Boudon affirme la prédominance de l'individu sur les contraintes structurelles. Dans *L'Inégalité des chances, la mobilité sociale dans les sociétés industrielles,* il démontre que les choix et décisions des individus entre les divers types de cursus, de filières, d'options ou de redoublement s'effectuent selon des calculs de risques, de coûts et de bénéfices. Or l'appréciation des coûts et des bénéfices, c'est-à-dire des chances de réussite de l'enfant, est liée à la position sociale des acteurs. A niveau scolaire égal des enfants, l'ambition des parents varie selon le milieu social et influence l'orientation et le destin des enfants. C'est ainsi que les familles modestes ont le plus souvent pour leurs enfants des visées limitées. Ces parents courent rarement le risque de prolonger la scolarité de leur enfant si l'école le leur déconseille. Face à l'incertitude et à l'inconnu des études longues, ils préfèrent la certitude et la rentabilité immédiate de l'apprentissage d'un métier. En revanche, les familles des milieux plus aisés exigent systématiquement la poursuite des études et font pression sur l'école pour éviter un redoublement ou une orientation non désirée, déployant de véritables stratégies pour favoriser la réussite de leurs enfants. Ainsi choisir le latin ou l'allemand au collège permet d'accéder aux meilleures classes de seconde (Compagnon 146). Au lycée, le choix entre les diverses filières est déterminant: les sections scientifiques, puis littéraires ouvrent plus largement les portes de l'enseignement supérieur que les sections technologiques. Les parents informés n'hésitent pas non plus à détourner la carte scolaire si l'établissement auquel est rattaché leur domicile ne présente pas de fermes garanties de réussite. En outre, leurs enfants ont la possibilité d'effectuer des séjours linguistiques dans les pays étrangers et de suivre des cours particuliers lorsqu'ils rencontrent des difficultés scolaires. Enfin, ces parents soutiennent davantage leurs enfants dans leur travail et entretiennent des contacts plus fréquents avec les enseignants.

Les enfants en échec sont issus de milieux à faible capital scolaire et leur culture familiale ne les aide pas à répondre aux exigences de l'institution scolaire. Les travaux menés depuis les années 1960 ont établi le fait que l'école reproduit statistiquement des différences sociales et culturelles pré-existantes. Mais l'analyse des inégalités sociales devant l'école oublie les cas de réussite scolaire en milieux populaires. Bernard Lahire a étudié ce qui, dans ces milieux, pouvait rendre raison de l'échec mais aussi de la réussite des enfants à l'école élémentaire *(Tableaux de familles)*. Il s'avère que des familles à faible capital scolaire peuvent très bien montrer qu'elles accordent une place importante aux études en manifestant devant leurs enfants un intérêt pour ce qui est fait à l'école. En effet, on ne peut pas vraiment prouver que les enfants issus de milieux moins cultivés sont pénalisés par le système éducatif. Cependant, ces enfants appartiennent à des milieux qui, traditionnellement, ne valorisent pas les performances scolaires et ils sont donc moins encouragés que les autres à persévérer dans ce domaine (Goux et Maurin 103).

B. L'âge

Après l'origine sociale, le choix de la série du baccalauréat est généralement lié à l'âge des lycéens. A cet effet, les séries générales qui conduisent à des études longues accueillent généralement les lycéens les plus jeunes qui n'ont jamais redoublé et ont donc effectué un parcours scolaire aisé. En revanche, les élèves qui ont redoublé une ou deux fois avant l'entrée en seconde sont plutôt orientés vers les séries technologiques ou professionnelles. Dans les séries générales, les lycéens sont de plus en plus jeunes: environ 50% sans retard dans les années 1990 contre 30% au milieu des années 1960. Cette différence s'explique en partie par le fait que la sélection s'effectuait autrefois avant l'entrée en sixième, alors qu'aujourd'hui elle se fait davantage en fonction de l'âge des élèves. Dans la filière scientifique (S), voie royale d'accès aux grandes écoles, on compte généralement trois fois plus d'élèves en avance qu'en série littéraire (L) contre seulement deux fois plus dans les années 60 ou 70.

C. Le facteur sexe

Le facteur sexe est un autre élément digne d'intérêt. C'est seulement à partir de 1962 que les filles rattrapent les garçons pour l'obtention du bac (11,7% à l'époque). Les filles dépassent vite ces derniers et, en 1975, elles sont 29,9% d'une classe d'âge contre 22,2% des garçons. Si elles restent aujourd'hui majoritaires, on remarque des différences dans le choix de la filière et le taux de réussite. Les séries littéraires et tertiaires sont plus féminisées. S'il y a pratiquement égalité en sciences, on compte deux tiers de garçons en mathématiques-physiques et technologie et 90% pour les spécialités proprement industrielles. Seules les filières économiques présentent un taux équilibré de gaçons et de filles. Quant au taux de réussite au baccalauréat, les filles dépassent les garçons d'environ 3% dans les séries générales, mais l'écart est plus faible dans les séries technologiques. Enfin, les filles sont plus jeunes que les garçons en séries générales: 55% ont 18 ans ou moins contre 49% des garçons. Bien que les filles obtiennent de meilleurs résultats scolaires que les garçons et qu'elles soient plus nombreuses à faire des études longues, elles choisissent des filières moins valorisantes et, plus tard, dans le domaine professionnel, elles occupent des postes moins importants ou moins bien rémunérés. En fait, les différences dans le choix des filières sont liées à des pratiques éducatives et à des attitudes sociales. Des études ont montré que, à résultats égaux, les filles sont moins souvent orientées par leurs professeurs vers les filières scientifiques; seules les filles qui ont des résultats supérieurs à ceux des garçons sont orientées vers un bac S, ce qui correspondrait au même consensus social implicite dans le domaine professionnel où « l'on exige des femmes des performances supérieures à celles des hommes pour ne leur accorder que l'égalité » (Duru-Bellat, L'Ecole des filles 41). Il semble également que l'auto-sélection des filles en matière d'orientation soit le résultat d'une sorte de compromis entre les disciplines qui les intéressent davantage (lettres, santé) et celles qui sont plus valorisantes sur le plan professionnel (sciences et technologie); sur ce point, les garçons sont naturellement attirés par des disciplines valorisantes et n'ont pas de dilemme à résoudre (Duru-Bellat, op.cit. 42). Quant au choix d'une carrière, les lycéennes manifestent une préférence marquée pour les professions liées à la santé et à l'éducation et les professions commerciales liées à l'administration et à la gestion. Plusieurs études ont montré que certaines professions apparaissaient comme plutôt masculines (filières techniques et industrielles) ou plutôt féminines (filières littéraires, administratives, commerciales, sociales et médicales); par ailleurs, on trouve beaucoup plus d'hommes aux niveaux de qualification les plus élevés, même dans les carrières qui s'apparentent aux domaines ressentis comme plutôt féminins. Dans l'enseignement, par exemple, les femmes sont 76% au niveau primaire, 56% dans le secondaire et 30% dans le supérieur dont seulement 13% parmi les professeurs des universités (Cacouault et Fournier 87-88). Un autre facteur intervient dans le choix d'une carrière: la situation familiale. Les femmes célibataires ont des salaires de 20 à 30% supérieurs à ceux des femmes mariées et sont moins nombreuses à chômer. Dans les années 1980 déjà, François de Singly avait démontré que ce n'était pas le fait d'être une femme qui représentait un handicap, mais bien le fait d'être une femme mariée *(Fortune et infortune de la femme mariée).* Cette situation n'a guère changé dans la mesure où les femmes célibataires ou divorcées sont plus nombreuses dans les catégories professionnelles occupées par les hommes, telles que l'enseignement supérieur. Par ailleurs, les quelques femmes mariées que l'on retrouve dans ces même catégories ont généralement un partenaire masculin qui travaille dans le secteur public ou dans l'enseignement et qui les soutient (Cacouault et Fournier 89). Or les choix futurs sont déjà anticipés à l'école où les filles montrent, par les filières sélectionnées, le besoin de « concilier » vie professionnelle et vie familiale; il s'agit là d'un deuxième compromis que ne font pas les garçons qui n'envisagent pas les préoccupations familiales dans le choix d'une carrière (Duru-Bellat, *L'école des filles* 60). Cependant, les dernières évolutions sont optimistes et enregistrent une importante progression des femmes dans le système éducatif et sur le marché du travail. De plus, les Françaises ne semblent plus interrompre leur vie professionnelle lors des maternités. Enfin, l'inégalité liée au sexe est moins marquée dans les professions où l'accès est fortement réglementé par le diplôme et la qualification, c'est-à-dire l'enseignement et les professions libérales (Cacouault et Fournier 87).

D. L'orientation scolaire

L'orientation des élèves, au niveau de l'établissement, est un facteur non négligeable. Sa conception et son organisation actuelles datent de 1973 et s'inscrivent dans l'objectif de démocratisation qui est devenu dominant après la réforme de 1959 lorsque l'obligation scolaire a été portée à 16 ans (Esquieu 57). Ces procédures d'orientation ont été instituées dans le but de développer l'information, d'améliorer le dialogue entre l'équipe éducative et la famille et de simplifier les démarches. Puis en 1975, c'est l'avènement du collège « unique » qui devait permettre à tous les élèves de suivre un enseignement commun jusqu'en fin de 3e. Une consultation nationale sur le collège, lancée en 1999 par le ministère de l'Education nationale, a cependant constaté que le collège « unique », avec ses classes hétérogènes, répondait aux besoins des élèves moyens. « Les enseignants ne parviennent pas à enseigner. Les mauvais élèves ne progressent pas, les bons perdent leur temps. Certes, tout le monde arrive au brevet, mais dans quelles conditions! » (Chartier 18). Le rapport de cette consultation (Dubet) n'a fait que confirmer le fait que l'égalité des chances ne passe pas par un enseignement commun mais par des pédagogies différenciées, des études dirigées confiées à des professeurs, des activités de soutien et une remise à niveau dès l'entrée en 6e pour les élèves en grandes difficultés (Auffray). En conséquence, des mesures ont été annoncées pour améliorer l'égalité des chances au collège et limiter l'échec scolaire (Gurrey).

Plusieurs études révèlent l'existence de différences d'orientation: à résultats identiques, des élèves se verraient proposer des orientations distinctes en fonction de l'impression qu'ils font aux professeurs (capacités, facultés, comportement), de la sévérité de certains conseils de classe et de l'environnement particulier. Par ailleurs, les élèves qui n'ont jamais redoublé en premier cycle vont généralement en seconde générale ou technologique, alors que ceux qui ont rencontré des difficultés scolaires vont plutôt en lycée professionnel. L'origine sociale intervient également dans la mesure où les parents ambitieux peuvent influencer les conseils de classe. On enregistre aussi des disparités géographiques: les régions ouvrières du Nord et de l'Est, la Picardie et la Normandie diffèrent de l'Ile-de-France, de la région Rhône-Alpes et du midi méditerranéen qui comptent davantage de cadres. Les demandes en faveur du second cycle général et technologique sont toujours plus fréquentes dans le Sud-Est et en région parisienne que dans le Nord ou le Centre-Ouest, ce qui indique que l'opposition Nord-Sud a évolué sans toutefois disparaître (Esquieu 65-67). Il y a aussi des disparités sociales variables d'une région à l'autre: l'excellence d'une académie, où les proportions réelles de bacheliers dépassent les proportions attendues, peut bénéficier à l'ensemble des catégories sociales (Casabianca et al. 15).

E. Le type d'établissement

Le type d'établissement dans lequel est scolarisé un élève peut également avoir une influence sur sa carrière. Les conséquences sont généralement modérées pour les élèves brillants et faibles, mais l'influence de l'établissement s'avère importante pour les élèves moyens, en particulier lorsqu'il y a hésitation sur leur orientation. Si le taux de passage des élèves moyens est globalement de 63%, il varie de 27% à 87% selon le collège fréquenté. Le choix de l'établissement est aussi une cause non négligeable d'inégalité sociale à l'école. On remarque ainsi que les transitions vers le second cycle long sont plus fréquentes dans les établissements de grande taille et dans ceux qui sont regroupés avec un lycée alors que les petits collèges, qui comptent un plus grand pourcentage d'élèves de milieux populaires, orientent plus souvent ces derniers en lycée professionnel (Duru-Bellat et al, « Les scolarités » 57-58).

F. Interactions

L'orientation scolaire dépend aussi des interactions auxquelles participent les élèves, leurs parents et les agents de l'institution. Ces interactions sont déterminées par les caractéristiques de la population scolaire, le corps professoral, les filières offertes par l'établissement et les facteurs circonstanciels. Par exemple, des éléments liés à la structure familiale peuvent en partie définir les choix des familles en matière d'orientation (Masson 130-131). C'est ainsi que la carrière scolaire d'un élève est parfois dépendante d'une modification des caractéristiques de la famille telle que l'agrandissement de celle-ci, ou le chômage du père (Lahire, *Tableaux de familles)*. Cela explique le fait que des enfants d'une même famille peuvent connaître des carrières scolaires très différentes. De même, la nature des relations avec les agents de l'institution scolaire peut être déterminante.

Les élèves peuvent s'orienter vers une filière particulière pour éviter un professeur, pour se retrouver dans la même classe qu'un camarade ou pour rester dans leur ville (Masson 141).

II. Le recrutement social de l'élite scolaire

La réduction des inégalités devant l'éducation a toujours été, en France, un des objectifs de l'Education nationale. Cependant, la sélection de l'élite scolaire n'est pas proportionnelle à l'enseignement de masse (Euriat 3). En effet, la principale difficulté que doit affronter l'Ecole est le déficit de reconnaissance sociale des diplômes et donc l'absence de récompense sociale du succès scolaire: 40% d'une classe d'âge disposent aujourd'hui d'un diplôme équivalent ou supérieur à bac + 2^2 alors que 20% seulement des emplois offerts requièrent une embauche à ce niveau. La disproportion est même plus grande lorsqu'il s'agit des diplômes de niveau bac + 4. Or l'Ecole ne joue aucun rôle dans cette situation. Elle se contente de répondre à une demande accrue de formation mais elle ne peut garantir la reconnaissance professionnelle des diplômes qu'elle décerne. En ce sens, elle est impuissante à appliquer le principe d'égalité des chances puisque la reconnaissance du diplôme dépend essentiellement de la voie d'acquisition de ce dernier, grande école ou université, qui est déterminante dans l'obtention d'un premier emploi (Chacornac 128-30). On constate donc un malaise général devant l'incapacité des diplômes à garantir l'insertion sociale.

Si l'on observe l'évolution générale des inégalités sociales devant l'Ecole, on remarque que la promotion des enfants de cadres et d'enseignants n'a guère changé alors que celle des enfants d'ouvriers s'est beaucoup améliorée, contribuant ainsi à une certaine réduction des inégalités. On peut attribuer ce progrès à la suppression du palier d'orientation en fin de classe de 5e, à la diminution de l'ampleur des redoublements et aux transformations du baccalauréat depuis les années 60. Toutefois, même si le bac est aujourd'hui accessible à un plus grand nombre, l'origine sociale des étudiants détermine les chances de suivre un enseignement supérieur: les enfants de cadres et d'enseignants ont 17 fois plus de chances d'être dans une classe préparatoire aux grandes écoles et 7 fois plus de chances que les enfants d'ouvriers d'être à l'université. Si la longueur des études supérieures est différente, les chiffres sont inversés entre la proportion des jeunes d'une certaine origine dans une classe d'âge et leur proportion dans certaines structures d'enseignement, ce qui se manifeste par des sections de techniciens supérieurs avec beaucoup d'enfants d'ouvriers par oppositon au 3e cycle universitaire[3] où ils sont présents en très faible proportion (Euriat et Thélot 4-6). Dans les années 60, les enfants d'ouvriers avaient 28 fois moins de chances d'être à l'université contre 7 fois aujourd'hui, ce qui indiquerait que l'évolution est quantitative plutôt que qualitative puisque l'accès à l'élite scolaire (et donc à l'élite sociale) semble être tout aussi fermé qu'autrefois. C'est ainsi qu'on entend dire parfois que « l'ascenseur social que constitue l'Ecole ne fonctionnerait plus aussi bien aujourd'hui à partir d'un certain niveau » (Euriat et Thélot 8). L'étude de Michel Euriat et Claude Thélot a retracé l'évolution du recrutement social de l'élite scolaire depuis quarante ans en examinant le profil des étudiants inscrits dans quatre grandes écoles parmi les plus prestigieuses: l'Ecole polytechnique (aussi appelée l'X), l'Ecole nationale d'administration (ENA), l'Ecole normale supérieure (ENS) et l'Ecole des Hautes études commerciales (HEC). Ces quatre écoles représentent en effet le passage obligé pour atteindre les sommets de la société française dans différentes catégories (administration, politique, enseignement, économie, commerce). Le nombre de places dans ces écoles a augmenté mais le pourcentage des jeunes qui y sont admis n'a guère changé depuis 40 ans, soit environ un jeune Français sur 1.000. Cette enquête montre que les jeunes d'origine populaire dans les quatre grandes écoles a beaucoup diminué en 40 ans (de 29% dans les années 50 contre 9% aujourd'hui, donc trois fois moins). L'évolution est donc très différente de ce qu'elle est à l'université où cette proportion était constante (environ 50%). Même si la part des jeunes d'origine populaire dans l'ensemble de la génération correspondante a également beaucoup diminué (de 91% à 68%), les chances d'accès des enfants d'origine populaire dans les grandes écoles sont aujourd'hui pratiquement identiques à ce qu'elles étaient il y a 40 ans.

Si l'on considère les autres types d'enseignement supérieur, on constate que le recrutement est de plus en plus sélectif lorsqu'on passe des sections de techniciens supérieurs (STS) à l'université, puis aux classes préparatoires aux grandes écoles (CPGE) et, enfin, aux grandes écoles. Les étudiants des STS sont aussi souvent issus des milieux populaires que l'ensemble des jeunes de 20-24 ans (69% contre 74%), nouvel indice de la très grande démocratisation de cet accès à l'enseignement supérieur. Les jeunes d'origine populaire ont aujourd'hui deux à quatre fois moins de chances d'être à l'université contre sept à dix fois il y a trente ans et l'inégalité d'accès à l'université s'est donc beaucoup réduite; cependant, leur présence dans les grandes écoles reste stable (Euriat et Thélot 7).

En conclusion, l'accès au collège, au bac et à l'université a augmenté pour les enfants d'origine populaire. Toutefois, le fossé s'est creusé entre d'une part, les grandes écoles et universités prestigieuses et, d'autre part, le reste de l'enseignement supérieur. Ce dernier a été modifié par l'enseignement de masse du second degré et n'est plus sélectif. Ainsi, l'ouverture du second degré et du supérieur aux couches populaires ne signifie pas nécessairement celle de l'élite scolaire car les deux phénomènes relèvent de mécanismes différents (Euriat et Thélot 15).

III.   L'égalité des chances serait-elle une illusion?

Malgré toutes les réformes récentes, l'école, par ses dispositifs de sélection à plusieurs niveaux, ne se différencie guère de la hiérarchie sociale. « L'école pour tous n'a jamais produit une école de tous: l'extension de la scolarisation s'est toujours accompagnée de nouvelles exclusions, partage en filières étanches ou échafaudage de sorties précoces. L'échec scolaire sanctionne, en dernière échéance, un vécu socioculturel » (Plenel 102). L'augmentation du nombre des titulaires du baccalauréat n'a pas réussi à produire une meilleure orientation professionnelle, ce qui semble indiquer que la prolongation généralisée des études ne ferait que différer la sélection qui avait lieu autrefois à l'entrée en classe de 6ᵉ. Sous une apparence égalitaire, l'entrée dans le second cycle long reste toujours très sélective, notamment dans les séries de l'enseignement général qui mènent à l'enseignement supérieur long. Les enfants ont plus de chances d'obtenir le bac aujourd'hui mais la valeur sociale du diplôme baisse avec la démocratisation de l'examen (Plenel 130).

Ainsi, le système scolaire a évolué plus vite que les divisions sociales. Avec la massification de l'enseignement, les diplômes se déprécient très vite. Pour obtenir le même poste, il faut posséder un diplôme toujours plus élevé. Or on sait que le diplôme ne suffit pas et que les relations, l'origine familiale et la personnalité de l'individu prévalent. Les désillusions s'accentuent avec le développement de la crise économique qui a entraîné un taux de chômage particulièrement élevé chez les jeunes. Même si les non-diplômés sont beaucoup plus touchés que les autres, le chômage étudiant, même s'il demeure faible, est un phénomène nouveau. Et, de plus en plus, les diplômés de l'université occupent des emplois de cadres moyens dans le secteur tertiaire, plutôt que de cadres supérieurs ou de professions libérales. Cette situation explique les déceptions devant l'école et ses promesses car les diplômes n'apparaissent plus comme un passe-port automatique de promotion sociale. L'allongement de la scolarité et l'ouverture de l'enseignement secondaire ont bien permis l'élévation du niveau d'instruction. Toutefois, les inégalités demeurent et les élites se perpétuent sous des formes nouvelles (Compagnon et Thévenin 150-151).

Le plan Langevin-Wallon[4] consacrait en 1947 le terme de démocra-tisation de l'enseignement et les Français ont cru que cette égalité des chances était possible (Robert 17-24). Jusqu'à la fin des années 60, la démocratisation est réelle: la scolarisation se développe de façon specta-culaire en France, à tous les niveaux. Par ailleurs, la démocratisation a réduit les inégalités entre les sexes. Mais, au-delà de l'école unique, le sys-tème se diversifie après la classe de 3e entre les filières générale, technologique et professionnelle qui mènent à des positions sociales et à des emplois dont la reconnaissance et la rémunération accusent des diffé-rences marquées. Les sections littéraires et scientifiques restent la voie royale empruntée par les enfants de cadres supérieurs et de membres des professions libérales, alors que les enfants d'ouvriers sont davantage orien-tés vers la filière technologique dont le discrédit perdure. L'enseignement de masse n'est donc pas le même pour tous dans la mesure où la sélection se fait toujours par les voies étroites qui mènent à la formation des classes dirigeantes. Par conséquent, il est indéniable que les inégalités sociales devant l'enseignement subsistent (Compagnon et Thévenin 137-140).

Dans *La Scolarisation de la France,* Jean-Pierre Terrail confirme cette situation en établissant un parallèle entre le système éducatif de la IIIe République et celui de la fin du XXe siècle. Il montre ainsi que, sous la IIIe République, chaque ordre d'enseignement (primaire court ou secondaire long) répondait aux besoins de reproduction de chaque classe sociale. Sous la Ve République, l'éducation a évolué sous la pression du développement économique et des revendications en faveur de l'égalité des chances. Toutefois, les changements opérés ont donné pour résultat un itinéraire divisé en filières différenciées selon une hiérarchie conforme à la division en classes sociales tout en donnant l'apparence d'offrir un enseignement commun:

La voie courte — sortie sans diplôme ou diplôme professionnel, bac compris [...] — recrute dans les classes populaires et alimente les emplois d'exécution; la filière technologique recrute dans la fraction supérieure de ces classes et dans les classes moyennes, et prépare aux fonctions semi-qualifiées ainsi que l'encadrement immédiat du travail d'exécution [...]; les terminales d'enseignement général sont la voie d'accès aux formations supérieures longues et aux emplois de cadres supérieurs et professions libérales [...]; la voie royale des plus grandes écoles [...] demeure quasiment inaccessible aux classes populaires (Terrail 35).

Conclusion

L'école et les familles portent chacune leur part de responsabilité dans la situation scolaire des enfants car l'échec et la réussite sont le produit de l'interaction entre des configurations familiales déterminées et des formes de vie scolaire particulières. De ce fait, un plan de lutte contre l'échec scolaire doit tenir compte de facteurs politiques, économiques et familiaux autant que culturels et scolaires (Lahire, « La réussite scolaire »).

La création des zones d'éducation prioritaire (ZEP) en 1981 avait pour objectif de « donner plus à ceux qui ont moins » en accordant davantage de crédits, et donc de personnels, aux quartiers défavorisés pour compenser une partie des inégalités sociales. Il en est de même des initiatives menées à la fin des années 90 telles que l'affectation de milliers d'emplois-jeunes dans les établissements scolaires où les élèves avaient besoin d'un encadrement plus structuré, et toute la série de mesures d'urgence prises par le ministre Claude Allègre à la même époque. Au vu de tous les travaux récents, il semble que les réformes éducatives aient réussi à favoriser l'accès d'un plus grand nombre à l'enseignement secondaire et supérieur. Mais il s'avère que l'inégalité des chances en matière de réussite est fortement liée aux inégalités sociales. Or « les seuls pays où une certaine démocratisation des carrières scolaires a été observée (Pays-Bas et Suède) sont ceux où se sont réduites les inégalités sociales de niveau de vie et de sécurité économique » (Duru-Bellat, « Les inégalités sociales » 48).

Il n'existe pas de solution unique à la question de la démocratisation qualitative de l'enseignement. On possède bien certains éléments du problème et le ministère de l'Education nationale a mis en place toute une série de dispositifs destinés à favoriser l'égalité des chances. Mais l'application de ces mesures exige des crédits considérables et la bonne volonté des personnels et des familles. La fin du XIXe siècle avait vu l'accès à l'enseignement primaire pour tous; la fin du XXe siècle s'est caractérisée par une véritable massification de l'enseignement secondaire. Il reste un long chemin à parcourir si l'on veut atteindre un jour un semblant d'égalité des chances en matière d'éducation. Mais cette égalité passera nécessairement par une modification de la structure sociale. Peut-être la fin du XXIe siècle sera-t-elle couronnée par une véritable démocratisation de l'enseignement qui se traduira par l'accès aux filières sélectives d'un nombre toujours croissant de jeunes, sans distinction d'origine sociale ni de sexe.

Notes

[1] En France, l'enseignement commence par trois années d'école maternelle pour les enfants de trois à six ans, suivies de cinq années d'école primaire ou élémentaire, de 6 à onze ans (cours préparatoire ou CP, cours élémentaire première année ou CE1, cours élémentaire deuxième année ou CE2, cours moyen première année ou CM1 et cours moyen deuxième année ou CM2). L'enseignement secondaire est divisé en deux cycles: le premier cycle ou collège dès l'âge de 11 ans (classes de 6e, 5e, 4e et 3e) et le second cycle ou lycée pour les jeunes de 15 à 18 ans (classes de seconde, première et terminale).
[2] En raison de la variété des diplômes qui existent en France, on désigne géné-ralement le niveau des études supérieures en précisant le nombre d'années effectuées après le bac. C'est ainsi que « bac + 2 » signifie deux années d'études supérieures.
[3] Le cursus des universités françaises est divisé en trois cycles. Le premier cycle concerne les formations équivalentes à deux années d'études, dont le DEUG (diplôme d'études universitaires générales); le deuxième cycle concerne la licence et la maîtrise; le troisième cycle comprend, entre autres, le DEA (diplôme d'études approfondies), le DESS (diplôme d'études supérieures spécialisées) et le doctorat.
[4] Cette commission avait été chargée de conduire une réflexion sur les problèmes de l'enseignement. Le rapport de cette étude insistait sur le principe de méritocratie (égalité des chances en fonction des aptitudes) et proposait la réorganisation du système éducatif à tous les niveaux, des mesures sociales et une meilleure formation des enseignants en cinq ans. Ce plan paraissait révolutionnaire à l'époque et n'avait pas été adopté. Mais ses idées continuent à inspirer les réformes de l'enseignement.

Références

Auffray, Alain. « Le collège fait l'unanimité sur son échec », *Libération,* 19 mai 1999, <www.liberation.fr/quotidien >.
« Le baccalauréat 1998 », Ministère de l'Education nationale, de la Recherche et de la Technologie, février 1999, <www.education.gouv.fr/actu>.
Boudon, Raymond. *L'Inégalité des chances. La mobilité sociale dans les sociétés industrielles.* Paris: Armand Colin, 1973.
Bourdieu, Pierre et Jean-Claude Passeron. *La Reproduction.* Paris: Ed. de Minuit, 1971.
---. *Les Héritiers. Les étudiants et la culture.* Paris: Editions de Minuit, 1964.

Cacouault, Marlaine et Christine Fournier. « Le diplôme contribue-t-il à réduire les diffé-
    rences entre hommes et femmes sur le marché du travail? ». *Egalité des sexes en
    éducation et formation,* sous la direction de Nicole Mosconi. Paris: Presses
    Universitaires de France, 1998, pp. 71-97.
Casabianca, Marthe, Michèle Thaurel-Richard et Paul Esquieu. « Notre école vue du
    bac », *Education et Formations,* n° 35, juillet 1993, pp. 3-19.
Chacornac, Georges. « Egalité des chances et équité sociale », *Revue des Deux Mondes,*
    septembre 1996, pp. 124-32.
Chartier, Nicole. « Collège unique: la fin d'une utopie? », *L'Express,* 13 mai 1999, pp.
    18-19.
Compagnon, Béatrice et Anne Thévenin. *L'Ecole et la société française.* Paris: Com-
    plexe, 1995.
Dubet, François (sous la direction de). « Rapport sur le collège de l'an 2000 », *Le
    Monde,* 18 mai 1999, <www.lemonde.fr/education>.
Duru-Bellat, Marie. *L'Ecole des filles. Quelle formation pour quels rôles sociaux?*
    Paris: L'Harmattan, 1990.
---. « Les inégalités sociales à l'école: les théories sociologiques à l'épreuve des faits »,
    Le Système éducatif, n° 285 de *Cahiers Français,* mars-avril 1998, pp. 44-49.
---, Jean-Pierre Jarousse et Alain Mingat. « Les scolarités de la maternelle au lycée.
    Etapes et processus dans la production des inégalités sociales », *Revue
    Française de Sociologie,* Vol. XXXIV, 1993, pp. 43-60.
Esquieu, Paul. « L'orientation des élèves au sein de l'enseignement secondaire depuis
    vingt ans » in *Education et Formations,* n° 48, décembre 1996, pp. 57-70.
Euriat, Michel et Claude Thélot. « Le recrutement social de l'élite scolaire depuis
    quarante ans », *Education et Formations,* n° 41, juin 1995, pp. 3-20.
Goux, Dominique et Eric Maurin. « Origine sociale et destinée scolaire. L'inégalité des
    chances devant l'enseignement à travers les enquêtes Formation-Qualification
    Professionnelle 1970, 1977, 1985 et 1993 », *Revue Française de Sociologie,*
    vol. XXXVI, 1995, pp. 81-121.
Gurrey, Béatrice. « Les mesures de Ségolène Royal visent à mieux gérer la diversité des
    élèves au collège », *Le Monde,* 26 mai 1999, <www.lemonde.fr/education>.
Lahire, B. *Tableaux de familles. Heurs et malheurs scolaires en milieux populaires.*
    Paris: Gallimard/Seuil, 1995.
---. « La réussite scolaire en milieux populaires ou les conditions sociales d'une schizo-
    phrénie heureuse » in *Ville-Ecole-Intégration,* n° 114, « Les Familles et l'échec
    scolaire », septembre 1998, <www.cndp.fr/savoirscollege >.
Lemaire, Sylvie. « Qui entre en lycée professionnel, qui entre en apprentissage? Profil
    des élèves qui intègrent une filière professionnelle à l'issue du collège » in *Edu-
    cation et Formations,* n° 48, décembre 1996, pp. 71-80.
Masson, Philippe. « Elèves, parents d'élèves et agents scolaires dans le processus
    d'orientation », *Revue Française de Sociologie,* vol. 38, n° 1, janvier-mars
    1997, pp. 119-42.
Plenel, Edwy. *La République inachevée. L'Etat et l'Ecole en France.* Nlle éd. Paris:
    Stock, 1997.
Repères et références statistiques sur les enseignements et la formation.. Paris: Ministère
    de l'Education nationale, de la Recherche et de la Technologie, 1997.
Robert, André. *Système éducatif et réformes.* Paris: Nathan, 1993.
Singly, François de. *Fortune et infortune de la femme mariée.* Paris: PUF, 1987.
Terrail, Jean-Pierre. *La Scolarisation de la France: critique de l'état des lieux.* Paris:
    Dispute/Snédit, 1997.

9

Voices for the Voiceless: Graffiti and Social Issues in Contemporary France

Ann Williams-Gascon
Metropolitan State College of Denver

It appears that as France nears the end of the twentieth century everybody wants to make a mark, to change the face of the country. Presidents build monuments, political groups write new definitions of who does and does not belong, and institutions of all types are responding to the pressures of changing demographics and technological capabilities. Everyone wants to be heard, including those people who do not have access to mainstream means of communication, who are not a part of the system, whose voices are simply perceived as background noise. However, they too can *faire signe* and some of them do. They write on the walls. They plaster those walls with unofficial posters.[1] They paint murals. They create graffiti, thereby reframing their position within the social order, both taking control of social space and defying the general public to ignore their voices.[2]

Out of the myriad definitions of graffiti come some terms that allow the inclusion of all of the forms that graffiti takes in France today. Graffiti is *visual*, whether using letters, drawings or a combination of the two. Graffiti is found in *public* places; on walls, on construction fences, in and around public transportation; anywhere that the writers or artists find the space to make their mark.[3] And for the most part, graffiti is *anonymous*. It is a crime to appropriate public or private property for personal expression and thus even the signatures that are "tags" paradoxically remain anonymous, to the uninitiated in any case. Is graffiti vandalism, as the French penal code states in Articles 257 and 434? Or is it art, as is implied by the 1991 exhibit at the Musée National des Monuments Français entitled "Graffiti Art: Américains et Français, 1981-1991"?[4] Whether one considers graffiti to correspond to one or both of these categories, it is most certainly a phenomenon that can serve well in the study of contemporary France.

Often regarded, and rightfully so, as evidence of unrest and social change, graffiti and the posting of unofficial bills *(l'affichage sauvage),* or "stickers" *(les affichettes)* as they are now called, have long been a part of the cultural landscape in France.[5] Considering the twentieth century alone, the unofficial bills posted during World War II to denounce Nazism and the graffiti taking both sides in the Algerian war set a clear precedent for the high point in graffiti writing which was Mai 1968. Traces of *O.A.S.* or *Organisation de l'armée secrète* from the Algerian War (Riout 76) and "Il est interdit d'interdire" are still visible, reminding passers-by of those turbulent times.

During the following decades typical hand-written graffiti continued to express issues of importance, such as a "Nixon Assassin" left over from the Vietnam War period which survived until at least 1993 (Kleinberg F02). It has been suggested that graffiti writers with a political or social message to communicate were and are frustrated by the system and feel as though they have "no other outlet for their thoughts" (Reisner and Wechsler vi). The seemingly never-ending strikes and demonstrations so commonplace in the 1980s and 1990s have thus been complemented with writings on the walls. According to the introduction to *French Graffiti,* by Imbach and Grindard:

> La rue est un des derniers lieux de communication et de rencontre. Le graffiti demeure un exutoire, un moyen de défoulement. C'est le cri de celui que personne n'écoute. Cri de la rue, cri du coeur: un mot, une bombe de peinture, c'est le circuit le plus court de l'expression pour tous ceux, une majorité, qui n'auront jamais accès aux médias. (1)

Handwritten graffiti and the stickers that are becoming more and more prevalent are often the exteriorization of unresolved social conflict, much as they were in 1968. But, naturally, the issues in question have changed in response to changes in the dominant social themes. Gone are the pro-Maoist slogans and few are the harsh criticisms of *les flics.* And even the idealism apparent in the 1968 graffiti that was highlighted in the book *L'Imagination au pouvoir* by Walter Lewino is lacking in this last decade of the twentieth century. By and large the graffiti is pragmatic, confronting concrete problems rather than calling out for a shift in thinking.

And yet in looking at these practical concerns that find their way onto the walls of France, many of them can be seen as social commentary. They allow us to have a sense, if not of all the specific issues, at least some of the desires that are being thwarted by contemporary society. Some include a secondary characteristic, taking the form of a dialogue, where these issues are "argued," anonymously, yet in a public forum.[6] In looking at examples of graffiti, it is important to note the general place and date of each instance. And since content takes precedence over form in handwritten graffiti, it is the text that is significant. Thus, an understanding of the social context of the writing is crucial. As with other cultural artifacts, the process of observing, analyzing, and verifying intracultural consistency is important prior to offering an interpretation of the graffiti.

One of the major types of social commentary that is expressed through graffiti is that concerning *l'appartenance* — who belongs and who does not belong in France and to France. Distasteful as they are, racist statements abound, reflecting the rise of new French nationalistic tendencies. For verification of this trend, one has only to look at the rising popularity of the *Front National* (whose racist discourse is somewhat muzzled by French law) and the growing visibility of groups such as *Action Française* and *L'Œuvre Française* (far-Right movements) [Figure 1].

Directed predominantly against North African immigrants, possible motivations for authors of racist graffiti are the high unemployment rate in France in the 1990s, the fear of even more immigration resulting from the *régularisations* of the early 1980s (when male immigrant workers were allowed to bring their families to France), and constantly vacillating government policies. These policies, fluctuating with the changes in government, demonstrate that political parties consistently used the issue of immigration as a political tool (Weil).

Figure 2, a similar statement, was located at a bus stop near the Mayor's office in Strasbourg. The proximity to Germany and the heavy influx of Turkish immigrant workers in that country makes the specificity of this graffiti particularly significant. No longer is the subject of racist discourse a general ethnic group. Because of its location a sub-group is singled out as victim [Figure 2].

But the large amount of racist graffiti, relative to other types, also speaks of another trend in contemporary society: the importance of the anti-racist movement. Racist graffiti underscores one characteristic of almost all graffiti: since the graffiti is anonymous, the authors are not subject to outside censorship,[7] nor to the auto-censorship that might keep them from saying out loud what they are willing to write in secret. Taboos no longer regulate the discourse, and as is the case with scatological or sexual graffiti, the writer is able to ignore social rules usually without recrimination. And yet recrimination there is, for although the writer of *"Arabes dehors"* in Figure 1 remains anonymous, he is criticized indirectly by the violent crossing out of his message. Furthermore, the addition of a kinder message to cancel out the hatred makes this palimpsest of particular interest as we analyze the type of discourse each writer is manifesting. The writer of *"Arabes dehors"* is calling for change and venting hostility. The shortness and brutality of the comment imply that it was created in seconds, perhaps less for a reader than for the writer himself. [8] There is no specific interlocutor; we do not know if he is telling an entire people to leave or asking for individual expulsions. It is a shout, not unlike the slogans of a demonstration, and like them, it is limited in scope.

Figure 1. Paris, *XIVe arrondissement,* January 1990.

In looking at the response to the initial graffiti, it seems that it was written in two phases. First is the crossing-out of the offending words, and a quickly scrawled *"HONTE."* But then, contrary to the writer-oriented initial statement, the length and complexity of the rest of the response make it consistent with reader-oriented writing. The French woman apparently has a specific reader in mind and she takes the time to write a letter. For although there is not a specific salutation, the closing *"Ami-calement une Française"* clearly points to an epistolary form. The change from *"Arabes"* to *"travailleurs étrangers,"* a reformulation of part of the original message, drastically changes the connotation attached to the group in question. The *"Arabes"* are assimilated into the wider group, further contradicting the *"dehors."*

Figure 2. Strasbourg, 1992.

Other graffiti dealing with *l'appartenance* approach the issue from the opposite direction. Not only are there those who want France to exclude certain groups, there are those who want to exclude themselves from France. Movements for regional autonomy are well represented on the walls, both in the form of posters and handwritten graffiti. The messages are almost always written in or contain some use of the regional language. *"Ober Breizh Dieub"* (*Action Bretagne Libre*) calls for the freeing of Brittany and slogans like Figure 3 and *Occitans sem una Nacion* (*Occi-*

tans, nous sommes une nation) seek to unite the traditional regions of the south and separate them from France [Figure 3]. Denys Riout, in his book *Le Livre du graffiti*, writes that the use of regional languages serves to exclude non-speakers of the languages from the communicative process.

> Certains textes jouent, d'ailleurs explicitement sur la notion d'exclusion: rédigés en langue d'oc, corse, basque, bretonne, arménienne, arabe, etc., ils ne s'adressent qu'à des "cibles" choisies, là où la langue officielle est le français, et renvoient les autres lecteurs à leur qualité d' "étranger."(76)

Figure 3. Aix-en-Provence, August 1990.

However, the graffiti is there for public view and the writers know that French-speakers will read it. The exclusion of this group comes primarily from the fact that they are not intended to be able to read the graffiti, rather than from a lack of understanding of the language. It is there, in French-speaking public space, but it is not "for" them. Contrary to the racist graffiti, interestingly enough, no dialogues occurred in conjunction with this graffiti, which reinforces the indirect nature of the communication. How would one answer back?

Another type of graffiti containing social commentary is a rather recent development, and in fact came from an ancient type of wall art, the stencil. Negative handprints from the Cosquer cave illustrate this prehistoric practice and the Parisian graffitist who signs his works BLEK reintroduced the stencil as art around 1981. Stenciled graffiti, known in French as *le pochoir,* is a technique which involves cutting a stencil from cardboard or another stiff material and holding it up to the wall to be painted. Applying the paint by brush or, more commonly, by using spray paint, stencils allow the artist to create detailed graffiti, mixing images and text, in part because the lengthy work of creating the stencil is done prior to the foray into the streets. Unlike handwritten graffiti, for stencils form does count, and in fact many stencils are of images only. They are often playful, with the playfulness coming in part from the repetition of the image in various parts of the city [Figure 4].

Denys Riout considers stencils to be art: *"Il va de soi qu'alors, nous ne sommes plus en présence de graffitis, mais d'un nouvel art urbain sauvage et illicite"* (82). Traditionally, there are specific areas of Paris where stencils are found, in particular between the Place de la Bastille and Les Halles (Huber 10). This is also popular for other street arts such as music, dance and theater, and the artistic nature of many *pochoirs* seems to complement these *arts de la rue,* popularized by Jack Lang during his tenure as Minister of Culture in the 1980s. The fact that many *pochoiristes* have become part of the mainstream art world indicates that this form of graffiti is tolerated better than others. An example of this is the case of Miss-Tic, a Parisian woman some forty years of age who creates stencils with poetry and self-portraits. Only some of her works are removed from the walls, which implies that they are not considered vandalism and may be recognized as art [Figure 5]. Postcards of her stencils have been on sale in Paris for several years, and she has collaborated in the publication of her work which includes several books. There are even Web sites devoted to Miss-Tic.

Pochoirs can also express social issues. In the 1980s, many stencil art graffiti had political overtones, as can be seen in *Graffiti'art: Pochoirs politiques* by Eric de Ara Gamazo. While Miss-Tic and other artist/poets still decorate the streets, stencils, like the simpler graffiti, bring to the fore problems in the France of the 1990s. Individuals who feel they have no recourse through official channels resort to writing on the walls and because of the repetitive nature of stencils, these make effective calls for change. Although many of the original *pochoiristes* are entering middle age, at the height of the stencil craze they were a part of that age group that in France has traditionally been the most expressive — *les 18-25 ans*. And now, more than ten years later, French youth are still *des bombeurs*.[9] Names of political figures and social issues make up much of what is stenciled [Figure 6]. Fear of unemployment, dissatisfaction with the educational system and a general sense of hopelessness seem to characterize the attitude of French youth in the 1990s. The *Contrats d'insertion,* the *stages,* the *emplois jeunes,* and the numerous reports from the Ministry of

Figure 4. Paris, 1994.

Education do little to alleviate the concerns of this alienated group. Other stencils focus on promises made to the youth and others request *"Bus gratuits"* signed *"des chômeurs."*

Figure 5. Paris, 1992.

Another related issue is that of housing for the poor and homeless [Figure 7]. In the early 1990s people supporting the organization DAL *(Droit au Logement)* had a stencil campaign *"Promoteur de malheur, si je t'attrape tu meurs"* (Gamazo 90) around the time that l'Abbé Pierre was leading 10,000 people through the streets of Paris in a demonstration against unfair relocations. The 1995 *Rue du Dragon* issue involving the requested expulsion of over a thousand inhabitants of a building in the chic sixth *arrondissement* created a similar hue and cry. The empty buildings of Paris and other cities have long been home to squatters, and the "right to housing" has prompted the occupation of several vacant buildings over the past ten years. In a mix of the whimsical and the critical, there is social commentary [Figure 8].

As any visitor to Paris has seen, there is one more form of urban iconography that speaks loudly of the situation in France today. Prior to the appearance of stencils in the early 1980s came the development of the tag *(le tag),* which is now by far the most predominant and most culturally significant form of graffiti in the 1990s. Stencils and tags are quite different in origin and in appearance and are not created by the same writers; nonetheless the two forms co-exist, often on the same walls, but rarely do artists from one group write over the work of the other.

Figure 6. Paris, 1994.

Tags began appearing on the walls of Paris not long after their birth in the Hip-Hop movement in the Bronx in 1974. American taggers *(les taggers* or *les taggeurs)* marked their passage through sections of New York, much like pilgrims in the Middle Ages, by using a combination of their "tag" or nickname and the number of the street on which they lived. Tags, far from being the gang-related territorial claims that many feared, were signs of both individualism and unity. Taggers were working to ameliorate the dangerous zones of their ethnic minority ghettos. One of their goals, as seen in this quote from the exhibit on Graffiti Art in Paris (1991), was to "lutter contre la violence, la drogue et le racisme qui font rage au sein de la jeunesse des ghettos, en 'transformant l'énergie négative des gangs en énergie positive et créatrice'" (Calzeda 7).

Figure 7. Paris, 1995.

Imported to Paris by two artists, BANDO and D. NASTY, the tagging phenomenon took hold among the *caille-ra* or delinquants (Gilot 1), including the characteristics and practices that had been developed in New York. In the case of tags, unlike stenciled graffiti and traditional graffiti where the *message* is expressive of certain facets of French culture, it is the very fact that tagging exists that is a significant cultural phenomenon. A simple tag (although an indecipherable piece of calligraphy for the uninitiated) is usually written with a spray can or a fat-tipped indelible magic marker and is no more than a sign that indicates "I was here"[10] [Figure 9].

More elaborate is the "throw," or "throw-up" which involves bubble letters or other lettering that requires filling in. These are colorful and in theory should show evidence of a personal style. Of these, "Wildstyle" where all letters are intricately connected is the highest form. The serious tagger, one who works hard to develop an artistic tag, is looking for approbation from others of his kind. Taggers often unite in "crews" where the more experienced "writers" serve as mentors for "toys" (new members). They sketch and practice in "books" or "bibles" and offer help and criticism to others. As in other art forms, there are conventions that regulate how tags are done: never steal another tagger's name or style (Sonik 3), don't allow dripping paint, never cover up another tagger's work. According to most graffiti studies, taggers were originally between the ages of 14 and 20, although one states that 17 to 35 is the current age range (Tessier 1). In the mid-1980s tags were predominantly found in the ethnically diverse Parisian suburbs to the north and east of the city, with two notable exceptions being Jim Morrison's grave in Père Lachaise cemetery and Serge Gainsbourg's house in the fifth *arrondissement,* where tags and graffiti abound [Figure 10]. Now they are found in almost every part of the city.

Figure 8. Paris, 1991.

Tags also invade the Paris *Métro*, especially the subway cars left in the suburban stations overnight. It gives particular pleasure to taggers to see their "names" go by and it is rewarding for them to know that people throughout the city are seeing their signature, even if they do not recognize it. The voyage towards self-esteem and the group dynamics that tagging permits make it an experience of great value for young people in search of a sense of worth and of a voice. As "Jef Aérosol" states, tagging is *"une manière de balancer ma carte de visite dans la ville"* (Tessier 1)

Tagging is one answer to some of the same questions brought to the fore by other forms of graffiti. Young people, especially the poor, do not even have the luxury of mass demonstrations. Students and workers might be able to call for *des manifs,* but the unemployed youth from the projects do not belong to a group whose demands can be heard. Alain Vulbeau, in his important analysis of the tagging phenomenon, clarifies this motivation:

> Vouloir être vu, vouloir exister dans un registre fantasmatique, revendiquer une appartenance de groupe à géométrie variable, occuper symboliquement des espaces publics ou publicitaires, tels les ingrédients d'une forme difficilement cernable, parce que non réductible à un modèle éprouvé, de mobilisation d'un groupe social. (Vulbeau 93)

Figure 9. Paris, *XVIIe arrondissement,* 1994.

Figure 10. Paris, 1992. Photo by Judy Ranger.

This is one source of tags. The fact that individuals can *"carton-ner"* or spraypaint large surfaces (Gilot 2) and *"arracher," "déchirer,"* and *"retourner"* to paint large numbers of tags (Lani-Boyle 120) gives a sense of ownership in cities where they own nothing. However, it would be erroneous to imply that tags are solely the creation of the disenfranchised. Taggers come from all social classes and from a variety of levels of education. Between two interviews with taggers conducted by the author it was possible to see a (socio-cultural) world of difference. GENIUS apologized for his lack of education[11] whereas EXTREM wrote a lyrical explanation of the art in *"graff'art"*.[12] In her psychological analysis of tags (based on Rorschach), Martine Lani-Bayle determined that rather than being confused delinquant types, taggers, especially those who do mural paintings (see below), are of a type that is *"à la fois créatif et actif, avec une bonne intégration sociale."* (97). For proof of this social integration we can refer back to the mentor/protégé relationships of taggers, and even more telling are the huge collective creations known as "pieces." Some are created with as many as twenty *graffeurs* working together, but EXTREM comments that such collaboration is unusual in his circles: "Ça nous arrive de peindre en groupe mais c'est rare car les graffeurs français qui sont bons 'se la pettent' (ça veut dire qu'ils se prennent pour des kings...)."[13] EXTREM paints with friends from childhood and in fact the piece below was done with a friend DEZI to celebrate DEZI's second anniversary as a graffiti artist [Figure 11]. *"Le perso"* (term for human figures in this type of graffiti) is, in fact DEZI. Note the mask used by such artists to protect them from the noxious paint fumes.

Short for "masterpiece" "piece" is translated into French as *"graff"* or *"fresque,"* and is sometimes called simply *"graffiti"* as if the other, traditional writing on the wall no longer counts. These are works of art, (whether one agrees with their aesthetic value or not) requiring time commitments prior to execution and excellent coordination of the crew members who join efforts for the work. French graffiti on view at the 1991 exhibit *Graffiti Art* were predominantly of this type, and some crews even negotiate with cities and cultural organizations to paint schools and other public buildings (Tessier 8). Artists are often invited to create pieces in the controlled setting of workshops and pre-designated sites; for example *"Usines Ephémères"* sponsored by the Ville de Paris (Tessier 9) and *"Des artistes dans la cité. . ."* in Pantin. A part of the experience sought by these illegal artists resides in that illegality. The thrill of creating art under the constraints of the legal system remains part of the process. According to RAMIREZ, a Parisian *graffeur,* "Le graffe est un coup de poing dans la gueule de Monsieur-Tout-Le Monde. C'est aussi la renaissance des quartiers décrépits. C'est dangereux, compétitif et excitant" (Gilot 1). The piece in the photo above was done across from the police station and a mayor's office on the west side of Paris and thus not one of the poor northeastern suburbs often associated with gangs. EXTREM indicated that other artists have been arrested working near the same site, and in fact this *fresque* was covered not long after its creation, not by the city but by other artists.[14] Speed is thus of the essence and the piece above was done in three hours, with pre-sketching done by DEZI. EXTREM describes his motivation.

> Le graffiti est pour nous le premier moyen de subsister dans les résidus de l'art contemporain. La création a disparu dans bon nombre de domaines et la seule direction encore créative (avec le dessin sur l'ordinateur) est le remplissage et les décors des graffitis puisque l'influence et la culture de chaque artiste lui est propre et en constante évolution. [...] Mais mon plaisir principal dans le graffiti est la couleur par-dessus la grisaille de nos villes et de son urbanisme.[15]

Graffiti artists perceive their work as beautifying the walls of their city, and they are proud of what they do. Numerous websites, the best and most comprehensive of which is *ArtCrimes,*[16] and magazines *(Outline,*

Figure 11. Paris, June 1998. Photo by EXTREM.

Paris Conexion, Molotov Coctail) bear witness to the growth of this movement and to the creativity that keeps it moving forward. But it must be recognized, too, that not all people feel the same way about graffiti. Early tags in New York were considered "scars" on the face of the city (Pijnenburg 15). Lani-Bayle suggests that tags and pieces are intimidating to adults because they represent the freedom of adolescents (53). In the *Métro* tagging is seen as a threat, a sign that the *RATP (Régie autonome des transports parisiens)* has no control over its space (Kokoreff 13), and the city of Paris spent 17,000,000 FF in 1996 to clean 410,000 square meters of walls *("Le Chiffre"* in *Le Petit Bouquet)*. Even other "writers" criticize taggers [Figure 12]. (This group, *Action Jeunes,* seems to forget that the removal of posters such as theirs is included in the cost of cleanup).

Figure 12. Paris, 1992.

Graffiti writers of all types send out a challenge. They call into question social class, property ownership and what constitutes a valid contribution to society. They are both the product of their culture and producers of a new culture. Graffiti in France are instruments of change and at the same time they are concrete manifestations of fears and failures, ideals and dreams both of the individual and of society. Different forms of graffiti tell the story of the decade in different ways and serve as guideposts in the study of social issues. They allow us to hear the voices of the (perhaps not so) voiceless.

Notes

[1] Even Post-its with *"Tibéri, ça suffit"* were used in 1997 criticizing Jean Tibéri's financial dealings as Mayor of Paris.

[2] Two forms of contemporary wall communication will not be considered here: "latrinalia," or the writing on bathroom walls, and posters created by major political parties and groups. The former are more indicative of individual psychological issues than of socio-cultural questions and the latter are organized campaigns rather than spontaneous expression.

[3] Pancel formulates it well, saying that graffiti "is about the usurpation of public space for private needs." (Page 1)

[4] This exhibit, which was designed to attract more young people to the museums of France, was controversial from the start, and became more so when some of the artists exhibiting also took credit for tagging the Louvre-Rivoli subway stop, an act considered by most to be vandalism.

[5] Most studies of political graffiti note widespread graffiti production in times of political and social instability. See Brown, on graffiti in Hungary; Sluka on mural painting in Northern Ireland; and, in particular, Peteet on the graffiti of the occupied West Bank in the 1980s.

[6] As with any study of graffiti, it is impossible to be exhaustive. The conclusions drawn here, based on graffiti photographed from 1990 to 1998, are limited to what the author saw.

[7] The city of Paris has special provisions for the immediate removal of racist graffiti, considered more serious than others, although the French penal code does not have a special provision for racism in its sections on graffiti. See Riout 105-106.

[8] Jonathan E. Bush applies Linda Flower's conclusions on "writer-based" and "reader-based" prose to graffiti (p. 94). The former are not an attempt to communicate a message, whereas the latter demonstrate a clear effort to do just that.

[9] Term used by the artist FRED to avoid confusion with the graffiti writers who scribble by hand (Riout 119).

[10] This differs from the "Kilroy was here" found in Europe at the end of World War II, in that the tagger is signing his name, or at least a name that he has attributed to himself.

[11] GENIUS Interview done through electronic mail, August 5, 1998.

[12] EXTREM Interview through electronic mail, August 6, 1998.

[13] EXTREM Interview through electronic mail, August 11, 1998.

[14] EXTREM Interview through electronic mail, August 24, 1998.

[15] EXTREM Interview through electronic mail, August 6, 1998.

[16] See http://www.yahoo.com/Arts/Visual Arts/Graffiti/Exhibits/ for a list of sites.

References

Brown, Jennifer C. "The Writing on the Wall: The Messages in Hungarian Graffiti," *The Journal of Popular Culture*, 29, 2 (Fall 1995) 115-118.

Bush, Jonathan. "Anonymous Dialogic Graffiti and the Rhetoric of Anonymity." Master's Thesis, Northwestern State University, 1996.

Calzeda, Rémi, "Le mouvement Hip Hop." *Graffiti Art: Artistes américains et français 1981-1991 au Musée National des Monuments Français.* Paris: Acte II,1991, 7-9.

"Le Chiffre," in *Le Petit Bouquet: Le quotidien électronique de l'actualité française,* No. 142, 25 septembre, 1997. New York: La Mission Scientifique et Technologique de l'Ambassade de France aux Etats-Unis.

De Ara Gamazo, Eric. *Graffiti art. Pochoirs politiques: Chronique d'une décennie.* Paris: Editions de l'Aube, 1992.

Flowers, Linda. "Writer-Based Prose: A Cognitive Basis for Problems in Writing," *College English* 41 (September 1979): 19-37.

Gilot, Louis. "Le Graffiti." Online Posting. *Cry-lon The Graffiti Cyberzine* <http://www.crylon.com/parisf.html>, July 30, 1998.

Graffiti Art: Artistes américains et français 1981-1991. Paris: Musée National des Monuments Français, 1991.

Huber, Joerg. *Sérigraffitis.* Paris: Fernand Hazan, 1986.

Imbach, Jean-Pierre and Gilles Grindard. *French Graffitis.* Paris: Editions du Guépard, 1982.

Kleinberg, Howard. "These Vandals Belong to the Ages," *Sacramento Bee,* July 18, 1993, p. F02.

Kokoreff, Michel. "La propreté du Métropolitain: vers un ordre post hygiéniste?" Online posting. *Annales de la recherche urbaine,* <http://www.equipement.gouv.fr/dau/cdu/datas/annales/kokore.htm>, August 8, 1998.

Lewino, Walter. *L'Imagination au pouvoir.* Paris: Eric Losfeld, 1968.

Lani-Bayle, Martine. *Du Tag au Graff'art.* Marseille: Edition Hommes et Perspectives, 1993.

Peteet, Julie. "The Writing on the Walls: The Graffiti of the Intifada," *Cultural Anthropology,* November 2, 1996, 139-159.

Pancel, Antonia Antoinette. "Graffiti: Its Aesthetic Origins and Legal Ramifications in Contemporary Society." Master's Thesis. University of Notre Dame, April 1994.

Pijnenburg, Henk. "Du métro au monde de l'art." *Graffiti Art: Artistes américains et français 1981-1991 au Musée National des Monuments Français.* Paris: Musée National des Monuments Français, 1991, 15-24.

Reisner, Robert and Lorraine Wechsler. *Encyclopedia of Graffiti.* New York: Galahad Books, 1980.

Riout, Denys et al. *Le Livre du Graffiti.* Paris: Editions Alternatives, 1990.

Sluka, Jeffery. "The Politics of Painting: Political Murals in Northern Ireland." *The Paths to Domination, Resistance and Terror.* Carolyn Nordstrom and J. Martin, eds. Berkeley: U of California Press, 1992.

Sonik. "Style, Technique, and Cultural Piracy: Never Bite the Hand that Feeds." Online posting. *Art Crimes: The Writing on the Wall.* Susan Farrell and Brett Webb, eds. <http://www.graffiti.org/faq/sonik.html>, August 24, 1998.

Tessier, Yvan. *Paris: Art libre dans la ville.* Paris: Herscher, 1991.

Vulbeau, Alain. *Du tag au tag.* Paris: Institut de l'Enfance et de la Famille, 1992.

Weil, Patrick. "Pour une nouvelle politique d'immigration," *Esprit,* Avril 1996, 136-154.

III. Identity - Identité

10

France in Trouble or Just in Transition?

Edward C. Knox
Middlebury College

How to sort out the state of France today? A look at several articles and two major books published during the period between mid-May 1998 — whatever day it became clear that the thirtieth anniversary of *mai '68* did not galvanize great interest — through President Chirac's July 14 statements, inevitably inspires a few thoughts about the discourse on contemporary France in the French and American press.

Journalists and authors write of course at different levels. One could identify and distinguish among, for example, event, sector and system. *Event* identifies the everyday but often non-scheduled occurrences that sometimes end up serving as a touchstone or source of resonance for the state of a society, e.g., the islamic scarves incident (1989), the strikes of November-December 1995, the World Cup victory in summer 1998, etc. *Sector* refers to such spheres as the family, education, leisure, the economy, etc., the contexts of the ebb and flow of national life, and trends rather than discrete events — most of the articles in this volume are sectorial in that sense. Writings that seek to identify at a deeper level what is specific to the French way or French identity are dealing with *system*. The period under review carried examples of all three levels.

During these several weeks France moved from concern about itself to a general euphoria about the World Cup that carried over into the best attended July 14 celebration in many years. Significantly, the World Cup events brought out general impatience with a strike by persons (the Air France pilots) considered to be well off and part of the protected sector, plus a keen sensitivity to how other countries would react to what risked being perceived as "typical" French behavior, a "blocage à la française" (*Libération*, 2 juin); and a multicultural lovefest inspired by the victory of the so-called "Black-Blanc-Beur" French World Cup team, with concomitant vaunting of the republican model of integration and "la France qui gagne."

Another large share of the discourse, particularly on the French side, continued to be a function of the situation analyzed in an earlier article, i. e., a striking pace of publication with a special focus on what characterizes France as a nation and social system: "who are we and what are we becoming?" (Knox 91). The explicit and widespread current concern about French identity stems from the sense of many that France is caught up in transnational movements (immigration and globalization) that force it to wonder about its future, not least because it has had so strong a sense of its own identity and traditions, the so-called *exception française*. To the extent the latter is intimately bound up with the overarching role of the State across many centuries, and with the strongly held view that national life and the general good, *l'intérêt général*, are to be politically determined (in the best sense) rather by the play of economic forces (à la the U.S., in French eyes), the loss of confidence in politics, politicians and the State can only feed those concerns mentioned. The constant critical attention from American commentators only exacerbates the situation. (See, however, Spinrad on the *exception française* defined as setting ethical and cultural values above economic imperatives.)

During the two-month period in question, two special pieces appeared: the *Science & Vie* "Dossier France," and the "Spécial France" in the *Nouvel Observateur*. The former looks at geography, history and the economy, and feels obliged to explain this uncharacteristic departure from more standard content: "au moment où la France va lier plus fortement encore son destin à ceux de ses voisins d'Europe, la connaissons-nous?" ("Dossier France" 1). It concludes reassuringly that France is fortunate in its geographical bounty and the diversity of its space, and that as a nation it remains one of the planetary powers (ibid.).

Le Nouvel Observateur strikes at first a more defensive (and somewhat exaggerated) note, particularly with respect to what Americans have to say: "Nous sommes, dit-on, anachroniques, accrochés à un étatisme, à une organisation du travail et à un modèle social que la mondialisation, le recul des Etats-nations et le déclin de la classe ouvrière condamneraient ("Spécial France" 4)." There is much in this issue that is more than familiar, but there are also several moments worth underscoring. In his editorial ("Comment vivre avec Gulliver? "), Jean Daniel does a brilliant comparison of American and French viewpoints, to try to get at the source of the antipathies:

Il est bien connu que la France et les Etats-Unis sont les deux seules nations à s'être investies d'une mission universelle . . . Ils sont à la fois chauvins et univer-salistes. Ils ont chacun leur manière — débat essentiel — de concilier la liberté et l'égalité. Ils veulent imposer un universel imprégné pour les uns par la tradi-tion et pour les autres par la modernité. (Daniel 64-65)

This overview becomes almost serenity in Daniel's interview with Foreign Minister Hubert Védrine, who sees America as the only superpower in the world, with France and six other nations grouped in a second tier.

Le monde change, mais il change en anglais et sous l'influence d'autres facteurs — CNN, Internet — , d'où une vraie mélancolie. Pourtant, nous sommes par-faitement capables d'agir dans ce monde-là, mais par la négociation, le com-promis, le troc entre ceci et cela, un travail de bénédictin, la technicité, l'ingéniosité, l'investissement dans la durée. Des choses qui n'ont rien à voir avec les formes habituelles de notre "génie". Mais il y a une autre conception de la grandeur. Il faut nous adapter. (Védrine 108)

An opinion survey in the same issue seems to bear out this new-found circumspection, as responses to several different questions paint a picture of a flexible, market-oriented (*libérale*) public opinion, albeit within recognizable French limits: "Les Français sont fidèles à leurs valeurs, mais conscients que les règles du jeu économique ont changé. La mondialisation, ils sont prêts à faire avec. Mais donnant donnant: oui à la modernité, non à la fin de la cohésion sociale' ("Spécial France" 124). Furthermore, Daniel Cohen develops at some length a plan for a new "so-cial contract" and throughout the issue we have awareness of how other countries do things (including an insert on the limits of the famous *modèle hollandais,* 116), or what those countries think about France, with a paean to Europe by Joseph Weiler of Harvard, who sees it as placing limits on the erosion of national sovereignty and therefore good for France (ibid. 86-90).

A sensitivity toward what foreigners have to say continues in French pieces, i. e., not just a reference to the content of what is said but the fact of foreign observation (e. g., Chocas during the period at hand, but also Louyot, Spinrad, the creation of such periodicals as *Courrier International* and *L'Européen).* Richard Cohen's February 1997 piece proved particularly grating to the French, but American journalism in general continues to stoke that fire. On the eve of the World Cup, the international editions of both *Time* and *Newsweek* saw fit to devote many pages to France today, albeit with considerable contrast. *Time* did a sympathetic profile of the several provincial cities playing host to matches (Rafferty), preceded by a decidedly unanxious overview in which Theodore Zeldin does his own historian's sorting out:

> After listening to what the French say about themselves, it is hard to decide whether this is a country moving forward toward suicide, or a country very successfully managing change behind a smokescreen of complaints. I, for one, think the patient has nothing more than a headache and a case of amnesia. (Zeldin 01)

Notably more strident, the cover of the June 15 *Newsweek International* — "France Welcomes the World. Just Ignore the Strikes and Riot Police" — was illustrated by an archival photo of strikers demonstrating, and ran a single article (Warner) deriding French preparations: public transportation, the Stade de France, ticket sales policy, lack of enthusiasm for soccer, intimidating presence of state police (*CRS*), etc. (Interestingly, the stadium received universal acclaim from players and fans, and the police were if anything chided later by the press for not intervening promptly enough against hooligans.) A week later, Michael Elliott responded to Alain Frachon's reading of the issue with the kind of intercultural condescension the American press usually sees as typically French. His basic ploy is to assert that in its alleged prickliness and defensiveness France is its own worst enemy:

> Imagine — it's hard to do, but try it anyway — a France that wasn't continually telling the world what a wonderful place it is. You'd then see a society that valued tolerance; that took intellectual pursuits seriously; that valued social cohesion. You'd find a nation that, though with high-population densities, protected its countryside, and that had built a successful modern economy. In fact, you've just discovered the Netherlands... The problem is, it's difficult to have a sensible discussion about the merits of different types of capitalism when the noisiest advocates of the European view are the French. (Elliott 2)

In other words, France gets taken to task not only for contaminating its own strengths, which somehow becomes an even greater failing than if it lacked the qualities cited, but also for obscuring the valid elements of the European approach. Moreover, Elliott opens and closes the article with praise for the good life in France: not only the kind of praise that he would deny the French about themselves as arrogant self-centeredness, but in effect little more than a variation on the old saw about how nice France would be if only there were no French people there.

During the same period but unconnected to the World Cup, *Business Week* ran a cover story on "France. A Quiet Revolution" aimed at identifying what it sees as modernizing trends in the economy.

> The country is far from embracing U.S.-style capitalism. But advocates of reform . . . want to free up the country's formidable resources to produce more efficiently, through decentralization. That means removing barriers to entrepreneurship, lowering taxes and social charges, and cutting the fat from state spending. (Edmondson 20)

Aside from a few familiar terms ("fat subsidies," "crowd-pleasing handouts," "fat pay increases," etc.) the article is relatively free of carping or the "one approach (American) fits all" rhetoric still prevalent in so many journalistic treatments. Moreover, a new interest in economic Europe may have been awakened in the American press with the realization during the spring of 1997 that the common currency would indeed come into being, and during the period in question the skillful intercultural work of Ambassador Rohatyn came in for high praise in the French press (Delafon).

A few weeks earlier, *Marianne* had run a look at the American model, in which unlike most American articles it at least cited some pro's (low unemployment, and to a certain extent reform of welfare) before it went about underscoring all the con's (poverty, precarious employment and health coverage, rate of incarceration):

> Repris par la plupart des médias, cet hymne au "miracle américain" poursuit, selon ses adversaires, deux objectifs: d'abord présenter comme futile car vouée à l'échec toute tentative de résistance ou même d'aménagement du néolibéralisme. Le montrer, ensuite, comme débarrassé de tout parti pris idéologique en escamotant son coût social. (Dior 34)

> On aime les Etats-Unis tant qu'ils ne prétendent pas ériger leur mode de vie en norme universelle et faire du hamburger l'égal du tournedos Rossini. Un travers d'autant plus haïssable que nous y avons nous-mêmes cédé pendant deux siècles. Du temps où la France avait encore des prétentions à l'universalisme. (Dior 38)

(See also Merlin's "L'Amérique revue et corrigée.")

Once we get past *Marianne's* reductive hamburger, we have an interesting take on evangelical universalism, now seen as American and no longer French. We also have here an example of one of the fundamental issues in the discourse, namely how infrequently views of France (or the U.S.) today have tried to weigh both sides, to see both positive and negative in the same picture. Yet something may be changing, as indicated for example by Daniel's and Merlin's pieces and embodied in Prime Minister

Jospin's visit to the U.S. during this same period. Jospin announced quite candidly that he now felt that it was worth looking at job creation in the U.S., that it now appeared not all of them were "petits boulots." His advisers might of course have informed him of that earlier, but he did have the forthrightness to say it, and thus to call into partial question the French approach to employment, now often referred to as "le traitement social du chômage," or a preference for unemployment. One also begins to see accounts of French poverty that counter somewhat the smugness once reserved for the ("disastrous") social effects of America's *ultralibéralisme* or unfettered capitalism (see Merlin; "Nouveaux visages;" de Closets, 53-59).

This new openness contrasts with Elliott's apparent disinclination to cite good elements without an immediate ironic overlay. Other examples of journalistic imbalance include the favorable coverage of Jospin's visit to the U.S. due to the perception he is not a typical French ideologue but a pragmatist (read: he was coming around to American ways). Treatment of the *modèle hollandais* is partial (in both senses), devoting insufficient attention, for example, to the salient differences in demography or work patterns there (most notably: fewer women working, more part-time employment). Moreover, the articles by Ahrens (the loudspeaker played American music to celebrate the French victory) and Kelly (the French as champions will not be more insufferable than ever, since nothing could make them more so) are simply embarrassingly chauvinistic humor, hardly better than the satirical image of France that appears on the Internet from time to time. Compare with Gopnick's piece, in which he moves subtly through a process that takes him from a self-satisfied scorn for soccer to an appreciation for the sport and for those who appreciate it.

At the systemic level, De Closets is once again full of examples that he says constitute the French model (chap. II): the unspoken collaboration surrounding social and economic privilege, the immobilism and conservatism that are barriers to meaningful change and modernization; the "socially correct" thematic (102) that provides a rationale for it all, the State budget that funds it (109). In that light, Viviane Forrester (179-180) and especially the 1995 strikes ("La France du refus,"), which he sees as the starting point of his "countdown" (61), come in for especially rigorous scrutiny.

As de Closets' title indicates, what is different here from his earlier work is that he situates all this in a process. He sees three Frances: the protected one, the competitive one, and the exposed one (96), and his pages on the working poor and the unemployed who have exhausted their benefits are compelling (e. g., 53-59). He claims that if change does not come soon, the *Front National* will only be consolidated in its position by providing a haven for the disgruntlement of the disadvantaged (319). On the other hand, he holds out for and believes in a better, more modern France, not a non-French imitation of the U.S., with a role to play in Europe and in the world (49-59) provided it takes the initiative (e.g., 29, 60, 179).

> . . . la mondialisation n'impose pas un modèle unique de société réduite au marché et à son Etat gendarme; (49) . . . je crois au modèle français, au vrai, celui de la réalité, pas des apparences, celui qui instaure la solidarité entre les hommes; (59) . . . dans un univers concurrentiel, l'alternative de la modernisation s'appelle la disparition. (141)

Lesourne is equally concerned and calls for an effort of the national will, but is working at a deeper level than de Closets. For him, the French model is the centralized, top-down, State-controlled one that brought modernization and prosperity to post-war France in the *Trente Glorieuses* (1945-1974), relying as well on a set of shared values, a favorable demographic situation, technical progress and the competence of its elite, etc. (119-120). He thus sees misunderstanding and underestimation by the French of the effects of the information society and of globalization, together with the difficulties inherent in the current demographical situation, as standing between France and the mastery of its future. His further concern is that the French may conflate the values that underpin the model and the model itself (169), or try to get off too easily by refusing to see itself as the source of its problems or seeking to maintain the "exception française" by reworking the model only at what he calls the margins (reduced public expenses, better control of Social Security, reduced work week, no change in retirement age, etc.). His sorting out is radical enough to be quoted at some length.

> (la société française) feint d'espérer que ces accommodements lui permettront de résorber le chômage, limiter l'exclusion, maintenir intact l'appareil d'Etat et soutenir la concurrence internationale . . . Un mirage plus qu'un espoir, qui risque de se terminer en cauchemar.
>
> Le mal français est plus profond. Il est dans la conception de la fonction publique, dans la confusion du politique et de l'administratif, dans la sclérose de la représentation sociale, dans l'incompréhension du rôle des prix, dans les modalités du système de prélèvements, dans les méthodes auxquelles il a recours pour combattre l'insécurité et l'inégalité. Il est dans la conviction partagée par la majorité de la nation que les valeurs fondamentales d'efficacité et de justice so-

ciale ne peuvent pas être poursuivies grâce à d'autres instruments que ceux élaborés en France après la Seconde Guerre mondiale. (189-90)

One could hardly ask for a better illustration of the difference between a sectorial and a systemic approach, although short of a revolution it is hard to imagine any society, much less one steeped in (successful) tradition, starting with systemic change. At the same time, a reading of de Closets and Lesourne leaves one convinced that the passage into the new Europe and a globalized world is the step that will make or break the process of French modernization begun after World War Two. Equally striking is the degree to which such changes would be dependent on unpacking and recasting of concepts, better information and understanding, less rhetoric and more value clarification. In a word, on a new discourse.

Two days after France's World Cup victory, President Chirac saluted in his July 14 interview "la France qui gagne... nous sommes sur le bon chemin" (*Le Monde,* 16 juillet 1998, 5). Some commentators wondered how long the euphoria would last, especially in light of an opinion poll — admittedly a delicate one to interpret — to which 40% of the French had responded they feel "racist" or "somewhat racist" (Cayrol). Chirac cited many necessary reforms, but the closest he came to proposing radical change concerned reforming political representation (more noncivil servants in the legislature) and the justice system (stronger presumption of innocence, less preventive detention, independence of magistrates). A six-part series in *Le Monde* less than a month earlier on the problems of the French state ("Voyage indiscret...") had left little doubt that things need to be in some sort of transition lest they end up in trouble, but about the same time, Moisi concluded, after a detailed review of the challenges to be faced (globalization, American hegemony, merging into Europe, assorted internal shortcomings), that "France will endure" (104). Rather than, say, *prevail,* as in "la France qui gagne"? Does one endure a transition, or an ordeal? In enduring does one evolve or remain the same? Is this a new, more modest perspective, or does the issue lie with the translation?

To sum up: the volume and pace of discourse on France not only continued unabated during this remarkably fertile two-month period, partly as a function of the World Cup but also due to a continuing self-consciousness and some new-found sensitivity bordering on attentiveness to the opinion of others. Signs indicated a new willingness (even beyond *Le Figaro* and the business magazines) to consider non-French approaches to things, and to see the downside of business as usual. At least two new critical studies laid out in depth what it will take to modernize *and* remain French, and a survey confirmed French readiness to do so.

On the other hand, anyone hoping for an objective view of France in the major American press of the period found that — with the exception of a few editorialists — little had evolved. International coverage is increasingly problematic overall, and when it elects to deal with France, the selection of content is often tendentious. We still get the provocative headlines, the supercilious tone routinely reserved for things French (and paradoxically ascribed to the French themselves as one of their irritating traits), the gratuitous comment or parenthesis reminding the reader "you know how those French are."

> Strikes, demos and riot police welcome the world's fans. A fiasco? No: France. Enjoy it. (Warner 32)

> . . . virtually everyone who came to France arrived with some heartfelt grievance — inconvenience due to strikes, ticket shortages, or simply the French being themselves. (Starr 41)

To explain this discursive phenomenon, one would have to sort out whether the U.S. press reacts too often to or through specific events rather than seeking out sectorial issues, with the resultant coverage drawing too heavily on the spectacular, the picturesque, or indeed the stereotypical. One source of its attitude is surely in great part frustration deriving from French independence in foreign relations (NATO, Yugoslavia, nuclear testing, policy in Iraq and Africa, etc.), fueled by a centuries-old cultural antipathy derived from the English (see Arnaud, for example).

A question for another study would concern whether this is the Americans' primary source of "information" on France, and what is likely to change the situation? Less brutally jingoistic than the English tabloids, but also less deftly cutting than, say, the *Economist,* the great majority of American journalistic discourse on France appears to seek reassurance in the other's difficulties, as though to quell one's own uncertainties in the face of a civilization that has always seemed — often smugly — to call American ways into question. But could it be that on the eve of the twenty-first century "even" the French were learning better than Americans how to ask openmindedly and internationally, "Compared to what?"

References

Ahrens, Frank. "Soccer Bleu! U.S. Culture Triumphs at World Cup." *Washington Post,* July 14, 1998, D01.

Arnaud, Jean-Louis et al. "Pourquoi les Anglais nous détestent." *L'Européen,* 8 juillet 1998, 18-43.

Cayrol, Roland et al. "La société française reste taraudée par le racisme." *Le Monde,* 2 juillet 1998, 14-15.

Chocas, Viviane et al. "Les étrangers séduits par la France." *Le Parisien,* 23 juin 1998, 2-3.

Closets, François de. *Le Compte à rebours.* Paris: Fayard, 1998.

Cohen, Roger. "Liberty, Equality, Anxiety: for France, Sagging Self-image and Esprit." *New York Times,* February 11, 1997, 1-2.

Daniel, Jean. "Comment vivre avec Gulliver?" *Le Nouvel Observateur,* 28 mai 1998, 64-65.

Delafon, Gilles. "Felix Rohatyn, un Américain à Paris." *Journal du dimanche,* 5 juillet 1998.

Dior, Eric. "Vérités et mensonges sur le modèle américain." *Marianne,* 1er juin 1998, 32-38.

"Dossier France." *Science & Vie,* hors série juin 1998, 156 pages total.

Edmonson, Gail. "A Quiet Revolution." *Business Week,* June 29, 1998, 20-24.

Elliott, Michael. "A Letter to the French." *Newsweek International,* June 22, 1998, 2.

Frachon, Alain. "Les Etats-Unis profitent du Mondial pour ausculter la France." *Le Monde,* 11 juin 1998, 30.

Gopnik, Adam. "Paris Journal: Endgame." *The New Yorker,* July 13, 1998, 28-33.

Kelly, Michael. "Causes for Celebration." *Washington Post,* July 15, 1998, A17.

Knox, Edward. "Regarder la France: une réflexion bibliographique." *The French Review* 72 (October 1998), 91-101.

Lesourne, Jacques. *Le Modèle français.* Paris: Odile Jacob, 1998.

Louyot, Alain et al. "Comment le monde nous juge." *L'Express,* 26 février 1998, 50-58.

Merlin, Albert. "L'Amérique revue et corrigée." *Le Monde,* 24 juin 1998, vi.

Moisi, Dominique. "The Trouble with France." *Foreign Affairs,* May/June 1998, 94-104.

"Nouveaux visages de la pauvreté." *Dossiers & Document du "Monde"* 266 (juin 1998).

Rafferty, Jean et al. "Focus on France: Host to the World." *Time International,* June 15, 1998, 70-83.

"Spécial France." *Le Nouvel Observateur,* 28 mai 1998, 70 pages total.

Spinrad, Norman. "L'exception française." *Le Monde,* 18 août 1998, 8.

Starr, Mark. "Le Jour de Gloire." *Newsweek Atlantic Edition,* July 20, 1998, 41.

Védrine, Hubert. "Les intérêts et le rang de la France. Entretien avec Jean Daniel." *Le Nouvel Observateur,* 28 mai 1998, 108-111.

"Voyage indiscret au coeur de l'Etat." *Le Monde* 23-28 juin 1998.

Warner, Judith and Christopher Dickey. "Perfectly Natural." *Newsweek International,* June 15, 1998.

Zeldin, Theodore. "*Les Misérables* on the Mend" in Focus on France, *Time International,* 15 June 1998, 00-02.

11

France's National Identity and the French Press

Jacqueline Thomas
Texas A&M University-Kingsville

France's self-image was so poor in February of 1997 that it was making the front pages of the American press. *The New York Times* ran the following headlines on February 11: "For France, Sagging Self-Image and Esprit," and "With Global Challenges, Identity Crisis Dampens France's Esprit." What was causing the French to question their sense of identity? This essay will examine threats to Frenchness and analyze the image of France which the French press portrayed between February 1997 and July 1998.

France is the largest, though not the most populous country in Europe and was once among the most powerful. France's linguistic unity and its natural boundaries flanked as it is by water on three of its six sides and by mountains on two others have contributed to a clear identity and an uncontested nationalism.

The State is all-powerful. No matter the form of its government, the state has regulated, subsidized, and more importantly, standardized its citizenry. In fact, the state is synonymous with the French way of life, employing five million of its sixty million inhabitants. More than half of the families in France depend on income from the state. Public services such as railroads and postal and telephone systems make up well over one third of the economy. *L'Etat-providence* has traditionally provided a cradle-to-grave security blanket for citizens: pre-school child care; education and medicine; decent minimum wages; job security, especially for civil servants; and attractive retirement benefits. In the nation state cultural identity becomes inseparable from national identity.

After the liberation of the French from German occupation in 1944, there followed *les trente glorieuses,* thirty years when France enjoyed its *liberté, égalité,* and *fraternité* and became a major industrial and exporting power. However, in the mid-1970s cracks began to appear in the system. Unemployment, which was at 2.7% in 1973, began to climb and reached 12.5% by 1997. Foreign immigrants, largely from France's former colonies, began to be blamed for the slowing economy. Voters looked to their leaders for solutions but successively became disenchanted as the changes in government attest: left wing, 1981-1986; right wing, 1986-1988; left wing, 1988-1993; right wing, 1993-1997; left wing, June 1997. What is more, the lack of a clear majority led to three periods of cohabitation beginning in 1986. Gradually the optimism which marked the end of the dark years of the Vichy Government (1940-44) was undermined and led to what American print media characterized as self-doubt, a feeling of drift and decline, and national discontent (Hoffmann 45).

Several measures of France's social climate confirm the presence of malaise: a rise in the suicide rate, especially among young people; interrupted sleep patterns reflected in increased sales of tranquilizers and sleeping pills; increased racism and xenophobia; feelings of insecurity; and growing anxiety about the future (Mermet 201). Mirroring the malaise was the publication of a flurry of social novels and non-fiction such as Vivian Forrester's *L'Horreur économique* in 1996-97.[1] What is of more interest here, however, is what the French press published in the eighteen-month period beginning in February 1997 and ending in July 1998.

Threats to "Frenchness"

Toward the end of the century, two ghosts of France past reared their ugly heads, the repercussions of which were discussed frequently in French daily newspapers and magazines: the role played by the French during the Vichy government and the Algerian War.

More than 50 years after World War II, the French Resistance myth was still a popular topic of feature films, documentaries, and fiction. Lucie and Raymond Aubrac were long considered heroes of the Resistance. They published books about their experiences, including one which inspired Claude Berri's film *Lucie Aubrac.* In April 1996 a book by Gérard Chauvy called *Aubrac, Lyon 1943* challenged the accuracy of their version of events. A panel of historians questioned the Aubracs on the premises of the left-wing daily *Libération,* but they were unable to categorically exonerate the couple. The experts attributed the shady areas of the Aubracs' testimony to the fallible nature of memory. The debate continues and, with it, national soul-searching about the extent of French collaboration during the German Occupation persists.

A headline in the center to center-left *Le Monde* underscores the weight of the Vichy period on France's collective conscience: "Tout concourt aujourd'hui au souvenir obsédant de Vichy" (Solé and Weill 1), and suggests a kind of "Vichy fixation." The article was written at the beginning of the six-month trial of Maurice Papon in 1998. An administrator in the Vichy government which passed retroactive legislation aimed largely at recent Jewish refugees, revoking French nationality from anyone who had acquired it after 1934, Papon was being tried for complicity in crimes against humanity in the deportation of 1,560 Jews. Set up as a discussion between Robert Solé and Nicolas Weill (1), the article analyzes why the wound that was caused by French collaboration "n'arrête pas de s'ulcérer au lieu de cicatriser: la constitution d'une identité juive particulière, et la constitution d'une identité proprement générationnelle; . . . l'effritement de la version gaullienne 'unanimiste' de la Résistance; . . . la mise en cause de la responsabilité directe ou indirecte de Vichy dans la 'solution finale'."[2] The discovery of Mitterrand's friendship with René Bousquet, the murderous Vichy police chief, further compounded the issue. Just as Papon's trial was a trial of the Vichy administration and its politics of exclusion,[3] the moral ambiguity of Mitterrand's experience echoed that of the nation's.

The blemish on society of Vichy's antisemitic policy, "cette tare indélébile de notre histoire," and its devastating effect on national identity were recalled by a journalist in the right-of-center weekly news magazine *L'Express* on the anniversary of France's capitulation to the German forces. He wrote, "En quelques jours, [la France] subit l'anéantissement collectif de ce qu'elle nommait nation, fierté" (Gluckmann 17). André Gluckmann, for whom the only important date in French history in the twentieth century is June 18, 1940, admonishes his readers to remember the possibility of saying "no." He congratulates those naturalized citizens who "emportent la patrie à la semelle de leurs souliers." He adds that whenever a Frenchman hears about refugees fleeing from Bosnia, Rwanda, or Kosovo, he can savor his freedom but "il lui demeure interdit de penser que cela n'arrive qu'aux autres." The debate about nationality, immigration, and naturalization endures.

Following the loss in 1962 of the Algerian War, 650,000 French Algerian immigrants were repatriated to France. Subsequent waves of immigrants from Algeria and Morocco continued to be welcome in France as long as the economy needed manpower, particularly in the mines in the north of France. The men worked and lived together in miserable conditions without their families. When the French economy began to slow down in 1974 immigration policies were tightened. The doors were closed to new immigrants and an effort was made to stabilize the existing population by bringing over their families. This immigrant population lived in ghettoes, largely excluded from mainstream French life. Whereas the percentage of foreigners living in France remained stable from 1975 on, the proportion coming from the Maghreb increased while the proportion coming from other European countries decreased. These facts combine to make immigrants of Arab origin highly visible. Moreover, these immigrants are associated with more complicated problems of integration than their European counterparts, for example, different religion and very different mores, and also with terrorism by militant extremists as the civil war in Algeria spilled over into France.

The National Front, France's ultra nationalist party headed by Jean-Marie Le Pen, capitalized on citizens' reactions to these problems. The Front's most famous poster said, "Three million unemployed, that's three million immigrants too many!" (Gourevitch 110). But it was Jean-Louis Debré, Chirac's minister of the interior in 1997, who stirred up bad memories of Vichy. He called into question France's national identity by including a provision in proposed immigration regulations that would have required French residents to get written permission for overnight visits from foreigners needing visas and to inform their mayor's office after their guests left. There followed a protest movement which culminated in a demonstration in the streets of Paris on February 22, a petition signed by intellectuals (including famous movie directors) known as le Manifeste des 121, and a lively polemic in the press about France's treatment of foreigners.

Under the heading, "Un débat sur la France," François Léotard, then leader of the Union pour la démocratie française (UDF), was quoted on the front page of *Le Monde* as saying that France should still be perceived as "un grand pays, fier de sa langue, assuré de son destin et attaché au respect de ses lois" but that the protesters were guilty of "une fuite étonnante devant les enjeux de notre cohésion nationale, et devant la réalité dangereuse de l'immigration illégale." For Léotard "le débat sur l'immigration, c'est un débat sur la France. La question n'est plus: 'Qui héberge-t-on?', ou bien 'qui intégrons-nous?', mais 'pourquoi héberger' et 'à quoi intégrer?'" (Léotard). Three days later *Le Monde* ran on its front page an article about fears that France was increasingly being seen abroad as xenophobic. Needless to say, a comparison to "les lois raciales de Vichy" was made. Michel Rocard, former prime minister, went so far as to say, "J'ai honte de mon pays en ce moment" (8). The day before, *Le Monde* had published a piece by a Moroccan exile on the same topic, titled "Vive la France!" After living the "dualité entre l'accueil généreux et chaleureux du peuple français et l'ombre grandissante du lepénisme," the writer reported being comforted by the public protests, which allowed him to conclude that "[la] société française, dans ses profondeurs, n'est pas lepéniste, elle n'est pas raciste" (Abraham 11).

The immigration problem continued to inspire debate about France's self-image in the press over the next few days, some if it on the front pages of *Le Monde*. For example, under the heading "De la République," Alain Juppé, then prime minister, started his article with the following words: "Notre pays est en état d'émotion. Je le comprends, car la querelle n'est pas médiocre: il s'agit, au fond, de l'idée que nous nous faisons de la France." In addressing divided opinions about racism, antisemitism, and xenophobia, Juppé mused that "Nous n'avons pas encore exorcisé la honte . . . Nous avons encore beaucoup à faire pour assumer notre passé avec lucidité et nous réconcilier une fois pour toutes avec nous-mêmes" (1997). While condemning the attitudes of the extreme right and the new mayor of Vitrolles (without identifying either by name), Juppé did, nevertheless, draw a distinction between legal and illegal immigrants and defended the Debré law. He called for citizens to "faire de cette diversité, comme par le passé, une source de richesse, de créativité et d'intelligence" and called for solidarity in the fight against rising intolerance. His words did little to save the controversial provision, however, and only a few months later Juppé was forced to resign.

In the same issue of *Le Monde* a researcher at the *Institut d'urbanisme* addressed the topic of immigration, the inability of political leaders to solve the immigration problem, and the wider concern of demoralization from which the French were suffering. Albert Lévy identified a "crise multiforme" comprised of the following: "crise de la représentation politique..., crise de la classe politique..., crise des élites..., crise des structures centralisées..., crise de la citoyenneté" (19). Unlike Juppé and Léotard, Lévy saw the militant reaction to the repressive law as part of a larger, grass-roots movement critical of the status quo. For Lévy, the movement represented not a negative reflection of discontent but a light at the end of the tunnel of malaise: "Face aux dysfonctionnements de notre système politique et aux bouleversements qui affectent la société, l'émergence de cette sphère publique critique apporte, dans le pessimisme ambiant, quelques raisons d'espérer" (17).

While Daniel Vernet was less optimistic in an editorial on February 27 about what he called "cette onde de protestation," he congratulated those who had protested the Debré provision and said, "il leur reste le mérite d'avoir tendu un miroir à une société qui n'osait plus se regarder en face" (1). The soul-searching, lack of self-confidence, and identity crisis alluded to in the American press were reflected multiple times in the French press in those days surrounding the debate about immigration.

Further Threats to "Frenchness"

At the same time that France was struggling with internal threats to its self-image, external forces were challenging the French to ask themselves what it means to be French: the global economy and the European Union.

For France to continue to be competitive as the world's fourth largest exporter, it needed to make painful changes to the way it ran business and to its way of life. The challenge was to make sweeping reforms while retaining the strength of the nation state and without touching social entitlements. Restructuring was seen as inevitable but unwelcome. Renault, privatized in July 1996, sent shock waves through France when it closed its plant in Vilvorde, Belgium in March 1997, firing 3,000 employees. The headlines of the lead story in *L'Express,* "L'Horreur économique est-elle une fatalité?" echoed the title of the depressing "L'Horreur économique"[4] (Barbier 26). Hailed as "le baromètre de l'histoire sociale française," Renault was the first in a long line of French companies, formerly owned and run by the state, that were forced to restructure to become more competitive. The writer was quick to point out that, "C'est donc un accouchement dans la douleur que vit actuellement la France, pour entrer dans un monde où, trois jours après le coup de grisou de Vilvorde, le CAC 40 a franchi, pour la première fois, la barre des 2 700 points" (Barbier 27).

Under the subheading "Chacun s'interroge sur le prix de l'Europe et de la mondialisation," the article analyzed the problems facing France's move into the twenty-first century: "La crise, c'est quand le vieux meurt et que le neuf hésite à naître... Le neuf pour la France, c'est la mondialisation" and specified the need to sacrifice people's livelihood for economic viability. France, the writer Christophe Barbier suggested, was going through the pangs of childbirth. The word *déboussolé* was used to describe ordinary citizens' disorientation, the expression *horreur économique* was repeated, and globalization was equated with fear.

In a related article, "Les affres de la mondialisation," *L'Express* warned that if France was to catch up with its competitors, the country must modernize its plants, increase its productivity, and explore South American markets more aggressively. The article ended by quoting the researcher Elie Cohen who suggested that, painful though it might be, France should "se préoccuper du retard que nous sommes en train de perdre plutôt que de déplorer la perte des emplois manufacturiers" (Abescat 32).

An article in *Le Monde* picked up the same theme. Jean-Michel Billaut, in charge of *la veille technologique* at *la Compagnie bancaire,* attacked France's elite for not understanding the Internet. He criticized France for clinging to the Minitel after it had become outdated. Worse, he saw France's reluctance to get onto the information highway as a bad omen and forecast with irony "dans un siècle, on parlera l'anglais, et le français sera devenu un aimable patois" (Alberganti 14). His message reinforced the need for France to adapt to changing times.

Threatening the status quo and France's national identity from another direction is the European Union. Each member nation must give up part of its sovereignty in return for the protection afforded by the common market. Moreover, each nation must "qualify" for the common currency, especially challenging for a country where the state is all-powerful. Fiscal measures called for to balance the books cause the same problems as those caused by the demands of globalization. The social security system itself, the strength of which will soon be tested by France's baby boomer generation, has been called into question by compliance with the monetary standards. The challenge according to *L'Express* is: "Comment faire l'Europe sans défaire la France" (Barbier 27).

Changing over to the common currency, the euro, promised to be as traumatic as changing from old francs to the new was in 1960. Only one Frenchman in two welcomed the arrival of the euro, which made its official appearance on January 1, 1999. The European Commission therefore mounted a campaign to educate the general public.

Still, as Jean Daniel points out in his editorial entitled "L'Europe est derrière nous" in the left-of-center *Le Nouvel Observateur*, the euro is not going to *make* Europeans out of the French; "nous le sommes déjà" he says. Daniel contends that the euro will lead the French to become French citizens of Europe and he suggests that it should be viewed as a *grande aventure*. According to Daniel, "l'Europe existe dans mille aspects de notre vie quotidienne et nationale. L'Europe existe et les Européens font comme si elle n'existait pas. Et comme s'il fallait la faire. Alors qu'il ne s'agit que de la parfaire" (48). Daniel also reminds his readers that the original initiative for a united Europe was a French one. Moreover, "il ne s'agit pas du tout de choisir entre la France et l'Europe, mais entre l'Europe et les Etats-Unis" if the French do not want to be subjugated to what he calls *pax americana*. Nevertheless, as Daniel points out, the European Union is "une issue inéluctable" and even Eurosceptics are resigned to its inevitability.

The fact that France was able to "qualify" for the common European currency was hailed as a good economic indicator. Confidence in the stock market increased immediately following the summit in Brussels which announced in 1998 the list of eleven countries participating in the common currency and the compromise that had been reached over the issue of who would preside over the European Central Bank (Leparmentier and Delhommais). Investors in the stock market began thinking of their risk less in terms of individual countries and more in terms of the European Union, a move which benefited the Paris stock exchange, according to an article in *Le Monde* (Delhommais and Fay 17). A headline on the front page of *Le Monde* the same day (June 24), "Euro: les banques sont prêtes," established a positive mood and assured readers that the banks were ready for the transition to the euro. The article assured readers that the banks were not planning to increase bank charges.

A Better Outlook

References to an economic revival had actually begun to appear earlier in 1998. In March the term *renouveau économique* appeared in the headline of an article about the region between Paris and Strasbourg (Zappi). The region, which five years before suffered an economic crisis, was now benefiting from diversification and an improved infrastructure in the form of new highways and high speed rail connections. Later the same month another article about the north of France talked about "la fin d'un long malaise" (Cherruau). By April, France's self-image was clearly entering a new phase.

The opening line of an article on the front page of *Le Monde* reads "La France en panne? C'était il y a un an" (Kauffmann 1). The article analyzes the perception in the States that a European economic revival was taking place and the realization that France was a key economic and political player in the new Europe. Against the backdrop of a projected increase in the gross national product of 3%, reduction of the deficit, and the beginnings of a decrease in unemployment, not to mention having qualified for the euro, Dominique Strauss-Kahn, the minister for economy, finance and industry, is reported to have told the American media that France was ready for globalization, economic competition, and entrepreneurship.

Another headline in *Le Monde* reads "Un nouvel enthousiasme." The article echoed headlines that had recently appeared on the front pages of French newspapers. It explained, however, that "La croissance sera forte en France dans les deux prochaines années, mais le chômage ne baissera que faiblement" (Larrouturou). Optimism was still tempered.

By July 1998 optimism had turned into euphoria. Not only did the hosting of the World Cup that summer go smoothly, but France won the tournament. More than just a sporting triumph, the winning French team took the country's spirits to a new high. Fans particularly praised the French players for playing as a team. The fact that the team was multiracial allowed every Frenchman (and woman) to identify with the players

and the press was full of puns on the new colors of the tricolor: *black,*
blanc, beur. The headline of the cover story of *L'Express* read, "Ce
Mondial qui a changé la France" and was typical of the significance that
was attached to the win by the press. As the journalist of the lead article
said, "Une France métisse qui gagne, c'est un symbole. Fort, très fort"
(Haget 14). Suddenly the soul-searching was over. The French could no
longer be accused of being racist or xenophobic. Another journalist in *Le*
Nouvel Observateur expressed it this way: "Sous le maquillage
bleu-blanc-rouge, on distingue à peine la couleur des peaux" (Daniel, "Une
guerre?" 38). In the same issue, Jean Daniel described France's reconciliation with itself. He suggested that the French had had enough of malaise;
specifically "ce dont ils ont eu assez, c'est d'être moroses, d'avoir peur, de
se sentir humiliés et en somme de ne plus s'aimer eux-mêmes, et de ne plus
savoir qui aimer" ("Une guerre?" 33). Now the French could smile at each
other, speak to each other, in fact love each other and celebrate that "ils
étaient bien une nation, une nation unique, vivante et chaude."

On July 14 *Le Monde's* headline on the front page read "La
parabole Jacquet." Even though the article warned that "tout reste en
l'état. Tout, c'est-à-dire la somme de nos maux, qu'un match de football ne
saurait effacer," it echoed the optimism being expressed throughout the
land and commented on France's identity: "Quelque chose a changé, ou
peut changer, dans la conscience collective, ayant trait à notre propre identité" (Colombani 1). The self-image portrayed in the French press in July
1998 was very different from the one pervasive in February 1997, when
France could scarcely face itself in the mirror. For the time being the challenges facing France's move into the twenty-first century — living down
its dark past, confronting unemployment and racial tension, globalization
and the European Union — were being seen through the eyes of a people
with something to be proud of. A country's confidence level is by its very
nature cyclical and dependent upon circumstances. It remains to be seen if
the positive self-image reflected in French newspapers and magazines
during the summer of 1998 will endure or if moroseness, malaise, and
soul-searching will return to dominate the French press.

Notes

[1] This work, which deals with the problems of the unemployed and the horrors of capitalism, became a best-seller, selling 500,000 copies in 1996. See also Barreau, Jean-Claude, *La France va-t-elle disparaître?*; Bayart, Jean-François, *L'Illusion identitaire;* Domenach, Jean-Marie, *Regarder la France. Essais sur le malaise français;* Marchand, Stéphane, *French Blues. Pourquoi plus ça change, plus c'est la même chose;* Viard, Jean et al., *La Nation ébranlée;* Wieviorka, Michel, *Une Société fragmentée? Le multiculturalisme en débat.*

[2] See Robert Paxton's *La France de Vichy* which was published in French in 1973.

[3] Rouxel, one of the defence lawyers in the Papon trial, is quoted in *Le Monde*, March 25, 1998: "[Le procès] mêle indissociablement l'homme et son mythe."

[4] See note 1.

References

Abescat, Bruno, and Sabine Delanglade. "Les affres de la mondialisation." *L'Express* 13 March 1997: 30-34.

Abraham, Serfaty. "Vive la France!" *Le Monde* 24 February 1997: 11.

Alberganti, Michel. "Billaut, Jean-François, responsable de la 'vieille technologie' à la Compagnie bancaire 'La France est extrêmement en retard, car son élite ne comprend pas Internet.'" *Le Monde* 8 July 1997: 14.

Barbier, Christophe. "L'horreur économique est-elle une fatalité?" *L'Express* 13 March 1997: 26-28.

Cherruau, Pierre. "Nord: le basculement consacre la fin d'un long malaise; ..." *Le Monde* 24 March 1998 <http://web.lexis-nexis.com/universe/docum>.

Colombani, Jean Marie. "La parabole Jacquet." *Le Monde* 14 July 1998: 1.

Daniel, Jean. "L'Europe est déjà derrière nous." *Le Nouvel Observateur* 23-29 April 1998: 48-49.

---. "Une guerre? Non. Une réconciliation avec soi-même. La France en avait besoin." *Le Nouvel Observateur* 16-22 July 1998: 33.

Delhommais, Pierre-Antoine, and Sophie Fay. "Les prix des services seront les mêmes en francs et en euros." *Le Monde* 24 June 1998: 17.

Dumay, Jean Michel. "Me Francis Vuillemin brosse un panégyrique de l'accusé; Le plus jeune défenseur de Maurice Papon a affirmé que son client était tout entier fonctionnaire-résistant et qu'il n'a jamais joué double jeu pour demander l'acquittement." *Le Monde* 25 March 1998 <http://web.lexis-nexis.com/universe/docum>.

Etchegoin, Marie-France. "Nos ancêtres les Marseillais..." *Le Nouvel Observateur* 16-22 July 1998: 38-40.

"Euro: les banques sont prêtes." *Le Monde* 24 June 1998: 1.

Gluckmann, André. "Tous déracinés." *L'Express* 18-24 June 1998: 17.

Gourevitch, Philip. "The Unthinkable. How Dangerous is Le Pen's National Front?" *New Yorker* 28 April-5 May 1997: 110-149.

Haget, Henri. "Ce Mondial qui a changé la France." *L'Express* 16 July 1998: 12-19.

Hoffmann, Stanley. "Look Back in Anger." *New York Review* 17 July 1997: 45-50.

Juppé, Alain. "De la République." *Le Monde* 26 February 1997: 1.

Kauffmann, Sylvie. "La nouvelle France des Américains." *Le Monde* 30 April 1998: 1.
Larrouturou, Pierre, and Michel Rocard. "Un nouvel enthousiasme." *Le Monde* 21 May 1998 <http://web.lexis-nexis.com/universe/docum>.
Léotard, François. "Un débat sur la France." *Le Monde* 22 February 1997: 1.
Leparmentier, Arnaud, and Pierre-Antoine Delhommais. "Malaise politique et confiance des marchés après le lancement de l'euro; ..." *Le Monde* 6 May 1998. <http://web.lexis-nexis.com/universe/docum>.
Lévy, Albert. "Cette sphère publique critique qui emerge." *Le Monde* 26 February 1997:19.
Mermet, Gérard. *Francoscopie 1997*. New York: Larousse, 1996.
Rocard, Michel. "J'ai honte de mon pays en ce moment." *Le Monde* 25 February 1997: 8.
Solé, Robert, and Nicolas Weill. "Tout concourt aujourd'hui au souvenir obsédant de Vichy." *Le Monde* 1 October 1998 <http://web.lexis-nexis.com/universe/docum>.
Vernet, Daniel. "Décembre 1995-février 1997, les fractures françaises." *Le Monde* 27 February 1997: 1.
Zappi, Sylvia. "Le renouveau économique passe par l'autoroute et le TGV; ..." *Le Monde* 13 March 1998 <http://web.lexis-nexis.com/universe/docum>.

12

Multiculturalism in Debate: The Immigrant Presence as Social Catalyst in Contemporary France

Fred Toner
Ohio University

Even to the casual observer, France is in the grips of a crisis, "une déprime collective," "un nouveau mal français" that Gérard Mermet terms "le misérabilisme." The French media report evidence of the crisis daily and many of the titles of recent works by noted authors reflect the growing social malaise: *Une Société fragmentée?* by Michel Wieviorka, *La France éclatée* by Christian Jelen, and *Pourrons-nous vivre ensemble?* by Alain Touraine, to cite only three. Even if Mermet and others may be inclined to see the "nouveau mal" as a form of hypochondria unjustified by the facts, the general dissatisfaction and anxiety are nonetheless palpable, and theorists and the general public alike are looking for the roots of the problem. As French society continues to evolve and to become more diverse and multiethnic, and as *communautés* celebrating their ethnic, religious, or other differences proliferate, the *Français de souche* increasingly turn an accusing finger at what is *autre*. The immigrant presence is the most common target. To the ever-present accusations linking immigrants to problems of unemployment and crime is added a growing concern with the relatively high birthrate of immigrants: "Surtout, ils craignent que l'identité française ne se dissolve progressivement dans la mise en place d'une société pluriculturelle" (Mermet 207). At the heart of the matter, the "nouveau mal français" is a crisis of identity, of what it means to be "French." It is a crisis shared by the *Français de souche* and the immigrant, and is experienced to some degree by all aspects of French society. Can France continue to assimilate the immigrant population, forming them in the *moule* of the universal ideals of the French Republic, or should integration — a mosaic of cultural differences — rather than assimilation, be the goal? Will multiculturalism ultimately enrich or endanger the Republic?

Immigration is hardly a recent development in French history, as Gérard Noiriel amply demonstrates in his history of French immigration, *The French Melting Pot*. Noiriel estimates that one third of the population currently living in France is of "foreign" descent (Noiriel xxvii). Michèle Tribalat, researcher at the *Institut national d'études démographiques* (*INED*), maintains that roughly one Frenchman in five "a au moins un parent ou un grand-parent immigré" (Gamazic 14). Even so, the recent debates on immigrant policy often have xenophobic overtones, and violence against immigrants is not uncommon. In 1995, seven murders in France were attributed to racism and/or xenophobia (Mermet 206). Sadly, this phenomenon is also not a new development in French history, as José Cubero's study of a xenophobic rampage against Italian workers in the region of Aigues-Mortes at the end of the nineteenth century chillingly illustrates (Cubero).

In spite of the fact that immigration has been a constant in French history for well over a century, some might suggest that there are certain complicating factors that set the recent immigrants apart from their predecessors and that make their integration into French society more difficult. Whereas earlier waves of immigrants — notably the Portuguese and Spanish but also the Polish, Belgian, and Italian — were of European origin and from Catholic countries, more recently the immigrants have come from Africa or Turkey and are in the majority Moslem. In addition to these cultural and religious differences, the physical features of the new immigrants often set them apart and make them more visible to the general population.

The historical context is also obviously different from what it was in the nineteenth century. The "modern" societies of the Western world are now what Michel Wieviorka, of the *Ecole pratique des hautes études en sciences sociales*, would term "post-industrialisées" (Wieviorka 1995). That is, they are no longer organized around the opposition of workers and employers, an opposition which gave immigrant workers a role in a larger community — the larger "we" against "them" — and which furnished a context in which immigrants could be "socialized." In the post-industrialized societies, especially in moments of economic crisis, the immigrant lacks this means of integration (de Foucauld and Piveteau).

The obstacles to integration faced by first-generation immigrants are well known, but nonetheless imposing. The newly-arrived immigrants find themselves between two worlds, having rejected the former while not being completely at home in the new. Learning the language and learning to recognize the expectations of a culture and its core values are barriers to finding work and thus, also, to the socialization process. The constant and inescapable barrage of advertising, vaunting products beyond the reach of most immigrant families, aggravates the situation by highlighting the gap — economic, as well as social and spatial — between immigrant and mainstream. Deprived of the "French Dream" of economic success by the enduring economic crisis and often isolated in housing projects on the periphery of the city, many immigrants are pessimistic about their chances of ever gaining true equality in French society.

As Didier Lapeyronnie points out in his interesting analysis of "Les Deux Figures de l'immigré," even a second- or third-generation immigrant who has "succeeded" in French society, who speaks a native French, who has internalized the culture, and whose self-concept is "French" may be excluded from the mainstream: "il continue de porter le signe d'une 'différence' non intégrable par la majorité de la population" (260). The immigrant is "stigmatized" by name, religion, skin color, history, or ethnicity. The identity constructed and imposed by the *regard* of the general public is difficult to reconcile with the immigrant's idea of self. These "colonized" immigrants, as Lapeyronnie calls them, are all the more sensitive to this kind of conceptual dissonance because they have internalized the cultural values of the majority population and have "assimilated" the principles of *liberté, égalité, fraternité:* "Ainsi, plus l'immigré est intégré, plus il est stigmatisé, et plus le stigmate lui devient intolérable, au nom même des valeurs de démocratie et d'égalité entre les individus qu'il partage avec tous les autres membres de la société" (Lapeyronnie 262). Even the successfully integrated — but not assimilated — immigrant may eventually lose hope of ever being accepted as an equal by the dominant population. As a result, there is an increasingly common tendency for the immigrants to "celebrate" the very difference that sets them apart and to identify themselves by their ethnicity or religion. The famous incident of the "voile islamique" in 1989 — when female students wearing the Islamic veil were expelled from a middle school — may be seen, at least in part, as a demonstration and celebration of cultural difference, perhaps even more than as a display of religious freedom.

The presence of immigrant communities and the tendency to self-identify by ethnicity or religion have prompted much debate in the French press, some seeing it as an imminent danger and others as an inevitable sign of social evolution. On the positive side are those that see such communities as a necessary presence in the process of assimilation. Didier Lapeyronnie, citing studies of Polish immigrants in American society at the turn of the century by Thomas and Znaniecki, maintains that immigrant communities serve to ease the shock of the cultural and social change imposed by being uprooted from all that is familiar. The ethnic community facilitates the immigrants' survival and adaptation to the new culture: "l'assimilation des migrants polonais . . . était avant tout un processus collectif fondé sur la construction d'une sorte de sous-société polono-américaine permettant aux migrants d'évoluer individuellement et collectivement vers une assimilation complète" (Lapeyronnie 253). The presence of such communities helps first-generation immigrants make the transition to the new culture and overcome the immobilizing discouragement of total isolation.

For second-generation immigrants, the role of the community can also be to combat feelings of alienation. In a situation in which integration seems impossible, the community can offer a feeling of belonging for those living on the outskirts of the city, "hors légitimité," and who are thus multiply "stigmatized," by where they live as well as by their appearance, name, or religion: "Constat fréquent chez les jeunes: il suffit de signaler que l'on vit dans telle banlieue malfamée pour se voir opposer un refus de la part de l'employeur potentiel" (Khosrokhavar 136). According to Farhad Khosrokhavar, the type of Islam practiced by young people in certain suburbs is a religion of the *exclus* and "procède de la non-intégration sociale des jeunes dans la société française" (136). Islam, as a sociocultural institution, can provide a positive space in which to construct an identity, "non pas pour rompre avec la société française, mais pour pouvoir endurer cet état de fait aliénant et difficile à supporter" (Khosrokhavar 137). Khosrokhavar sees this kind of community as fulfilling the role played in the past by workers' unions or even the communist party, taking charge of the socializing process of immigrant youth.

By contrast, middle-class immigrants who have jobs and who have already been more or less integrated into the society may form Islamic communities as a way to separate themselves from a culture that is in the midst of an identity crisis and which has no clear set of values to offer. Such a phenomenon belies the theories of sociologists who wish to explain the multiplication of communities as the result of classic conflicts of interest or due exclusively to economic inequalities (Tabboni 229-31). For this kind of Islamic community, as Khosrokhavar explains, it is not so much a matter of abandoning hope of social and economic integration into French society as it is a conscious refusal to assimilate (Khosrokhavar 139). These individuals refuse the duality of the Republican *public/privé* and insist on proclaiming their faith publicly. Just as the young women in the "affaire du foulard" wanted to be recognized publicly as "franco-musulmanes," the members of these kinds of Islamic communities wish to be recognized publicly as both French and Moslem.

The debate brought about by the proliferation of ethnic and religious communities often concerns two opposing philosophical positions, each accusing the other of extremism. While *communautariens* maintain that the idea of democracy is based on the respect of differences, the *assimilationnistes* counter that universal rights and values should take precedence over any "particularités," which should be relegated to the private sphere. If France has been able to assimilate immigrant populations successfully in the past and preserve national unity by absorbing the subcultures, the *assimilationnistes* continue, why risk social ruin by granting "special rights?" For writers such as Christian Jelen, the idea of "le droit à la différence" can only lead to disastrous effects. He sees recent decisions in public policy, such as granting the right of polygamy to African immigrants in 1980 and permitting the Islamic veil in public schools in 1989 and 1992, as a betrayal of Republican ideals and as the first steps toward the disintegration of society, producing *la France "éclatée."*

For many, multiculturalism leads inevitably to ethnic conflict and racism. One has only to think of Lebanon, Bosnia-Herzegovina, or the newly independent states of the former Soviet Union, to see the violent result of prioritizing ethnicity or religion. The model of American multiculturalism is hardly more encouraging, according to these same thinkers: "le pays est en train de devenir une mosaïque de ghettos ethniques, religieux ou idéologiques" (Jelen 36). For these critics, the use of affirmative action (*discrimination positive* in French!) has "racialized" social relations, turning one community against another in a country that has a long history of interethnic conflicts (Lacorne).

Recent reports of gang violence near Paris, in areas with a large immigrant population, have been seen by *assimilationnistes* as proof that multiculturalism is a divisive force in society. A report of community tensions in Sarcelles in *Le Monde diplomatique* depicts the growing social schism: "Première constatation: le temps des 'potes' est bel et bien terminé. Les jeunes ne jurent désormais que par la 'communauté' ou la 'religion' et ne croient plus au métissage" (Ellyas 8). As described in the article, Sarcelles is a city "tentée par le repli communautaire," where the young people associate with those of similar racial or religious affiliations, rather than with those who share their neighborhood: "On reste délibérément 'entre soi' et, si l'on a affaire à un journaliste, on ne se prive pas d'accuser avec hargne les 'autres' d'être à l'origine des problèmes de la cité" (Ellyas 8). Many fear that the reigning "chacun pour soi — et contre les autres" mentality is the image of France's future.

Jelen even compares "le vrai visage du multiculturalisme" with the nationalism of certain right wing parties, notably the "national-culturalisme" of the *Front National (FN)*: "Comme [le Front national], [le multiculturalisme] renvoie chacun à son appartenance ethnique, à sa tribu, à ses coutumes, à ses traditions, à ses croyances religieuses, à sa communauté" (27-28). Defining individuals by their communities, Jelen continues, is to deprive them of their individuality. According to this line of reasoning, members of communities, by emphasizing their difference, sacrifice their ability to establish a separate individual identity. To use Lapeyronnie's term, they "stigmatize" and further alienate themselves.

Interestingly, the presence of the immigrant population in France and their increasing visibility has had the effect of bringing to the dominant population an experience of "alienation" in some ways similar to that of the immigrants. The changing demographic landscape, especially in urban areas where the change is most noticeable, has a disorienting effect. The multicultural aspects of the modern city transform the familiar into the unknown where, as Michel de Certeau suggests, citizens become "nomads" travelling between two cultures (42). In the space where First and Third Worlds collide, both worlds will be challenged and changed. While the immigrant population struggles with the restrictive identity imposed by the *regard* of the dominant population, these latter will be forced to see themselves through other eyes. Immigrant demands for "le droit à la différence" call into question the superiority of the French way of life and call for a reevaluation of core values. French natives, forced to discuss and defend their ideas of what it means to be French, are shaken from their comfortable self-satisfaction. The destabilization resulting from the contact with the "other" has been a source of anxiety in French culture and, along with other social pressures, notably economic, has led to a radicalization of approaches to immigration.

The *FN*, whose party platform calls for the expulsion of immigrants from French soil, is one of the most clearly anti-immigrant forces in France today. Some would maintain that the *FN* has made immigrants, and more particularly *Maghrébins*, the scapegoat responsible for all social problems, including unemployment and the Social Security deficit (Perrineau 72). Taking advantage of the anxiety of the general public, the *FN* has repeatedly attacked the government for its laxity in terms of its immigrant policy. The various French governments, immobilized by the lingering economic crisis and record unemployment, have allowed the *FN* to define the terms of the debate on immigration: "L'idée s'est répandue, à gauche comme à droite, que l'intégration des immigrés passait par la maîtrise des flux migratoires" (Tribalat 77). The growing success of the *FN* at the polls and its rhetoric of the "besieged citadel" were no doubt instrumental in the passage in 1993 under Balladur of *les lois Pasqua*, which tightened the controls on immigration. Aware of growing popular support for anti-immigration measures, even the traditional defenders of immigrant rights, the political left, have been loath to speak out against the tightening restrictions. It is revealing that Lionel Jospin did not offer to reconsider the *lois Pasqua* when campaigning for the last presidential elections. In matters of immigration, one might ask if there is any significant difference between the parties of the right and the left (Gaspard 203-18).

While the rhetoric of the *FN* has no doubt done much to fan the flames of xenophobia and racism, the effects of placing immigration and the immigrant presence in the national spotlight have not been entirely negative. One of the reactions to the anti-immigrant stance of the *FN* and its growing strength at the polls was the development of a number of "associations" seeking to combat racism, defend the rights of minority populations, and facilitate the integration of the immigrants into French society. Even if several of these organizations predate the beginnings of the *FN*, all were moved to intensify their efforts in the shadow of the perceived threat. The associations range from those targeting practical issues such as providing information on housing (*Droit au logement*) and legal or civil rights (*Ligue Internationale Contre le Racisme et l'Antisémitisme, Ligue des Droits de l'Homme, Groupe d'Information et de Soutien des Travailleurs Immigrés, Arabisme et Francité*), providing immediate aid to those in need (*Comité Inter-Mouvements Auprès Des Evacués*), or encouraging political engagement (*France Alternative Républicaine*), to other associations whose aim is more social or cultural (*Mouvement contre le Racisme et pour l'Amitié entre les Peuples, Agence pour le Développement des Relations Interculturelles*). Each of these organizations plays the important role of bringing immigrants in contact with non-immigrants and opening a dialog. Many of the associations offer training sessions for social workers, sponsor educational colloquia, and disseminate important information to the immigrant population and the general public alike. These efforts are publicized in traditional ways as well as on a number of impressive web sites.

While designed to help the immigrants, whether by meeting certain needs or by facilitating the socialization process, such associations are in fact beneficial to both sides. The non-immigrants are exposed to the complexity and diversity of the immigrant cultures and are able to supplant stereotypical images with human faces. Associations such as *ADRI* (*Agence pour le Développement des Relations Interculturelles*), by sponsoring exhibits of immigrant artists and by participating in exhibitions such as the *Rencontres des cultures urbaines*, help bring examples of immigrant art and music to the attention of the general public.

One could make the case that immigrant culture is in fact more present and admired in France than at any time in recent memory. In spite of the xenophobia evident in the recent successes of the *FN*, *la culture banlieue* — immigrant music, art, language, and style — has become the model for many youth in comfortable, wealthy neighborhoods across France (Ferhati 14-15). The Algerian music known as *raï*, is heard regularly in the best *discothèques* in Paris and on Skyrock radio. Certain artists, such as Cheb Khaled, the first Arab-language singer to be classified among the best sellers in France, or Cheb Mami, who mixes rap and *raï*, are international stars. Films dealing with the immigrant presence in France, including Mathieu Kassovitz's *La Haine* and its chilling but stylish portrayal of the painful reality of *la banlieue*, and Karim Dridi's *Bye-Bye*, with its depiction of life between two cultures, have inspired critical acclaim and gained financial success. In addition, immigrant sports figures — most recently Zinedine Zidane, hero of the 1998 World Cup — are widely admired models of discipline and skill.

The popularity of a culture, its success in sports or in the entertainment field does not equate, of course, to social equality, as the situation of the African-Americans in the United States illustrates. From all evidence, the massive anti-racism, anti "F-haine" campaign launched in France in the 1980s has done little to slow the growth of Le Pen's party. Pierre-André Taguieff states it clearly: "Tel est le fait devant lequel il n'est plus possible de rêver les yeux ouverts: scientifiquement réfuté et judiciairement réprimé, consensuellement tenu pour 'le Mal absolu,' ce qu'il est convenu d'appeler le racisme paraît poursuivre son cours, se développer, se transformer, surgir là où on ne l'attendait pas" (Taguieff 15). Still, there is reason to believe that the increasing contact among the various cultures in contemporary France will hasten the desired reconciliation of extremes. Michel Wieviorka, for one, insists on the importance of a continuing dialog to break through the stalemate between the rigid and seemingly irreconcilable positions of so-called "Républicanistes," "universalistes," or "assimiliationnistes," on the one side, and the "communautariens" on the other.

Can the understanding of what it means to be French be expanded to include those who insist on identifying themselves as Moslem and French, North African and French, gay and French? Can the good of the society take precedence over the interests of a community while still protecting the rights of cultural minorities? France is certainly now — and, some would say, always has been — a diverse, multi-ethnic and multicultural society. Cultural diversity will in all likelihood continue to be the rule, barring the unthinkable ethnic cleansing, as France makes its way through the twenty-first century. The central problem is, as Alain Touraine succinctly states, "comment combiner ce qui est séparé, comment faire vivre ensemble des individus et des groupes qui ont des cultures différentes?" (in Wieviorka 302). The immigrant presence in France, by challenging the sense of cultural homogeneity, is the catalyst of a process of mutual adaptation that is taking place not only in France, but on a global scale, wherever First and Third World cultures meet. In such contact, when there is a true dialog, change is probable on both sides. What each has inherited from a culture is reexamined and seen in the light of the other. As Edmond Jabès has said: "L'étranger te permet d'être toi-même, en faisant, de toi, un étranger" (quoted in Chambers 12). The way in which those on both sides react to the contact, the manner in which France resolves Touraine's fundamental question will determine in no small measure the country's own domestic tranquility and its relationship with other nations in an evolving political reality. It remains to be seen if the home of *les droits de l'Homme et du Citoyen* will continue to be considered a model of human rights.

References

Certeau, Michel de. *The Practice of Everyday Life.* Berkeley, Los Angeles & London: University of California Press, 1988.
Cubero, José. *Nationalistes et Etrangers.* Paris: Imago, 1996.
Foucauld, Jean-Baptiste de, and Denis Piveteau. *Une Société en quête de sens.* Paris: Odile Jacob, 1995.
Ellyas, Akram. "Replis communautaires à Sarcelles." *Le Monde Diplomatique* (Février 1996): 8. <http://www.monde-diplomatique.fr/md/1996/02/>.
Ferhati, Amo. "La Banlieue qui bouge et qui dérange." *Salama, le Maghreb dans tous ses états* 12 (juin-juillet 1998): 14-15.
Gamazic, Séverine. "Généalogie: le 'vrai Français' n'existe pas." *Journal Français* 19.10 (octobre 1997): 14.

Gaspard, Françoise. "Il y a trop peu de différences entre droite et gauche en matière d'immigration." *L'Antiracisme dans tous ses débats.* Condé-sur-Noireau: Panoramiques-Corlet, 1996: 203-218.

Jelen, Christian. *La France éclatée ou les reculades de la République.* Paris: Nil, 1996.

Khosrokhavar, Farhad. "L'Universel abstrait, la politique et la construction de l'islamisme comme forme d'altérité." *Une Société fragmentée?* Ed. Michel Wieviorka. Paris: La Découverte, 1996. 113-51.

Lacorne, Denis. *La Crise de l'identité américaine. Du Melting-pot au multiculturalisme.* Paris: Fayard, 1997.

Lapeyronnie, Didier. "Les Deux Figures de l'immigré." *Une Société fragmentée?* Ed. Michel Wieviorka. Paris: La Découverte, 1996. 251-266.

Mermet, Gérard. *Francoscopie 1997.* Paris: Larousse-Bordas, 1996.

Noiriel, Gérard. *The French Melting Pot: Immigration, Citizenship, and National Identity.* Trans. Geoffroy de Laforcade. Minneapolis & London: University of Minnesota Press, 1996.

Perrineau, Pascal. "Pourquoi le Front national séduit-il des millions de Français?" *Phosphore* (hors série, 1996-97): 72-73.

Tabboni, Simonetta. "Le Multiculturalisme et l'ambivalence de l'étranger." *Une Société fragmentée?* Paris: La Découverte. 229-231.

Taguieff, Pierre André. "Les Raisons d'un échec patent." *L'Antiracisme dans tous ses débats.* Ed. Lucien Bitterlin. Condé-sur-Noireau: Panoramiques-Corlet, 1996. 13-24.

Touraine, Alain. "Faux et vrais problèmes." *Une Société fragmentée?* Ed. Michel Wieviorka. Paris: La Découverte, 1996. 291-319.

---. *Pourrons-nous vivre ensemble? Egaux et différents.* Paris: Fayard, 1997.

Tribalat, Michèle. "Pourquoi l'Intégration des immigrés semble-t-elle si difficile?" *Phosphore* (hors série, 1996-97): 76-77.

Wieviorka, Michel, ed. *Une Société fragmentée? Le Multiculturalisme en débat.* Paris: La Découverte, 1996.

---. Conférence-débat d'"Alerte aux réalités internationales" du 18 octobre 1995. *Espaces: Conflits ethniques et culturels en Europe.* <http://www.geoscopie.com>.

IV. Culture

13

French Leisure: A Social Order in the Making[1]

Roland H. Simon
University of Virginia

"THERE IS LIFE AFTER WORK!" proclaimed a half-page banner running across the front cover of the March 11, 1998 issue of the French weekly *L'Express*. This is the kind of statement that seems to resonate well with the French and with the image that foreigners may have of prevalent French attitudes regarding work: the less the better, a necessity but not a way of life. The prevalent image is that of a people who enjoy spending a great deal of time on "frivolities;"[2] who flock to café terraces as soon as there is a ray of sunshine and take an hour to sip a cup of coffee; who love to spend hours at the dinner table just talking; who manage to celebrate more holidays[3] than any other people on earth; and whose school-children have the longest vacations in the world. After all, what could be more emblematic of how seriously the French value their time away from work than the creation of a Ministry of Free Time and Leisure in the first socialist cabinet formed under François Mitterrand's presidency in 1981? One might ask, then, whether the French really needed to be reminded in 1998 of something they had been obviously proving through their actions all along, or did *L'Express's* banner mean something entirely new?

It appears that the end of the twentieth century brought with it in France, and in most European countries, a set of social problems never confronted before in times of relative growth and robust competitiveness of the national economy.[4] Oddly enough, if work remains problematic, it is not because there is too much of it in the eyes of those who are employed, but because there is too little to occupy every potential worker, and an increasing number of social thinkers and political leaders believe that it needs to be redistributed so as to benefit everyone.[5] Thus the irony is that the French workers as a whole, *la population active,* are now confronted with the need to learn to work fewer hours a week and for a shorter span of their lives. This is perceived as the only way for the government to effectively tackle serious problems of long-term unemployment of roughly twelve percent of the potential workforce and all social ills that feed on joblessness.

In the chapter of *Les Français* devoted to leisure, Laurence Wylie and Jean-François Brière remind us that underneath the French stereotype of the pleasure-seeker lies the long-lived aristocratic tradition that "living free of work is much more enviable and carries more prestige than having to work for a living" (266). They go on to say that the immense majority of those who have to work for a living see it "as a sort of (divine) curse from which it is difficult to escape" (266). *In Fragile Glory: A Portrait of France and the French,* Richard Bernstein adds in the same vein that "to work less is part of the French worker's eschatological vision, his belief that the tide of history is supposed to bring less work, more time for leisure, and by God, if the capitalists won't let him have it, then the only solution is to get it through political action" (180). But all three authors are quick to point out that there is in France another — more recent — bourgeois, and mostly Protestant,[6] tradition that values work as "giving access to spiritual, social and economic salvation," a way "to better one's lot and that of society as a whole" (Wylie and Brière 267). In short, these conflicting traditions account for some apparent contradictions between a desire to succeed and a need to escape, with in-between a tenuous compromise which consists of working hard, and even depriving oneself of daily necessities in order to afford an expensive three-week vacation on a remote island in the Pacific, with nothing to do but soak up the rays and spend endless hours in the local bar trading stories about other exotic vacation spots. When all is said, leisure in France is practiced as an *art de vivre* that calls for a drastic separation from any sort of discipline in most instances, which goes a long way into explaining the formidable success of that most internationally famous French leisure institution of the twentieth century: "Club Med." In his irreverently funny and quite perceptive *Les Hexagons,* published in 1994, French journalist Alain Schifres made a remark that went to the heart of a major difference between the French people and the Americans, i.e., the people with whom they most love to compare themselves. He wrote: "They [the Americans] take seriously what is for us a laughing matter: cholesterol, God, sex. They have fun with some sort of fanaticism, but they work in a relaxed environment. They do everything contrary to us" (419).

First, some historical background. French workers officially "discovered" vacation time in 1936, when the short-lived socialist *Front Populaire* government of Léon Blum succeeded in pushing through a law guaranteeing a two-week paid vacation for every salaried worker. What had been up to that point a jealously guarded privilege of the bourgeoisie became a national symbol of the democratization of a nation famous for its rigid autocratic and paternalistic cast system. Even though most people chose in fact to stay home and rest, spend more time in their victory gardens in the suburbs or visit family, big industrial cities such as Paris or Lyon saw a sudden joyous exodus of people rushing in trains, cars, motorcycles, and even bicycles to go look at the sea for the first time or to go back to their provincial roots. Because of the major role some of its labor unions, especially railroad workers, had played in the Resistance, the French Communist Party was, after World War II, in a strong position to jockey for new social benefits. But the close alliance between labor unions and the political left at that time does not entirely explain the desire for more vacation time. It is true that General de Gaulle, who headed the Provisional Government from November 1944 until his resignation in January 1946, appeared to make enormous concessions to a party he fundamentally abhorred by appointing Communists to his cabinet, but it must be remembered that he would be credited some thirty years later for having been one of France's most progressive leaders in terms of labor and social laws. His first actions after the war were designed to avoid political strife in order to concentrate all the national energy on the task of rebuilding the country, and that meant, as we know much better now, morally as well as physically. If, for a short while, post-war France seemed to some foreign observers "to be languishing in a precapitalist warp" (Karnow 40), the next thirty years, later called by French historian, Jean Fourastié "the thirty glorious years," were a period of extraordinary economic growth for France, with an unprecedented across-the-board rise in the standard of living of every citizen. A few years after the war, France quickly became a major industrial nation at the forefront of technological innovation. This is all the more striking when one considers that, during the same period of the Fourth Republic, there was grave political instability, labor unrest, often violent and deadly, was rampant, and the French were militarily engaged in tragic post-colonial wars and conflicts. With more disposable income than ever, a very generous medical coverage, state-run family support, free education (or practically so) from kindergarten through higher education, and a safer future, people began to spend more on themselves. Nowhere is this better illustrated in fictional form than in Christiane Rochefort's novel *Les Petits Enfants du siècle,* in which the author describes how, in state-sponsored low-cost housing units sprouting up all over the French urban landscape at the time, the purchase of a second-hand car and two weeks of total idleness in a hole in the ground take precedence over the acquisition of a washing machine or repairing the television. True, older generations, especially in rural France, remained traumatized by the deprivations of the war and continued to perceive leisure and vacation as something for the rich, and now those "lucky" factory workers, but they eventually joined in the general move toward unabashed consumerism and associative life designed to run leisure activities for all.[7]   By the mid-seventies, there was little apparent distinction of social origins, professional past or financial means among the millions of senior citizens chartering buses and planes to go and discover their own country or the rest of the world all year round. They were only imitating the example of their own children, with the difference that they had more money to spend without worrying about retirement and sickness. France was getting younger culturally as a whole at a time when its population was growing increasingly older, with an average life expectancy among the highest in the world.

On February 24, 1956 the National Assembly approved a socialist-backed report of its Labor Commission asking for a third week of paid vacation for all workers "as a physical, moral and human imperative," noting that France was in fact only following the lead of the Netherlands, Norway, and Denmark, whose workers were already enjoying those benefits. The law this time extended the benefit to house employees, farm hands, and artisans. In recognition of an employee's faithful service, an additional clause granted two more days a year for every five-year period worked for the same employer. Of course, the measure could also be interpreted as an incentive for the employee to stay with an employer at a time when there was increased volatility in salary compensations due to economic growth.

By then, increasing numbers of women were joining the national work force, especially in low-paying industrial jobs, as employees in the fast expanding retail business, and in social services and education. This influx of women workers had an obvious impact on social and labor laws. Whether they chose to work or decided that they had to, in order to provide for themselves, for their children or for their household, and however exploited they may have been initially, their arrival on a famished job market-place meant a major cultural shift. In the male-dominant culture of the past, it had been expected all along for women to fulfill simultaneous responsibilities as coworkers in the fields, housewives, and mothers. However, once they were tied down to rigid work schedules at the factory, the office or the superstore, it became apparent that family values were at stake. As more and more women decided to pursue their education beyond primary school, with the full intention of securing a career more prestigious, if not necessarily more lucrative, than that of their parents (see Annie Ernaux's *La Place,* for a poignant case), the threat to the traditional image of the family was ever more palpable. A majority of the French people were quite unwilling to consider alternatives, but now that women had at last gained the right to vote (1944!) and were exercising it fully, concessions or accommodations were in the making. This is manifest in the 1956 debate over the proposal that workers be given two extra days of paid vacation per child under the age of fifteen, as long as they were solely responsible for the welfare of that child, a measure that was voted in. As puny or even insubstantial as this gain may have been in concrete terms, it nevertheless signals something quite important in French society: leisure is quality time often shared with one's family and friends to nurture and invigorate social bonds. One archetypal example comes to mind: if it is true that food occupies the center of the French table, not so much for the sustenance it provides as for its capacity to generate discourse, we cannot forget that often enough the table itself is also the privileged place where family matters are discussed and negotiated at length among all members of the family. The thought that children might gulp their food down, excuse themselves to rush to see a friend while dinner is still on the table, or worse not even sit at the table to eat it, is repugnant to most French parents to this day. Of course, it is undeniable that some leisure activities are by nature solitary activities, but it is the thought that they are in fact appreciated by one's partner, one's kin or friends that make them most valuable. The lone mountain-climber, the lone sailor, or the lone scholar lost in the depth of a library may very well be admired, but they are seldom if ever proposed as models to emulate in a culture that loves to talk things out, whether trivial or crucial.

Because labor laws in France were designed — some say wrenched — from within a very paternalistic social hierarchy, leisure periods throughout the year still carry their major birthmarks. Common wisdom early on decided that summer time was the ideal time for putting paid vacation into practice, that is when children are out of school and therefore able, but by no means free to decide, to follow their parents wherever the latter might wish to go. Therefore, when summer camps, in many cases state- or union-sponsored, became more common for all children after World War II, they were seen as in addition to, and not in lieu of family vacations. As late as 1994, James Corbett noted:

> The importance the French attach to family vacations is a major obstacle to re-organizing the school year, and the tourist industry exerts considerable pressure on the Ministry of Education when the negotiations on holiday dates take place. Already the midterm February and Easter vacation dates are staggered to ensure a longer season for the ski resorts which could not accommodate a holiday rush of all the French at the same time!" (Corbett 105)[8]

This explains why highways, train stations and airports during summer months look so congested that, were one of Montesquieu's Persians to observe France today, he would probably exclaim that at certain times, the French seem to ritually seek to escape some sort of solar apocalypse! One can easily assess the cost of such massive vacation departures and returns, for not only are they expensive in terms of fatalities on the highways, but because they also stretch transportation and traffic controls to the breaking point. This is what the 1956 law sought to avoid, when it was decided that the third week of paid vacation could be taken separately from the other two, but it never worked quite as expected, due in large part to the reluctance of employers to delegate the running of the shop to some responsible employees while others were away. It was either all or nothing, and since nothing was by now out of the question, entire plants would be shut down for three weeks, stores would close, law offices would do the same, pharmacies, etc., while hotels and camping grounds — often improvised and, as a result, under-equipped — were saturated, only to have to shut down for lack of customers during the rest of the year. Jacques Tati made a quite telling and delightful comic film on the summer vacation rush as early as 1953: *Les Vacances de M. Hulot.*

The construction and subsequent enlargement of a system of super highways in the 1960s gave renewed impetus to an old bourgeois tradition and extended it to whole new layers of urban executives and well-paid white-collar workers who were eager to renew their ancestral peasant ties, real or imagined. It had been the custom for centuries for the well-to-do to own a *résidence secondaire* in which to enjoy a retreat away from the bustle of city life. Stanley Karnow mentions that his French hosts, no less than Nathalie Sarraute and her husband, Raymond, indulged in such a tradition in the late forties, although he could not quite discern how their cozy-but-not-rich income allowed them such a fancy as the purchase and renovation of a "dilapidated farmhouse" in Normandy, fifty miles away from Paris. France has always enjoyed the densest network of roadways in the world, but the — albeit very expensive — *autoroute* made it soon thereafter possible to reach just about any point in France from anywhere within its borders in a few hours. Considering that the average French citizen at the wheel insists on driving at break-neck speeds,[9] regardless, it seems, of the size and condition of the car, it meant that one could reach any destination in the countryside on weekends by leaving home after the kids came back from school on Friday afternoon. A good number of people who continued to make do with tiny apartments and long flights of stairs in big cities were saving their money to purchase "that old shepherd house in Provence" or all imaginable variations according to regional origins. For people who felt basically estranged in office life under any guise, however remunerative it might be, the dream consisted of reaching out to the past for an identity they seemed to have lost. Whether it be for a few hours or a few weeks at a time, leisure for many French people means forcing that precious hiatus in their ordinary work life where they can gather again around their country-house's over-sized fireplace, share a meal made entirely of mythical "native" products, breathe the mythical fresh air drifting in from the mountain, drink mythical spring water that, depending on its source, is endowed with a thousand different medicinal virtues, and just smell the same mythical odors of the earth their ancestors smelled. In that they have not moved so far at all from the epitome of the seventeenth-century court lady, Madame de Sévigné, who wrote that haying was just as much fun as a ball at Versailles.

Entire villages that had been threatened with extinction throughout the fifties and sixties, in what the social historian and economist Jean-François Gravier termed "the French desert"[10] (1972), were regaining life in the eighties and nineties. There was enough to rebuild and renovate for all tastes and means, from the one-room farm house to the fifteenth-century priory or the castle to which it had been attached. *Bricolage* was more than ever a national pastime. The French spent fortunes and devoted every bit of free time they could steal from the work place straightening a crumbling medieval foundation, beaming and re-tiling a roof, weeding, and reading dozens of new magazines that gave them guidance on how to perform their labor of love, so as to preserve the historical integrity of their architectural gem without relinquishing on demands for twentieth-century comfort and amenities. For it must be said that most of the work in fact called for highly-skilled labor, and the owner's task was predominantly that of inspection. The craze for country retreats generated in turn quite a robust market for local artisans and antique dealers. As more and more people joined in the trend, it became financially viable for some young people to move back to their own once-abandoned-now-restored house and start a business closely tied to what was quickly becoming one of France's major industries and sources of national revenues: tourism. By the end of the eighties, there were an amazing 20 million secondary residences in France.[11] France's European neighbors had joined in and were playing a big part in the economic and human resurrection of those not-so-long-ago nearly deserted areas of the Vosges, Brittany, Périgord, Ardèche, and Haute-Provence. As if inspired by André Malraux who, as the first French Minister of Culture undertook in the sixties the immense project of erasing the grime of time off Paris's public buildings and, not unlike Viollet-le-Duc a century before, of preserving some of France's most precious architectural heritage, the French were frantically busy restoring a *France profonde* most of them had never known. Also in the sixties, the government had launched two very ambitious programs, whose goals were to facilitate and channel leisure in new creative ways: one was the creation of cultural centers *(Maisons de la culture)* throughout the country; the other was the opening and protection of natural parks, where hikers would have the opportunity to discover native landscapes in their original state.[12]

Something very important happened in the late fifties and early sixties whose effect could only be fully measured culturally a little less than a decade later: a sudden increase in demand for higher education on the part of post-war baby-boomers who started crowding ancient universities incapable of accommodating them. In 1960, for every one thousand French people a little fewer than eight teenagers entered the university system; in 1970, their number had doubled.[13] With more money available in the pockets of their parents, and pushed by the ambitions of their parents, more and more young adults sought and created a new way of life characterized by revolt against discipline and a burning desire to enjoy the good things of life, as was so superbly illustrated in Georges Perec's *Les Choses.* That is not to say that a majority of them were not driven by their own motivation to achieve a good life through academic prowess, but they were the ones with the extended weeks of leisure, and at least partially the means, to enjoy and sometimes produce most of the goods the new society of affluence was proposing. They traveled extensively, they discovered their own music, their own fashion, both of which were directly imported or quickly adapted from the United States; they went to the movies assiduously, they had radio shows designed especially for them, they organized themselves into unions and political clubs. All the while wholly dependent on the riches of their caretakers and the benefits granted them by a generous *État Providence,* they were demonstrably and vociferously acting out a youth culture whose model was slowly but inexorably permeating all of French society, starting with the younger workers and practically the entire education system. They battered the fissuring walls of political conservatism and embarked upon reforming the world through the Marxist-inspired ideology of "radiant tomorrows."

The so-called Revolution of May 1968 indirectly brought about the fourth week of paid vacation, but the seed had been germinating throughout the preceding decade. If only as symbols, it is worth noting that two of the most visible slogans scribbled on the walls of Paris during the sometimes violent events of the time were "Under the cobblestones [used historically to erect street barricades], there is a beach!" and "It is forbidden to forbid!" On July 17 were signed the Grenelle agreements between labor unions and the *CNPF* (French Business Leaders Union), whose goal was to work toward an effective reduction of the work week to its legal limit of forty hours, something that could not be achieved at a time of such intense economic activity. The national average number of worked hours was still 45.2 in 1968. In 1976 it had come down to 41.8. Meanwhile the fourth week of paid vacation became law on May 16, 1969, almost day for day a year after the initial student demonstrations at the University of Nanterre that ignited the general strikes of 1968, paralyzing the entire country for days on end. Even though enough books have been written about those events to fill the shelves of a large library, one is still entitled to ask without irony: what was 68 exactly? A recent thirty-year anniversary article in *Newsweek* may help us put it in a perspective closely related to the topic explored here. Entitling their piece "You Said You Wanted a Revolution," the authors open with the statement that "many years after their May revolt, France's students are members of a not-so-different ruling class [than they fought against]." The most telling part comes at the end, in the interview with one of the most famous veterans of the "battle," Bernard Kouchner, now secretary of State for Health: "'Sixty-eight was palpitating, sensual — a wonderful adventure,' he said. 'And what was most wonderful about it? That it happened.' He leaned forward conspiratorially. 'And that we didn't believe in it. It was the last great exercise in style.' You have to be French to get away with stuff like that" (Dickey and Warner 45).

Maybe the wisdom that Bernard Kouchner has gained with age also comes with selective memory, for in its own theatrical exaggerations sixty-eight did mark a high point in social and moral expectations about what France should be in the future. True, some of the pronouncements made at the time were far from realistic, but decisions were made subsequently that were inspired by the utopian generosity of those frenzied weeks. What emerged in the early seventies and continued to take shape throughout the eighties and nineties despite economic adversity was a much more relaxed, more liberal society than ever before. While everyone recognizes that the oil crisis of the mid-seventies had a crushing effect on the French economy, increasing the State social financial burden and sobering up youthful dreams of a better life for everybody, France was already diversifying and redistributing its resources in order to preserve its quality of life.

The big black spot on the record, and one that has grown so large and remained so for twenty years now is, of course, unemployment, which will bring us back to the introduction to this essay. The problem that France has addressed for the past twenty years is not how to cut down on social benefits, but how to protect and even expand them at all cost while trying to make sure that everyone has equal access to them.

As a matter of fact, the fifth week of paid vacation became law by executive order of President Mitterrand on January 16, 1982. To be sure, it provoked heated confrontations between labor union leaders and business leaders on the matter of salary compensation, especially since it was accompanied by a reduction of the work week to thirty-nine hours, but time has shown that it did not have any of the dire consequences that its detractors were forecasting. It is said that by acting out of executive privilege, François Mitterrand wanted to stimulate contractual negotiations in a country where the gap between the rich and the poor, and especially those unemployment figures were growing alarmingly. It is quite telling that Jean Auroux, then minister of Labor and arbitrator, reminded both business and labor leaders of their imperative duty to work for social justice and national solidarity. It is quite evident that "leisure" was thus taking on a totally different meaning from what it had had up to that point.

Whether by choice or by force, and with the exception of a few major industrial sectors that weathered the oil crisis storm with time and continue to this day to place themselves among the top worldwide, France has been restructuring its income-producing forces, particularly in the area of "services," or in other words in the "leisure industry." Now the word "leisure" is not quite right here, for the industrial sector of "services" includes an immense variety of professional identifications, from the waiter in a restaurant to the hotel manager, from the street cleaner to the retirement home orderly, from the tour operator to the hairdresser. What they and many more have in common is that their job is, put simply, to make life more enjoyable for everyone. Tourism attracts increasing numbers of foreign visitors, and more and more Europeans decide to settle and retire in France. In 1994, more than sixty million tourists passed through France, that was three million more than there were French people at the time, which may explain why an uninformed glance could give the wrong impression that everyone is constantly on vacation in that country.

It is striking to note, for example, that in 1994, fifty-eight percent of the French people took a vacation outside of their home, that is thirteen percent more than in 1970, even though they spent only (!) twenty-two consecutive days away rather than twenty-seven days in 1970, i.e., the year after the four-week paid vacation became law. Conversely, ten percent of them, most of whom go skiing, now take vacation time during the winter versus four percent in 1970. There are now 13.3 million of them officially registered in amateur sports federations, whereas there were only 5.5 million in 1970. They go to the movies less often than they used to, with only 130 million tickets sold in 1995 versus 182 million in 1970 despite vigorous state-run and industry-sponsored campaigns to promote cinema attendance, such as "Cinema Day." And if it were not for the great amount of support the State gives to finance French and Franco-European film production, especially but not exclusively via the Ministry of Culture, the making of movies would be mostly a thing of the past, eclipsed altogether by American commercial behemoths, which the French public tends to prefer to most home-made products anyway. One does not necessarily explain the other, but it is of no small significance that the total amount of money spent for the purchase of television sets has increased almost eight times during the same period 1970-1995, and money spent on cassette-players-recorders and VCR-camcorders was multiplied by more than twenty-five, both amounts reaching over twenty-four billion francs. Although they are still relatively expensive when compared with U.S. market prices, it can be estimated that ten to twelve million such items were purchased in 1995.

The audio-visual pastime reigns: the French of today purchase four times more CDs, tapes and cassettes and spend forty percent more money than they did twenty years ago on shows.[14] But it may be comforting to note that they also spend twice as much in sports facilities; they buy more sports equipment and visit museums more than ever before, and they have increased their consumption of printed news and books by ten percent. And yet when they compare themselves with their partners of the European Union, they may be chagrined to learn that they spend on average half as much as the citizens of tiny Luxembourg on the purchase of "leisure accessories" and only twice as much as their Spanish neighbors. They stand at eight points under the European one-hundred average, and they may be quite upset to discover that both the Germans and the British stand at thirty-eight and twenty-six points above the average respectively. In the category of "leisure services," they again fall five points short of the average, far out-distanced again by the British and the Danes. In the last category surveyed, that of books, dailies and periodicals purchased, they fare much better, standing at one hundred-and-twenty-eight points and in third position, but still behind Luxembourg and Denmark. Of course, it is difficult to give these numbers an absolutely clear meaning, for it is understandable that the purchase of leisure goods and services may not correlate with an increased amount of leisure time, as it does with new ways of utilizing already available leisure.[15] It may also suggest, however, that all Europeans are now sharing to various degrees in a common cultural model resulting from a need to confront similar economic and social problems.

So what is the situation now, and will the French learn to use their increased free time constructively and with felicitous results for the unemployed? The law now states that a thirty-five-hour legal work week will be the norm by January 1, 2000. Willy-nilly, since 1996 the country has already been at work putting its words into action, and hundreds of early "contracts" have been signed between business leaders and unions. As of November 1998, one out of five businesses was negotiating on a case by case basis the modalities of employees' compensation, with the added headache of designing a new workday and/or a new workweek. Inequalities abound among businesses, with the upper white-collar workers faring distinctly better than most common workers and much better than part-time workers, who are on the increase. Some early experiences have nevertheless been shown to work to the full satisfaction of the employees and their employers.

With the legal workweek limited at thirty-five hours, the three-day weekend is not, and certainly will not be, an exception anymore. The extension of paid vacations to five weeks a year has been fully absorbed so as to generate minimal disruption in the production of goods and services, especially as those who are employed have learned to take better advantage of opportunities to take time out from work throughout the year instead of taking all of their vacation time during the summer months, as was too often the case before. It remains to be seen what kind of impact all that extra leisure time will have on schooling. When one considers that practically one hundred percent of three-year old children are "schooled" at present, it might come as a benefit to them to have their parents more available for their emotional and general nurturing needs. It is another matter altogether in the case of school children, who already suffer from the stress of very demanding academic programs and schedules that conflict with their parents' newly acquired freedom, as Corbett pointed out.

The last compression of work comes with retirement, and that has seen dramatic changes too over the past ten years or so. There is now under consideration a mandatory retirement age of fifty-five, but as is true of the complexity of the system and discrepancies between professional categories regarding the application of the legal workweek, retirement has its own numerous special cases and volumes of regulations which result from long-established privileges or social benefits secured at various times in recent history by special sectors of labor, particularly civil servants and employees of State-run industries and services. Let it suffice to note that the legal retirement age at present is sixty for both men and women. In order to qualify for full retirement benefits, a French citizen first has to have worked for forty years, but to take only two examples of exceptions, railroad workers retire with full benefits at age fifty and primary-school teachers retire at age fifty-five. All civil servants must retire at age sixty-five (unless they belong to a "special status" professional category), but they may retire at age sixty with full benefits. The list goes on and on. Up to this point, an earlier retirement age coupled with a growing life expectancy has benefited the French society as a whole, in great part due to the buying power of the retirees themselves. "Presently the situation of retirees in France is satisfying overall . . . The standard of living of retirees is approximately equivalent to that of the employed work force" (Cordellier and Poisson 479). Sociologists have also been quick to note that the leisure gained through early retirement meant in many cases a return to a three-tier family, where grandparents are more available to take care of their grandchildren than they were throughout the past forty years or so. Once again, leisure proves to be good for the family.

In conclusion, the French will shortly work less than ever, at least as they step into the twenty-first century, but they will live longer and they will not be willing to relinquish any of the benefits they have gained throughout the second half of the twentieth century. They will have more leisure. If all goes as planned despite black storm clouds on the horizon, they will not only have the means to enjoy themselves, but they will also provide employment for their fellow citizens and their families now in dire need of some sort of steady income. We may some day come to realize that far from falling behind its industrialized peers in terms of economic and social achievements, France has been steadily at work over the past fifty years pioneering a new (revolutionary?) democratic model for the twenty-first century. There is only one obvious question remaining: will they continue to make of their extra freedom something of cultural benefit to society or will they all be acting mindlessly in a remake of another of Jacques Tati's movies, *Playtime* (1967)?

Notes

[1] In addition to sources referenced in the text, the information used in this article comes from the web, specifically <http://www.lexpress.fr/editorial/dossiers/35heures/ouverture.htm>. All translations of quotations from the French are the author's.

[2] See the chapter entitled "In Praise of Frivolity," in Richard Bernstein's *Fragile Glory: A Portrait of France and the French*.

[3] Catholic feast days continue to be observed nationally, even though only thirteen percent of French Catholics practice regularly. In addition, there are commemorative and 'cultural' holidays, for a total of eleven days out of the year. Depending on which weekday they happen to fall, they have been generally used over the past forty years to extend weekend periods over four and even five days. What had been called a "bridge" over a workday, when the holiday happened on a Thursday or a Tuesday, has by now become a 'viaduct,' when the holiday happens on a Wednesday. Of course, only a minority of professions may enjoy these extended holidays.

[4] Contrary to preconceived ideas, the French per capita Gross National Product has steadfastly remained among the top five in the world over the past fifty years, often enough in second position immediately behind the United States.

[5] This idea is certainly not as new as it might appear. Some American readers may be surprised to learn that, more than twenty years ago, their very own renowned economist, Kenneth Galbraith, had already formulated the thought that the most pressing duty of the developed industrial countries in the world should be to learn to work less and to enjoy themselves more. Recent history may have shown that Galbraith's proposition was way ahead of its time, but it may still come to be realized, as new technologies continue to allow for increased productivity while reducing demand for labor.

[6] By church denomination, it is well known that the Protestants represent only a tiny minority in France (just under one million people, only ten percent of whom attend religious services regularly). But it can be said that, despite the political and religious persecution to which the Protestant church was subjected throughout the *Ancien Régime,* the Protestant work ethic was at all times alive among a good part of business-oriented layers of French society. It grew stronger toward the end of the eighteenth century, and after the Revolution, many political leaders were its outspoken promoters throughout the new bourgeoisie. With his famous proclamation, "French people, get rich!", a political conservative such as François Guizot, born of an ardent revolutionary Protestant father, may be seen as one of the most illustrious forefathers of post-war generations of aggressive technocrats, self-made men and women, and business leaders who were learning to work long hours for a hefty return in consumable goods and the satisfaction of being instrumental in the country's general economic boom.

[7] Presently, there are an astounding six-hundred and fifty thousand "leisure" associations in France, whose legally registered activities cover every conceivable definition of culture, from stamp collecting and music appreciation to sports and civic-minded beautification programs. Quips an observer: "Every French person can be a president at

least once in a lifetime. All it takes is a project and two friends (one a treasurer, the other the president) in order to qualify under the non-profit organization status required by a 1901 law" (Brame 252).

[8] It is worth quoting Corbett at length here for his own enlightening interpretation of the phenomenon of vacations. He writes: "The right to vacations is not written into the constitution, but it is a privilege the French, with their more than five weeks of annual paid vacation, refuse to let anyone tamper with . . . A cultural explanation for the importance of holidays in the value system might lie in attitudes toward health care, where restorative vacations are deemed essential for 'charging the batteries again.' Of course, it is a vicious circle. Frenzied spurts of activity require 'time to decompress' as the popular saying goes, and then the lost time must be made up by investing even more in work which, in turn, requires a further break! Whatever the reason, it is strange that a nation so deeply attached to the welfare of the family and children should impose upon its youth a workweek that many adults would find exhausting" (105).

[9] It may be worth remembering that the speed limit is ninety miles an hour on super highways, but drivers going ninety-five or a hundred miles an hour are not uncommon. As leisure goes, driving fast is a sport in France, one from which people of practically all ages seem to derive a great deal of pleasure. It is, however, a costly pleasure, not only in terms of tolls and gas prices, but especially in terms of lives lost. Throughout the seventies and eighties, it looked as though it would be impossible to lower the number of road fatalities in France under the frightful number of ten thousand a year. This was finally achieved with great fanfare a few years ago.

[10] The full title of Gravier's study is *Paris et le désert français en 1972*. In it the author deplored the striking post-war imbalance between the vitality of Paris and its surroundings and the morbidity that had struck entire regions of France as their youths abandoned unprofitable farming and related activities in search of steady jobs and better standards of living in big cities.

[11] This was, admittedly, a middle and upper-class phenomenon at a time when, in the words of Michel Winock, "The steam-roller of economic evolution had turned the [French] dream of owning one's own house into a 'lost paradigm'" (Winock 93).

[12] Despite the astronomical cost involved, some high-voltage lines were taken down and buried underground, so as not to interfere with a full appreciation of unadulterated nature, but many such projects were scrapped for obvious economic reasons.

[13] And by 1990, it had grown to forty per one thousand, putting France in third position in the world behind the United States and Canada (Frémy and Frémy 1239).

[14] As they do, by the way, on the purchase of lottery tickets.

[15] On that point we should keep in mind that in the United States, as well as in Japan, leisure expenditures are fifty percent higher than in France, although Americans and Japanese work longer hours and have paid vacations roughly three times shorter. As in all cases of manufactured goods consumption, leisure expenditures depend much more on disposable income than on extended leisure time (Cordellier and Poisson 1996, 148).

References

Bernstein, Richard. *Fragile Glory: A Portrait of France and the French.* New York, Alfred A. Knopf, 1990.
Brame, Geneviève. *Chez vous en France.* Paris: Dunod, 1993.
Corbett, James. *Through French Windows: An Introduction to France in the Nineties.* Ann Arbor: The University of Michigan Press, 1994.

Cordellier, Serge and Elisabeth Poisson, eds. *L'État de la France 97-98.* Paris: Editions
    La Découverte, 1997.
---. *L'État de la France 96-97.* Paris: Editions La Découverte, 1996.
Dickey, Christopher and Judith Warner, "You Said You Wanted A Revolution?"
    Newsweek, 1 June, 1998.
Ernaux, Annie. *La Place.* Paris: Gallimard, 1983.
Frémy, Dominique and Michèle Frémy, eds. *Quid 1994.* Paris: Robert Laffont, 1993.
---. *Quid 1998.* Paris: Robert Laffont, 1997.
Gravier, Jean-François. *Paris et le désert français en 1972.* Paris: Flammarion, 1998.
Karnow, Stanley. *Paris in the Fifties.* New York: Random House Inc., 1997.
Perec, Georges. *Les Choses: Une histoire des années soixante.* Paris: Editions Jai Lu,
    1978.
Rochefort, Christiane. *Les Petits Enfants du siècle.* Paris: Editions Bernard Grasset,
    1961.
Schifres, Alain. *Les Hexagons.* Paris: Robert Laffont, 1994.
Winock, Michel. *Parlez-moi de la France.* Paris: Seuil, Collection "Points," 1997.
Wylie, Laurence and Jean-François Brière. *Les Français.* Englewood Cliffs, N.J.:
    Simon & Schuster Co., 1995.

14

Le dire-vrai du roman social contemporain

Marc Bertrand
Stanford University

Le roman social contemporain, ou mieux, selon la formule de Jean-Patrick Manchette, le « roman d'intervention sociale », est aujourd'hui d'une richesse et d'une variété remarquables, d'autant plus que ses auteurs sont d'origine sociale, et ethnique, très variée, et souvent proches de la matière sociale qu'ils mettent en scène, ajoutant une mesure d'authenticité supplémentaire aux sujets et situations qu'ils abordent (différence marquante avec les auteurs pratiquant ce genre dans les générations antérieures, quasiment tous issus du milieu bourgeois éduqué). La critique au jour le jour, qui évolue elle aussi, comprend l'intérêt de ces textes et les pousse en avant; certaines maisons d'éditions, telles les Éditions de Minuit (refuge, naguère, de Beckett, de Duras et du Nouveau Roman!), ont pris le tournant et ont admirablement championné ces voix venues d'en bas et des marges.

Chaque année sortent au moins une douzaine de romans à contenu social qui, du fait de leur qualité littéraire, rehaussent la tranche de vécu parfois pénible qu'ils découpent dans la réalité sociale contemporaine. Pour situer rapidement, un exemple récent parmi d'autres: *Viol* (1997) de Danièle Sallenave qui présente, sous forme d'entretiens imaginaires, la difficile confession d'un viol incestueux dans un ménage ouvrier, récit qui s'élargit pour dire aussi l'histoire d'une famille, d'un quartier et d'une grande cité du Nord depuis les Trente Glorieuses. Ce roman se présente presque comme un contre-discours sociologique, Danièle Sallenave préservant la part subjective de tout récit de soi, ainsi que la part de déformation de l'interlocuteur-questionneur prétendument objectif — relation délicate et complexe que ne saurait transmettre un rapport ou une enquête de sociologue.

Puisqu'un choix s'impose dans un domaine aussi foisonnant, il s'agira donc ici de textes romanesques (y compris des « polars » très engagés) qui tous s'organisent autour d'un des thèmes sociaux forts qui agitent, perturbent, et transforment la société française contemporaine: intégration/assimilation de groupes immigrés, minoritaires souvent réfractaires (première génération) puis déchirés (deuxième génération, Beurs et autres); ghettoïsation des grandes cités suburbaines où sévit petite (et grande) délinquance et où fermente l'intégrisme religieux et politique; spéculations de promoteurs sur des quartiers anciens, des villages, et déplacements de population qui s'en suivent; rapports sociaux et sexuels changeants; présence d'un « troisième âge » indépendant et actif; affaiblissement de l'identité ouvrière et syndicale; visibilité des chômeurs et des sans domicile fixe (SDF) et formation de nouvelles solidarités sociales au gré des difficultés et des grèves; rapports entre forces de l'ordre et citoyens; mimétisme de la télévision; intense désir de mobilité et d'échappée chez les jeunes bloqués dans les « quartiers d'exil »...

La provenance bourgeoise de la quasi-totalité des écrivains français a fait que la représentation du travail manuel a toujours été plutôt rare et de deuxième main, pour ainsi dire. Mis à part le lointain *Germinal* et l'œuvre du Réaliste mineur Charles-Louis Philippe au XIXᵉ siècle, quelques tentatives de tendance « populiste » ou « prolétarienne » des années 1930 (Henri Poulaille, Léon Lemonnier, André Thérive...), il a fallu attendre des écrivains beaucoup plus proches de nous pour que le travail en usine ou en atelier entre en littérature sans manifeste ni étiquette.

Il n'est que juste de rappeler ici la réussite éclatante de Claire Etcherelli dans *Élise ou la vraie vie,* évocation hyperréaliste et hallucinante de la chaîne de montage dans une grande usine automobile. Même atmosphère dans *Chaîne* de Saïdou Bokoum et dans *L'Établi* de Robert Linhart, étudiant soixante-huitard de milieu bourgeois qui, par fidélité aux idéaux égalitaires de Mai 68, entre en usine, au travail à la chaîne, chez Citroën (situation peu fréquente). Dans cette lignée, François Bon est devenu sans conteste le meilleur spécialiste de la vie quotidienne des travailleurs en usine, comme dans *Sortie d'usine* et *Limite,* ou encore en milieu dangereux comme dans son plus récent roman, *Prison,* traitant du quotidien d'un éducateur pour incarcérés, lequel nous fait pénétrer dans la réalité carcérale sans romantisme, mais aussi dans les fantasmes des prisonniers, leurs confessions déguisées et leurs aspirations pour « l'après », à partir des travaux écrits et dessins de ses élèves.   L'écriture « blanche » de François Bon (phrases courtes; mots précis; images modestes) renforce l'impression d'authenticité de la réalité sociale décrite, effrayante parfois; mais plus effrayants encore sont la solitude et le manque de solidarité des personnages de Bon: biais d'écrivain ou réalité sociale?   On pourra compléter l'évocation de François Bon par celle de Frédéric Boyer dans *En Prison* dont le sujet est très proche, mais son petit prof des prisons pousse la compassion si loin qu'il s'y englue psychologiquement et finira par se fondre dans la masse des prisonniers et s'y faire enfermer avec eux. Un mouvement semblable d'extrême empathie anime l'infirmière de Sylvie Caster, dans *Bel-Air,* soignante à domicile dans une de ces banlieues où l'entrée des immeubles sent l'urine et le désinfectant; l'auteur ne nous épargne rien de la misère intime, de la souffrance souvent solitaire, dans une suite de petites notations sèches, sans mièvrerie, mais d'autant plus insupportables de souffrance et de solitude.

Certains de ces romanciers savent évoquer de façon notable (parce que rare) la douleur physique du travail manuel dur et répétitif (Etcherelli; Bon) et les conséquences de la fatigue: l'accident du travail, mortel parfois, comme dans ce passage du roman de Jacques Chatain, *Bliche ou l'herbe rance,* lors de la construction d'un barrage:

> De là-bas, le béton est transporté; des bennes le descendent et le déversent, au-dessus du plot 6, en travail; une équipe le vibre; il faut le rendre homogène avant qu'il ne fasse prise. Du haut en bas de la station de concassage, le vacarme règne et l'on ne peut communiquer que par signes. [...] Il était environ huit heures et, plusieurs minutes après, le débit devint anormal et le tumulte changea de ton; le concasseur s'engorgeait. Paddas se mit en rogne, se demanda « ce qu'ils foutaient »; puis, se rappelant que Smaïl était seul là-haut, il décida de monter voir. [...] Il jura contre Smaïl qui avait quitté son poste; et puis il se souvint que Smaïl n'aurait pu quitter son travail que par cette seule échelle de fer qu'il venait de gravir, et au pied de laquelle lui-même, Paddas, se tenait depuis le début du travail. Et Paddas hurla: « Nom de Dieu! », et se précipita en bas en gueulant: « Les gars! l'Arabe est tombé dedans! » (18-19).

Le nom de la victime de la bétonneuse, Smaïl, nous rappelle la présence nombreuse des travailleurs immigrés, à majorité maghrébine, dans le paysage industriel français depuis la fin des années cinquante. Le récit éponyme de cette première vague de travailleurs immigrés — en général paysans incultes et célibataires forcés — reste l'admirable *Ligne 12* de Raymond Jean, récit des journées difficiles, des va-et-vient en autobus d'un terrassier algérien: le travail harassant dans les petits matins frigides; l'interminable retour jusqu'au taudis banlieusard; les sous-entendus racistes et les insultes dans le bus; la frustration de ne pouvoir communiquer correctement: tout cela dit de manière sobre et émouvante. En livre de poche, ce texte relativement court a fait beaucoup pour la prise de conscience de nombreux Français d'alors sur le genre de vie que menaient ces hommes que l'on voyait partout creuser des tranchées ou des fondations d'immeubles ou bien promenant leur esseulement dans le silence des dimanches provinciaux: « Seuls des ouvriers expatriés, des Arabes séparés de leur famille, arpentant les rues, en groupes exclusivement masculins, désœuvrés, trouvant dans le repos d'une religion étrangère un triste répit à leurs travaux de force » (Béquié,13).

Situé dans cette Bretagne mini-industrialisée depuis peu, *Le Voyage à Paimpol* de Dorothée Letessier fut un excellent premier roman-témoignage qui mettait l'accent sur le travail de jeunes femmes en usines provinciales, phénomène nouveau en Bretagne et toujours plutôt mal vu, et sur leur vie démultipliée d'ouvrière et de militante, d'épouse et mère. L'héroïne subit tout: tâches répétitives, sécurité du travail douteuse, brimades masculines, surveillance pointilleuse, etc., jusqu'au jour où elle craque, et fait une fugue d'une journée et d'une nuit, à Paimpol, à 40 km de chez elle! De lecture aisée, le roman de Letessier rend très bien les conditions du travail féminin dans un milieu encore très « masculin », pour être gentil, mais aussi dans un milieu géographique ancestralement peu ouvrier et qui cherche de nouvelles façons de vivre ensemble et de se valoriser socialement. L'effort de « resituation » (fonction et valeur) de tout un groupe social auquel sont astreintes les jeunes ouvrières bretonnes de Letessier pourrait susciter une discussion ou des projets de recherche d'étudiants, surtout si ce roman est mis en comparaison avec d'autres où sont montrées avec force la tradition syndicale et la solidarité ouvrière (Etcherelli, Linhart, Bon).

De nos jours, la peinture du travail appelle aussi son contraire, le chômage, thème de plus en plus fréquent, hélas, et dont François Bon a su bien rendre le taraudage mental:

> Le chômage, si tu ne penses qu'à ça, tu deviens chèvre. Et va penser à autre chose. Tu te forces. Et pourtant quoi faire. Quoi faire qui ne te demande pas d'argent. Les coudes sur la table, le menton pendu au-dessus de la toile cirée rouge, tu regardes l'autre côté de la rue, la section opaque de mur que découpe sur la maison d'en face ta fenêtre sans rideaux. Un tuyau de gouttière en patte d'oie, sur la gauche, fait de ton rectangle une photo d'artiste, la chance que t'as. Assez, de se retrouver là. Et c'est encore là, accoudé, que tu te retrouves pour penser que t'en as assez. [...] Se forcer à penser, à n'importe quoi, les autres, les choses. Mais ne pas penser demain, ne pas penser l'attente, ne pas te souvenir de ces cinq mois pour rien, ne pas te rappeler tes vingt-trois ans qui viennent. Ressasser plutôt tout le reste, même cela aussi dont tu as marre, cela dont tu sais que c'est fini, que cela ne peut déboucher sur rien (*Limite*, 44-45).

L'aboutissement ultime, et dégradant, du chômage de longue durée est la clochardisation: c'est le sujet à la fois de *Jours chômés,* d'Anne

Lasserre, version féminine du quotidien d'une demandeuse d'emploi et de son ras-le-bol, et de *Zone,* de Jean-Louis Degaudenzi, où un journaliste sans travail apprend à parcourir le Paris de la dèche, celui de la péniche de l'Armée du salut et des SDF perpétuellement transhumants: pas de lyrisme de la marginalité ici. Même ton persuasif et sans effets de manches, chez Dominique Fabre dans *Moi aussi un jour, j'irai loin,* dont le personnage, Lômeur, la quarantaine, au chômage depuis trois ans, subsiste de petits boulots, de distribution de gratuits et de « bonnes adresses », mais refuse le désespoir et la perte de sa dignité: rester propre pour susciter et maintenir des contacts heureux avec quelques compagnons et êtres de rencontre. Lômeur, dont le nom suggère, par contraction, « l'homme meurt », en prend presque une dimension symbolique car le personnage fait tout pour éviter cette fatalité. Ce qui n'est malheureusement pas le cas de l'engeance qui peuple les parkings souterrains de *Comme ils vivent* de Christine Spianti; les rampes hélicoïdales des parkings sont autant d'accès à un nouvel enfer dantesque où se débattent SDF, toxicomanes et délinquants. Le Virgile de cette descente infernale est un mécanicien nommé Ange, qui semble connaître tous les détours de ces bas-fonds version 1998 et sait nous faire entendre les lamentations des damnés de la mondialisation qui en disent l'exclusion (heureusement d'ailleurs, parce qu'économistes néo-libéraux, énarques et patrons aspirant au fructueux rapport multinational, ont réussi à faire avaler aux politiciens de tous bords la notion du chômage comme une bavure inévitable de nos sociétés avancées, toujours plus mondialisées et toujours plus inégalitaires!).

Depuis *Voyage au bout de la nuit,* grâce au talent de Céline, on sait l'effet catastrophique du premier après-guerre économique sur le niveau de vie et le statut social de la petite bourgeoisie, surtout commerçante et artisanale, effet de déclassement social qui nourrira le ressentiment de ce groupe, des années trente jusqu'au poujadisme et au lepénisme des années 90. Les héritiers de Céline expriment à leur tour, en littérature, leur expérience de déclassés, leur sentiment pénible d'éloignement, social et affectif, de leurs parents et de leur paysage d'origine.

Déjà Suzanne Prou, dans *La Petite Boutique,* avait amorcé le thème avec brio et compassion; plus intimiste, *La Dentellière* de Pascal Laîné, brodait avec finesse sur ce genre d'expérience entre deux jeunes gens qui se croyaient pourtant affranchis des préjugés de leurs parents. Suite à ces œuvres repères, ce sont naturellement le nom et les œuvres d'Annie Ernaux qui viennent à l'esprit sur ce sujet, en particulier *Les Armoires vides,* où était traité avec tact et lucidité ce passage de la boutique à la « Fac » et d'une certaine incompréhension qui en découle entre la jeune fille et ses parents. Depuis ce premier roman, Ernaux a fait paraître deux romans inspirés par la vie de son père et de sa mère, enquête toujours recommencée où les circonstances sociales sont interrogées au même titre que la psychologie.

Plus récemment, Éric Holder a révélé un talent remarquable dans *Mademoiselle Chambon,* qui traite lui aussi de rapports socio-amoureux difficiles, délicats, entre un maçon d'origine portugaise et l'institutrice de son petit garçon: langage, manières, allusions et références culturelles sont évoquées mais sans aigreur chez l'un ni pédantisme chez l'autre, lors de cet exercice toujours difficile de contact entre les êtres alors que les différences sociales perdurent (surtout en province) en dépit d'un nivellement important depuis cinquante ans. Quiconque apprécie cette approche où se mêlent psychologie et sociologie d'aujourd'hui, trouvera un plaisir fort à ce roman de Holder, ainsi qu'au suivant, *L'Homme de chevet,* centré sur un autre genre de contact humain, inattendu et difficile, celui d'une tétra-plégique (suite à un accident de voiture) à l'esprit vif, et de son « homme de chevet », ancien boxeur devenu soignant à domicile. Bien que la réalité phy- sique de la situation soit décrite avec franchise, l'essentiel du livre est évidemment dans l'évolution des rapports entre ces deux êtres, tous deux dans la trentaine, mais très fermés sur eux-mêmes tout d'abord, et pour des raisons naturellement différentes. Ce rapprochement s'accomplit avec pu- deur dans les gestes et selon les « tropismes » à la Sarraute dans les paroles échangées. D'une écriture subtile mais non précieuse, ces deux premiers romans de Holder satisferont les amateurs de document d'époque (situations sociales, langage...) qui découvriront du même coup un grand talent littéraire.

S'il est un groupe social qui a renouvelé en littérature la thématique des rapports de soi à l'entourage immédiat (familial, scolaire...) puis à l'en- tourage social plus large, c'est bien la génération beur (autonommée), fils et filles d'immigrés maghrébins, souvent nés en France, scolarisés et parfaite- ment intégrés à la culture d'âge, et qui vivent difficilement la faille culturelle qui s'établit entre eux et leur parentèle. Ceux qui ont conquis l'écriture littéraire nous ont donné des récits et témoignages qui touchent à tous les aspects de ce sentiment de décalage socioculturel. Parmi ces témoignages (directs, ou déguisés en « autofictions »), il n'est pas étonnant que les plus émouvants viennent de jeunes filles de ce milieu, lesquelles éprouvent avec le plus d'acuité le passage identitaire, étant donné les us et coutumes traditionnels touchant la femme arabe et musulmane.

Tel est le récit d'Aïcha Benaïssa, *Née en France. Histoire d'une jeune Beur:* née en région parisienne où ses parents algériens vivent et travaillent depuis de nombreuses années, Benaïssa décrit cependant un milieu familial au père tyrannique, au frère omnipotent, aux filles surveillées et à la mère passive; Aïcha et ses sœurs vont au lycée, cependant, jusqu'au jour où, au cours de vacances en Algérie, le père décide qu'Aïcha y restera, dans sa propre famille (pour la punir d'une passade avec un garçon non musulman): cette partie constitue un témoignage accablant sur la condition des femmes dans l'Algérie contemporaine, univers de l'enfermement où règnent l'ignorance, des préjugés insondables et des abus d'autorité de toutes sortes. La séquestration d'Aïcha durera plusieurs mois avant qu'elle ne réussisse à s'évader: d'où la dédicace « à toutes celles qui se battent pour leur liberté ». D'une langue facile et un peu maladroite, le récit d'Aïcha renvoie au dilemme des jeunes beurs déchirés entre deux cultures, ou plutôt projetés dans une culture (arabe et musulmane) dont ils se sont déjà détachés en France, s'identifiant pour le moment beaucoup plus à la « culture des jeunes », lycéens ou étudiants bien intégrés et, pour les filles, à mille lieues de la culture de sérail subie par Aïcha.

On trouvera également une dénonciation du patriarcat beur dans *La Voyeuse interdite* de Nina Bouraoui, et, plus forte encore, dans *L'Interdite* de Malika Mokeddem qui crie la malédiction de naître fille dans une société qui les marie à peine nubiles, vouées à faire enfant sur enfant, envoilées et enfermées... Malika Mokeddem se révolte et s'enfuit dès qu'elle le peut: devenue médecin à Montpellier, dans le milieu des immigrés, elle continue à ressentir la coupure du pays natal, éternelle bâtarde de deux cultures.

Mais il y a aussi des insertions heureuses, ou du moins à fin heureuse. Ainsi de l'histoire que développe Dich dans *Ernest,* entre un jeune Marocain beur étudiant à Paris et un vieil homme bougon « qui a fait la Libération, Dien Bien Phu et l'Algérie et qu'il ne faut pas emmerder... »; d'abord tendus puis, passées les préventions du racisme ordinaire, les rapports du jeune Beur et du vieil Ernest évoluent; Ernest se raconte pour la seule fois de sa vie; revit ses espoirs déçus d'être un grand peintre...: le passé de l'un pour l'avenir de l'autre. Écrit d'un style sobre, *Ernest* est le roman d'une amitié improbable mais réussie, et qui doit sa réussite au fait que certains non-dits sont dits, sans détours mais sans honte ni sans haine: un bon roman où l'on fait circuler l'air malsain.

Zaïr Kedadouche est né d'un père éboueur (ancien porteur de valises du Front de Libération Nationale) et d'une mère « analphabète trilingue », c'est-à-dire parlant arabe, kabyle et français mais ne sachant ni lire ni écrire dans aucune de ces langues. Son premier roman, *Zaïr le Gaulois,* est le récit d'une intégration plus réussie encore, en dépit de circonstances familiales difficiles, de rebellions juvéniles et de la tentation de la délinquance dans la culture de rues où il vivait et allait à l'école. Malgré tout, suivent les études brillantes, les concours, puis Sciences Po et, enfin, la politique (conseiller régional d'Ile-de-France): produit exemplaire d'intégration et de promotion sociale par l'instruction publique et les diplômes, on comprend la passion républicaine (laïque, égalitaire) qui anime l'auteur. Récit du héros comblé, certes, mais sans complaisance et grâce à des mérites conquis.

Tous les écrits beurs ne traitent pas les difficultés d'intégration ou les conflits culturels avec la véhémence ou le sérieux des textes cités ci-dessus. Celui qui écrit sous le nom de Chimo, dans *Lila dit ça,* choisit délibérément la gouaille mediterranéenne et le cynisme léger du vétéran des cités chaudes qui en a vu d'autres. Il est particulièrement caustique à l'égard des médias et de l'image qu'ils renvoient de la vie des cités; de leur exagération, parfois, quant à l'influence de religieux intégristes:

> La télé, tout ce qu'elle raconte sur la religion, c'est bidon, comme quoi les terroristes se recruteraient dans les quartiers chauffés par Dieu, ici en tout cas la religion elle progresse pas au contraire, si des filles se mettent le foulard c'est surtout pour tenir les mecs à distance. [...] Sûr qu'ici la religion elle fout le camp vitesse de pointe, on va encore à la mosquée mais c'est plutôt pour passer un moment, pour voir ceux qu'on ne voit pas les autres jours [...] les barbus ils se bagarrent pour que la tradition de la foi se perde pas mais ils ont beau souffler y a presque plus de voiles (111).

Chimo s'en prend aussi aux images de violence et d'émeutes qu'amplifie la télévision:

> Les journalistes ils crient de la gorge que les banlieues flambent, les soirs comme ça c'est vrai ça éclaire, après on en raconte le détail pendant des mois et tout se transforme, ça devient la grande guerre du monde, l'horreur et tout. Moi je dis que ça non plus je peux pas le croire. Tu brûles un bus quatre bagnoles et tu défonces une douzaine de vitrines, c'est pas la guerre que tu crois (100).

Lila dit ça est aussi un roman d'initiation à l'amour et à la sexualité entre Chimo le jeune Beur et une « Gauloise » (« Gaulois », « Gauloise »: utilisés dans les cités et les écoles pluriethniques pour ne pas dire: « Français de souche », employé par le Front National!) — Lila, jeune fille délurée, très affranchie sexuellement: sorte de Zazie adolescente, c'est Lila qui fait toutes les avances, initie certaines pratiques érotiques (aspect qui a contribué au succès du roman, bien entendu). Toutefois, au fil de cette trame amoureuse, nous sont données des vues, des instantanés, de la vie des jeunes en cité (oisiveté, machisme primaire, petite délinquance; trafics et violence soudaine) ainsi que le spectacle d'une conscience exacerbée des différences ethniques et raciales.

Bien qu'appartenant pleinement à ce milieu, Chimo se sent différent et aimerait pouvoir développer sa différence hors les limites de la cité; pour l'instant, il vit autre chose avec Lila (fille de la cité elle aussi mais qui semble d'ailleurs grâce à sa désinvolture). Mais l'impatience gagne Chimo: le discours officiel lui dit qu'il est « exclu » mais lui voudrait bien l'être! « Exclus ils disent. Ils en font là-dessus de la salive, de la pâtisserie! Putain, des colloques et tout. Mais exclus de quoi tu peux pas savoir. Tu peux même pas savoir de quoi tu es exclu. De Santa Barbara? De ces endroits qu'on voit à la télé avec des piscines et des monokinis bleu pétrole? » (73).

L'échappée de Chimo ce sera l'écriture, ce texte qu'il écrit sur des cahiers d'écolier, dans une langue très spéciale qu'il invente, peu argotique mais très parlée, avec des accents méditerranéens reconnaissables. Cette invention langagière devient symbole même de l'évasion souhaitée, ses camarades suffoquant dans la répétition, précisément, dans l'itération de mots grossiers, de verlan usé et d'expressions toutes faites:

> Résultat, ici les locaux, les filles et les mecs gaulois ou pas, ils se contentent d'une misère de langue, avec des beurgh et des tchao, des OK putain bordel keums connasse et nique-ta-mère, ils ont tout dit dans leur cage à paroles. Moi, naturellement je prends des sueurs pour ne pas écrire comme ils parlent, puis je recopie tout ici, le verlan aussi c'est la barbe et c'est limité, mais je suis pas sûr d'être dans le juste. Les mêmes mots sont pas donnés partout à tout le monde (72-73).

Les moments de doute chez Chimo ne se rapportent pas tous à la création textuelle; le spectacle de sa cité lui donne parfois des accents nihilistes très beckettiens: « Notre existence est arrêtée le matin et puis le lendemain elle se répète. C'est pas l'état de guerre, l'état d'alerte, c'est la longue attente de rien, tu vieillis chaque jour pour rien » (101).

Les Vieux, ça ne devrait jamais devenir vieux déclarait avec humour l'essai de l'anthropologue Pierre Sansot pour n'en reconnaître pas moins que la catégorie sociale du "troisième âge" est devenue, en France, un secteur de plus en plus large et qui a une visibilité inconnue naguère, lorsque les vieilles gens étaient absorbées dans le giron de la famille plus jeune. Ce n'est plus le cas, majoritairement; les personnes bénéficiant de la « Carte

Vermeille » sur les transports publics bougent, voyagent, appartiennent souvent a des groupes d'affinités, vivent en maisons de retraite... Bref, ce nouveau statut socio-économique des « anciens » , qui les a émancipés, a aussi transformé les rapports d'obéissance et de responsabilité entre les générations, phénomène progressif mais réel, et jusque dans les campagnes.

C'est un roman du tandem Boileau-Narcejac, *Carte Vermeille,* qui lança le genre, pour ainsi dire. Si les deux vieux complices sont fidèles à la formule para-policière qui a fait leur célébrité, il s'agit ici aussi d'un texte d'expérience vécue; outre la réalité sociologique des lieux de retraite, sont décrits également, ici et là, des états psychologiques sans complaisance sur le grand âge approchant:

> [...] j'essaye de comprendre ce que c'est que l'ennui. [...] Car c'est l'ennui, je l'ai déjà dit, qui me détruit. Il est fait de fuite, de dérobade, comme si l'on jouait à cache-cache avec soi-même. Mais, pendant qu'on s'évertue, il y a, pour ainsi dire par en-dessous, comme un grignotement continu de minutes, comme une lente hémorragie de temps. On vieillit imperceptiblement, sur place, sans changer. Le temps vit et moi je ne vis plus avec lui. Je suis écartelé au plus profond de moi-même. Agir, c'est coller à sa durée. Vieillir, c'est lui lâcher la main. D'où l'ennui (21).

Comme dans tout roman social français où se mêlent les généra-tions, l'Histoire, le sentiment historique, n'est jamais loin et certains au-teurs ne manquent pas au devoir de mémoire. Ainsi de Daniel Pennac, dans *La Fée carabine,* dont l'un des personnages rappelle ce poids de l'Histoire dans l'expérience de « [...] ces vieillards qu'on avait deux fois privés de leur jeunesse, une fois en 14, une autre en 40, sans parler de l'Indochine et de l'Algérie, sans compter les inflations, les banqueroutes, leurs petits com-merces balayés un matin dans l'eau des caniveaux, sans parler non plus de leurs femmes mortes trop tôt, de leurs enfants oublieux... » (192).

La Fée Carabine est un polar politico-social où sont dévoilées (sur le ton pince-sans-rire cher à l'auteur) des magouilles politico-policières pour droguer puis éliminer les personnes âgées qui vivent dans les vieux quartiers de Belleville afin de racheter ensuite les immeubles vétustes pour les revendre à des promoteurs tout prêts à reconstruire pour des loyers augmentés. L'élimination mystérieuse des gens du troisième âge à Belleville relève bien sûr d'une intrigue policière prenante, mais le thème social, celui du mercantilisme hypocrite et effréné derrière toute l'opération, est soutenu tout du long par l'auteur. Car outre l'immense escroquerie sociale qui sous-tend l'intrigue, la disparition des vieux immeubles et de leurs habi-tants (de tous âges d'ailleurs) va aussi modifier radicalement la composition et l'atmosphère d'un quartier de Paris où, depuis les années 1930, co-existent toutes les races et les ethnies, tous les métiers, toutes les langues, dernier refuge de la compréhension et de la solidarité populaires.[1]

On se souvient peut-être que c'est dans le roman de Joseph Joffo, *Un Sac de billes* (1973) et surtout celui de Romain Gary, *La Vie devant soi* (1975) qu'est apparu ce quartier parisien de Belleville, déjà centre de bras-sage social et havre des plus déshérités: Madame Rosa et sa « pension » pour enfants de prostituées de toutes couleurs, races et confessions; l'im-payable petit Momo (pour Mohamed), s'inventant une vie à l'aide de mots appropriés n'importe comment; le travesti sénégalais, ancien boxeur; Mon-sieur Hamil, ancien vendeur de tapis et homme de piété et de modération... C'est à ce grand texte de Gary que l'on peut faire remonter le « mythe bellevillois » qui est devenu presque un passage obligé du roman social contemporain.   C'est là encore que se situe le *Petit Prince de Belleville* de Calixthe Beyala, petit prince choyé qui est comme la réincarnation noire du Momo d'antan et qui, avec verve et drôlerie, nous fait participer au quotidien des familles africaines de Belleville, à leurs coutumes de là-bas et d'ici, à leurs malheurs et leur entraide... Dépaysés d'abord mais finalement retrouvant là un espace villageois qu'ils vont investir (dans tous les sens du mot), les Africains de Belleville sont le dernier avatar de ce qui semble de-venir un mythe socio-littéraire: Belleville comme site d'une idéale coexis-tence harmonieuse des races, ethnies et religions, comme espace quasi utopique aménagé pour l'exemple, et pour l'espoir, par quelques romanciers (et cinéastes, voir les films: *La Balance, Mécaniques célestes* et *Chacun cherche son chat*).

Contrairement à l'opinion péremptoire d'Angelo Rinaldi pour qui « le roman policier à la française ressemble, la plupart du temps, à l'explo-sion de hargne d'un chauffeur de taxi parisien » *(L'Express*, 25-12-1997, 70), c'est dans des collections policières, telle la cinquantenaire Série Noire, où s'est inscrit, ces dernières années, un très riche « polar social », et politique: de A.D.G. à droite jusqu'à Jean-Patrick Manchette à gauche. On trouvera sous la célèbre couverture noire et jaune un échantillonnage remarquable de ce que Manchette lui-même appelait le « polar d'inter-vention sociale » qui représente un canton de la littérature « engagée » d'aujourd'hui où, au fil d'une enquête policière, surgissent des réalités sociales bien documentées et nettement situées, et, parfois, des prises de positions morales sans équivoque.

Parmi les réussites récentes du polar engagé, on rangera *Total Khéops* de Jean-Claude Izzo: située à Marseille (ville fétiche de l'auteur), l'intrigue nous fait passer de la mentalité policière et de ses pratiques (pas toutes répréhensibles) à celle des habitants des zones franches, des banlieues chaudes et des quartiers louches, au racisme ordinaire des uns comme des autres, mais aussi au refus courageux de l'amalgame raciste chez certains. Pour Izzo, c'est Marseille, porte ouverte sur la Méditerranée et centre de brassage humain depuis des siècles, ville où l'on est chez soi, d'où que l'on vienne, c'est Marseille qui est le principe actif, le lieu guérisseur où se résorbera, dans sa lumière, toutes les haines et la difficulté d'être actuelles. Il y a chez Izzo une tendance très camusienne à faire confiance au soleil, à la mer et à son sel pour blanchir et arrondir les aspérités humaines. On trouvera dans *Total Khéops* (titre venant de la langue des rappeurs signifiant « Bordel immense » !) des descriptions très fortes de la réalité vécue dans une grande ville française de cette fin de siècle, mais aussi quelques recettes marseillaises succulentes symbolisant, chose rare, une confiance qui réchauffe le cœur[2].

D'autres collections de romans policiers (Fleuve Noir; Fayard Noir; Engrenage; Rivages/Écrits noirs; Cabinet noir; Crime...) fourniraient tout autant d'exemples de polar social où sont mis au jour les problèmes sociaux les plus brûlants; ainsi chez Ricardo Matas dans *Mauvais sang* (Fayard Noir), José Varela dans *Spécial Purée* (Engrenage), dans *Banquise* (Fayard Noir) d'Hervé Prudon, ou encore dans *Le Roi des ordures* (Fayard) de Jean Vautrin, orfèvre en la matière, et qui annonce sans ambages, dans le préambule à son livre, que « le roman noir, à l'envers de nos nombrils de Français bien nourris, continue à porter les germes d'une critique sociale comme il n'en existe à aucun étage de notre littérature en col blanc ». Opinion à laquelle fait écho Évelyne Pieiller:

> Ce n'est pas au Fleuve [Noir] qu'on découvrira des stylistes. Mais c'est peut-être bien au Fleuve qu'on découvrira de drôles de mondes, inquiétants, bancals, tordus, qui racontent à leur manière les troubles de notre fin de siècle. La littérature véritablement populaire trouve alors sa beauté: comme naguère dans les feuilletons, elle est « brut de coffrage », mais elle a des audaces saisissantes que lui permet son indifférence aux critères de la belle littérature (60).

Ce qui est certain, c'est que le polar social « [...] compose un paysage strictement français [...] où passent des paumés ordinaires, travaillés par les crises du social et les crises des menus désirs » (Pieiller 60).

Dans une société qui fabrique plus d'exclusion que d'inclusion, le spectacle le plus affligeant est celui de « personnes déplacées » nouveau genre, sans domicile fixe pour cause de chômage mais aussi parfois délogées de leur quartier ou de leur communauté par des promoteurs avides. La dislocation d'un groupe social peut être aussi douloureuse que la dislocation d'un membre et c'est cet arrachement social que dénoncent avec véhémence plusieurs romans, tels les romans « bellevillois » de Daniel Pennac déjà mentionnés, mais aussi *Brocéliande-sur-Marne* de Jean-Hugues Oppel narrant la lutte d'une communauté de banlieusards contre les promoteurs-démolisseurs, ou encore *La Rénovation* de Dominique Rolin décrivant le refus d'expulsion pathétique d'une vieille dame alors qu'on « rénove » l'immeuble tout autour d'elle, sachant bien qu'elle ne pourra payer le loyer augmenté.

Parmi ces romans de la dislocation, le plus original de ton est *Kérosène* de Claire Frédric, décrivant l'existence de quelques familles pauvres et déracinées qui squattent les maisons abandonnées sur les terrains entourant l'aéroport de Roissy:

> [...] dans notre bled, la campagne se trouvait ratatinée à quelques lopins de maïs avec d'énormes pylônes électriques au milieu. D'immenses câbles haute tension labouraient le ciel de leurs lignes sombres décorées de boules rouges ou argentées pour éviter à un Boeing miraud de s'y emmêler (56).

Paysage d'enfer baignant dans l'odeur du kérosène et le bruit des avions qui passent au ras des toitures:

> Nous parlions fort par nécessité, rapport au raffut des zincs de Roissy. Notre beau ciel habité non-stop par des décollages, des atterrissages, nos cumulus au Kérosène, nos nimbus crevés de cockpits composaient une bande-son inlassable, éreintante, un taux de décibels à vous rétamer les esgourdes (6).

La narratrice, Réjane Pic, est une gosse de neuf ans à la langue bien pendue et douée pour l'accordéon, talent qu'encourage vivement sa mère célibataire, grande gueule mais aussi grand cœur. Réjane a un frère attardé, mais travailleur et habile de ses mains: il se livre à la taxidermie la plus surréaliste, fabriquant des animaux empaillés qui ne sont pas dans la nature, comme des lapins aux ailes de hiboux! Par l'activité du frère taxidermiste, par les jeux et les rêves des enfants dans ce livre, on est presque dans l'univers merveilleux d'Alice, où tout est possible grâce à l'imagination, quelles que soient les circonstances. Mais par la vie quotidienne des adultes, squatters sédentaires ou en transit, par les histoires de SMIC et de Sécu, on se retrouve vite dans l'univers précaire des marginaux sociaux actuels qui doivent « se débrouiller ». Et qui y parviennent grâce à la solidarité de tous les « permanents » pour s'entraider. L'esprit de résistance, agrémenté d'humour noir, qui est en fond de cette histoire, est bienvenu, mais l'on sent bien que cela ne peut durer: les enfants non scolarisés, les branchements illicites d'eau et d'électricité, l'hygiène douteuse, les dangers permanents venus du ciel, tout ceci ne saurait longtemps échapper à la sollicitude implacable des autorités diverses... L'intention de l'auteur était bien entendu de nous laisser pressentir cette éventualité en suspens, ce nouvel arrachement, vers quoi?

La dislocation sociale au centre de *Kérosène* et la reformation, de bric et de broc, d'une communauté forcée chaque jour d'inventer ses moyens de survie, cette thématique a une résonance particulière dans la sensibilité collective française: exode, réfugié, expulsé, déplacé, déporté, sinistré, sont des termes maudits depuis la guerre et dont la malédiction est entretenue par la *doxa* familiale et nationale. L'euphémisme administratif: « Sans domicile fixe » n'atténue nullement la colère, la honte et la peur mêlées qu'éprouvent la plupart des gens à l'idée et au spectacle de cet état dans nos sociétés de surconsommation. Puisque l'on reproche souvent de nos jours aux intellectuels de ne pas prendre position contre ce genre d'abus, signalons au moins une tentative dans ce sens, celle du Collectif Adret, qui publiait en 1997 un ouvrage de témoignages intitulé, précisément, *Résister.* Ces quelques lignes de l'Introduction à *Résister* pourraient servir d'exergue au roman de Claire Frédric:

> Ce livre parle de la résistance qu'opposent des gens ordinaires à la grande machine qui happe le sujet, le broie et le réduit à n'être plus qu'un objet interchangeable, sans voix et sans avenir. [...] Chacun des hommes et des femmes qui prennent ici la parole témoigne de son refus de se laisser traiter et de se vivre comme un objet, [témoigne] de sa façon de vivre avec d'autres dans la société en l'aménageant localement ou en inventant les moyens de faire avec (1).

Dans un article intitulé « Quand les romanciers disent le malaise », Norbert Czarny signalait déjà le roman social comme lieu d'un engagement rare dans la production artistique contemporaine:

> [même si l'on ne peut parler] d'engagement au sens où d'autres pétitionnaires, ceux qui se réunissaient dans les années soixante, envisageaient à la suite de Sartre, l'engagement. Ne serait-ce que parce que le monde n'est plus bipolaire, que l'horizon n'est plus aussi visible qu'il paraissait l'être l'époque et qu'enfin la culture politique n'est plus la même. [...] Il est toutefois remarquable que de nombreux romanciers se font, plus qu'auparavant, en ces années quatre-vingt dix hédonistes et narcissiques, l'écho de ce que vit la société française. Que des écrivains fassent de leurs livres le « reflet » de ce qui se passe autour d'eux, est-ce si étonnant? Le miroir stendhalien reflète la boue du chemin (70).

Jadis, *Les Misérables* de Victor Hugo et le roman naturaliste eurent une influence reconnue sur la pensée et l'action des hommes politiques de la Troisième République lorsqu'ils tentèrent d'établir enfin un sentiment et une pratiques démocratiques dans une collectivité moins égoïste. Espérons que certains de leurs homologues d'aujourd'hui jetteront un œil sur le genre d'ouvrages dont il a été question ici. Et qu'ils entendront la voix de ce personnage du roman de Louis-Stéphane Ulysse, longtemps Africain de Paris qui, rentré à Bamako, évoque avec humour et vérité sa vie en cité banlieusarde: « Il y a de tout là-bas sauf des gens normaux. Oui, mon cher, c'est comme je le dis: des Occidentaux accidentés, des Orientaux désorientés... C'est à cause de leur peur à vivre... C'est déjà très difficile d'être un arbre là-bas, alors pensez: être un homme ! » (138).

Notes

[1] Daniel Pennac a par ailleurs très bien analysé ce phénomène-Belleville dans un entretien avec Kirsten Halling et Roger Célestin dans le premier numéro de *Sites,* 1 (Spring 1997): 342-43. On trouvera également des allusions au sujet dans *Paris la Grande* de Philippe Meyer.

[2] A côté du symbole de réconciliation qu'est Marseille dans les romans d'Izzo, ajoutons la « Mère Méditerranée », dans un ouvrage collectif d'écrivains réunis par Michel Le Bris et Jean-Claude Izzo, *Méditerranées* (1998) où est décliné un amour partagé pour cette mer « qui nous sépare et nous assemble », comme le disent les préfaciers; Amin Maalouf, lui, en parle comme « d'un laboratoire idéal pour une identité de rassemblement, pour une identité globale ».

Références

[Sauf indication contraire, le lieu d'édition est Paris]

Beau, Nicolas. *Paris capitale arabe.* Seuil, 1995.
Begag, Azouz. *Les Chiens aussi.* Seuil, 1995.
Benaïssa, Aïcha, et Sophie Poncelet. *Née en France. Histoire d'une jeune Beur.* Pocket, 1994.
Benguigui, Yamina. *Mémoires d'immigrés; l'héritage maghrébin.* Albin Michel, 1997.
Béquié, Jean-Michel. *Charles.* Minuit, 1993.
Beyala, Calixthe. *Le Petit Prince de Belleville.* Albin Michel, 1992.
Boileau-Narcejac. *Carte vermeille.* Denoël, 1979 et Folio.
Bokoum, Saïdou. *Chaîne.* Denoël, 1974.
Bon, François. *Sortie d'usine.* Minuit, 1982.
---. *Limite.* Minuit, 1985.
---. *Prison.* Grasset, 1998.
Bouraoui, Nina. *La Voyeuse interdite.* Gallimard, 1991.
Boyer, Frédéric. *En Prison.* Éditions POL, 1992.

Caster, Sylvie. *Bel-Air.* Grasset, 1991.
Cauwelaert, Didier van. *Un Aller simple.* Albin Michel, 1994.
Charef, Mehdi. *Le Thé au harem d'Archi Ahmed.* Mercure de France, 1983 et Folio.
Chatain, Jacques. *Bliche ou l'herbe rance.* Seuil, 1970.
Chimo. *Lila dit ça.* Plon, 1996.
---. *J'ai peur.* Plon, 1997.
Collectif Adret. *Résister.* Minuit, 1997.
Conchon, Georges. *Le Bel Avenir.* Albin Michel, 1983.
Czarny, Norbert. « Quand les romanciers disent le malaise », *Échos,* No. 83, 1997, pp. 68-71.
Degaudenzi, Jean-Louis. *Zone.* Fixot, 1987.
Despentes, Virginie. *Les Chiennes savantes.* J'ai Lu, 1997.
Dich. *Ernest.* Edtions Anne Carrière, 1997.
Echenoz, Jean. *Un An.* Minuit, 1997.
Ernaux, Annie. *Les Armoires vides.* Gallimard et Folio, 1974.
---. *La Honte.* Gallimard, 1997.
Etcherelli, Claire. *Élise ou la vraie vie.* Denoël et Folio, 1967.
Fabre, Dominique. *Moi aussi un jour, j'irai loin.* Maurice Nadeau, 1995.
Fauconnier, Bernard. *L'Être et le géant.* Deforges, 1989.
Frédric, Claire. *Kérosène.* J'ai Lu, 1997.
Gary, Romain. *La Vie devant soi.* Mercure de France et Folio, 1975.
Holder, Éric. *Mademoiselle Chambon.* J'ai Lu, 1997.
---. *L'Homme de chevet.* J'ai Lu, 1997.
Houellebecq, Michel. *Extension du domaine de la lutte.* J'ai Lu, 1997.
Izzo, Jean-Claude. *Total Khéops.* Série Noire, 1996.
Jean, Raymond. *La Ligne 12.* Seuil, 1973 et Points-Roman.
Joffo, Joseph. *Un Sac de billes.* Lattès, 1973 et Livre de poche.
Kedadouche, Zaïr. *Zaïr le Gaulois.* Grasset, 1996.
Lasserre, Anne. *Jours chômés.* Flammarion, 1997.
Le Bris, Michel, et Jean-Claude Izzo. *Méditerranées.* Éditions Librio, 1998.
Letessier, Dorothée. *Le Voyage à Paimpol.* Seuil, 1981 et Points-Roman.
Linhart, Robert. *L'Établi.* Minuit, 1978.
Livoir, Thierry. *Une Mort de printemps.* Plon, 1996.
Meyer, Philippe. *Paris la Grande.* Flammarion, 1997.
Mokeddem, Malika. *L'Interdite.* Grasset, 1993.
NDaye, Marie. *La Sorcière.* Minuit, 1997.
Oppel, Jean-Hugues. *Brocéliande-sur-Marne.* Éditions Rivages, 1994.
Pennac, Daniel. *La Fée Carabine.* Gallimard, 1987 et Folio.
---. *Messieurs les enfants.* Gallimard, 1997.
Pieiller, Evelyne. *Magazine Littéraire,* décembre 1991, 60.
Pilhes, René-Victor. *Le Christi.* Plon, 1998.
Prou, Suzanne. *La Petite Boutique.* Mercure de France, 1972.
Roche, Corinne. *Tout va bien dans le service.* Seuil, 1992.
Rolin, Dominique. *La Rénovation.* Gallimard, 1998.
Sallenave, Danièle. *Viol.* Gallimard, 1997.
Sansot, Pierre. *Les Vieux, ça ne devrait jamais devenir vieux.* Payot, 1995.
Seguin, Boris, et F. Teillard. *Les Céfrans parlent aux Français: chronique de la langue des cités.* Calmann-Lévy, 1996.
Soraya, Nini. *Ils disent que je suis une beurette.* Pocket, 1997.
Spianti, Christine. *Comme ils vivent.* Maurice Nadeau, 1998.

Toussaint, Jean-Pierre. *La Télévision.* Minuit, 1997.
Ulysse, Louis-Stéphane. *Toutes les nouvelles de mon quartier intéressent le monde entier.* J'ai Lu, 1997.
Wickham, Alexandre. *Salarié matricule 1437.* Calmann-Lévy, 1997.

15

The Cosmopolitan Tradition in French Film

Jeri DeBois King
Converse College

Although many writers and thinkers have used the word "cosmo-politan," few have committed to a full definition.[1] An examination of the *American Heritage Dictionary* reveals that a cosmopolitan might be defined as a citizen of the world. In his work, *The Renaissance Self-fashioning*, Stephen Greenblatt traces the concept to the Renaissance, defining a "bourgeois, mobile, cosmopolitan sense of self" as a cultural artifact (Clifford 35). Most French historians would posit that the term cosmopolitanism results from eighteenth-century revolutionary ideals, citing its pejorative usage early in this century when Barrès wrote of animosity in France between "nationalists and cosmopolitans" (Barrès 248).

France claims to welcome foreigners and people of all races as its citizens. De Gaulle said it best: "En Afrique, en Asie, en Amérique du Sud, notre pays est le symbole de l'égalité des races, des droits de l'homme et de la dignité des nations."[2] Today there are 4 million foreigners in France, approximately 6.5% of the nation's population (Edmiston and Duménil 176). These numbers remain relatively stable because France absorbs foreigners quickly as naturalized citizens. Over the years the complexion of these foreigners has darkened and their religions have differed from Roman Catholicism. In their consternation many French ignore this change in the manner of Michel Winock who describes Paris' "caractère cosmopolite" as a uniquely European mixture, ignoring the immigrants from the Maghreb or Africa. These latter groups take the blame for France's perceived problems of unemployment, crime, and illegal aliens (Winock 218-19). They are also reputed to inspire the success of Jean Marie Le Pen's *Front National* party and the creation of laws restricting immigration and naturalization, all of which fuel national debates and invite embarrassing accusations of racism.[3]

Film as Artifact

The concept that film is a cultural artifact starts with anthropologists and sociologists and was developed by semiotic critics. Max Weber and Clifford Geertz claimed to define cultures by reading the "thick description"[4] in a particular artifact.[5] These thinkers, in the tradition of interpretive anthropology, believe that we may read cultures as assemblages of texts by studying the synecdoches at work in all representations (Clifford 41). Literary critics such as Paul Ricoeur think that we may read a culture in nonverbal texts while Stephen Greenblatt, like the semiotic critics in the tradition of Roland Barthes, proposes that performances are artifacts fraught with cultural symbols. All of these scholars justify interpreting film as an artifact from which we may understand cultural values.[6]

In 1995, France celebrated the Lumière brothers' invention of the movie projector. For more than one hundred years, the genre has been carefully nurtured and claimed as France's gift to the world. Proud of its place in the international film industry, France is second only to the United States in production. Dudley Andrew claims that the French have inflated the role of cinema in their culture and their own role in the art. His criticism is an unwitting affirmation of the French awareness of film as a reflection of their culture.[7] For Andrew, film is not an unconscious reflection of France's culture, but a self-conscious monument erected for propaganda purposes in which France has embedded its culture to the point that creativity and change are impossible (Andrew 206).

France's self-conscious cosmopolitanism is apparent in the way it has nurtured its film industry and in the form and content of its films. Among the many that reflect this self-awareness three works stand out as milestones for their timeliness and for the unique blend of cosmopolitan characteristics that each embodies: *La Grande Illusion, Le Petit soldat,* and *Indochine.* These films incorporate different aspects of cosmopolitan themes, subsuming nationalist interest under a larger view, be it international understanding through a sympathetic portrait of traditional enemies, artistic preeminence over politics, or claims to a more humble view of France as a player on the world stage.

World War I

Co-written by Jean Renoir and Charles Spaak, *La Grande Illusion* recreates World War I in 1916 before the Americans joined the Allied forces. Ironic in its timeliness and its predictability, the film was directed by Renoir in 1937, three years before France's occupation. When two characters describe the hero, Maréchal's assertion that the war would last only months as an "illusion" in double-voiced discourse, they not only speak as characters to underscore the film's title, but also as Renoir who predicts the imminent time of World War II. This uncanny timeliness resonates throughout the film as we watch with the knowledge of World War II history.

The film tells the story of four individuals' experience with war as they meet in a prisoner of war camp.[8] Jean Gabin plays a middle class Frenchman, Maréchal, who is a lieutenant in the army. His fellow officer, de Boëldieu, (played by Pierre Fresnay) is a captain who belongs to France's vanishing aristocracy. Maréchal's good friend is Rosenthal (played by Marcel Dalio), the rich son of a Jewish banking family. Erich von Stroheim plays a cosmopolitan career officer in the German aristocratic tradition, von Rauffenstein, who speaks French, enjoys good food and music. In a table scene in which the major characters first meet, cosmopolitanism is introduced as a major theme. The French-speaking German aristocrat and de Boëldieu appear to have more in common than their respective comrades, while Maréchal and a young German discover that they share similar careers. The two pairs are reflecting mirrors, aristocrats discussing mutual acquaintances and middle class officers talking of their lives at home, Germans and Frenchmen finding more in common with each other than with their compatriots. Language here seems to be the key in defining the cosmopolitan theme. The two Germans and de Boëldieu speak French and English while the lower-middle class Maréchal is monolingual.[9]

Maréchal has problems communicating in the international theater that is war. When French prisoners are transferred to another camp Maréchal is unable to tell the Englishmen who take their place that he and his comrades have almost completed an escape tunnel because he cannot speak English. One critic sees this issue as constituting the film's most important and tragic theme: alienation, be it through nationalism, language, religion, or class (Triggs 70). Later in the film, Maréchal and Rosenthal are taken in by a German woman, Elsa, who treats them like family members while

Rosenthal recovers from an injury. Maréchal falls in love with Elsa and carries on an affair with her in spite of his inability to communicate in German. When he tries to speak German, he can only utter the same sentence: "Lotte hat blauen Augen." Even at the last meeting, Elsa has to correct Maréchal's pronunciation (Johnson 1285). Music is Maréchal's only means of communciation. He connects with his guard in solitary confinement through music and communicates his defiance of the Germans during a theatrical presentation for the camp. While performing in drag before the Germans, the French learn of a victory at Douaument. They then transform their burlesque performance into a rousing and patriotic rendition of "La Marseillaise, " and as ringleader, Maréchal ends up in solitary confinement.

Language is the tie that both binds and isolates the three French characters who have totally different backgrounds. De Boëldieu is distant with his comrades, refusing to abandon the formal "vous" form. When Maréchal mentions this to de Boëldieu, the aristocrat lets him know that he does the same with his family. In spite of the distance between them, de Boëldieu is willing to give up his life for his fellow Frenchmen by distracting guards during the escape attempt. The aristocrat rebuffs him when Maréchal entreats de Boëldieu to escape with them. He knows he will probably die, but in risking death, Boëldieu demonstrates that his identity as a Frenchman is more important than his class as an aristocrat. In spite of his class, de Boëldieu endorses republican values assuring von Rauffenstein that his compatriots' word of honor is just as good as his. Maréchal mirrors these republican values in an exchange during the escape attempt. When Rosenthal injures his leg and cannot keep up, Maréchal taunts him, saying that he never liked Jews. Rosenthal's religion notwithstanding, we know that Maréchal will never abandon him because he is a fellow Frenchman. In this film republican values take precedence over personal differences.

While most critics agree that the film is a masterpiece and still relevant today, few mention that the conflict of cosmopolitan and nationalistic themes in *La Grande Illusion* are as timely today as they were in 1937. When today's debates over the common market polarize "cosmopolitans" with a "libéralisme européiste" against "anti-Maastrichts" they really address the timeless issue of cosmopolitanism versus nationalism.[10] While today's cosmopolitan view has gained more support and nationalistic themes are in disfavor, *La Grande Illusion's* cosmopolitan values are amazingly timely. It is not surprising that *Capitaine Conan* (1996), directed by Bertrand Tavernier takes place during the same period in history and also treats the effects of war on several men, as in *La Grande Illusion*. In this film there is also a burlesque palimpsest of the rousing "Marseillaise" scene in *La Grande Illusion*. Only here, a ragtag band plays the "Marseillaise" off key, while soldiers break rank, taking turns to relieve themselves under the nose of oblivious commanding officers. Clearly, nationalism yields to the cosmopolitan view of France as a smaller player on the world stage in this scene, and one may infer in its cosmopolitan intertextual reference to *La Grande Illusion's* rendition of the national anthem, a rejection of her nationalistic past. With its combination of artistic excellence in camera technique, acting, directing, and the presentation of lofty ideals, *La Grande Illusion* presents international understanding against the backdrop of war and nationalism. Representative of France's golden age of cinema and what André Bazin called the "cinéma d'auteur," *La Grande Illusion* is probably one of the greatest films of the 1930s.

From World War II to the New Wave

The Nazis were flexing their muscles in Germany while Renoir was filming *La Grande Illusion*. During the early years of Germany's aggression, France became a temporary haven for film artists from all countries, primarily for Jews from Russia and Eastern Europe. It provided a cosmopolitan "culture" in which the film industry could take root and flourish. When the Germans occupied France and established the Vichy government they quickly took advantage of this established medium, and filmmakers engaged in what one critic described as "une collaboration plus que discrète" (Comes et al. 75). Ironically, many of these film artists and directors were Jewish. Because the Germans banned all American and British films, the French film industry worked hard to produce films to fill the void. The Vichy government established the *COIC* (*Comité d'organisation de l'industrie cinématographique*) in 1942, to keep censorship under French control. The years of 1942 and 1943 were highly productive years in the French film industry. During the Liberation France gave American filmmakers almost unlimited access to its market and ratified its surrender of the economic control of its film industry through the Blum-Byrnes accords of May 1946. Two years later, in January 1948, actors and technicians demonstrated in the streets. The *CNC* (*Centre national de cinématographie*) which replaced the *COIC,* encouraged the first coproduction agreement with Italy in 1946 and attempted to aid its film industry with a tax structure that would subsidize French productions and coproductions. In 1948, the *TSA (taxe spéciale additionnelle)* was enacted to raise money to subsidize French film projects. The ancestor of the *avance sur recettes*, ratified in 1953 and revised in 1958, provided funds for French productions by taxing the profit from American films.[11]

While the occupation created a renaissance in the French film industry by banning American films, the liberation inspired a retrenchment into what has been described as "purification" (Andrew 171). Whatever the name, censure was prevalent and arrests were made. This excess of nationalism to re-establish the "Frenchness" of the French film industry eliminated the Eastern European and Russian set designers and actors who had given an "international style" to French films (Andrew 171). This unfortunate climate created a cultural void for most of the fifties until the young directors of the New Wave crashed upon the international film scene. After this group swept the awards at the 1959 Cannes film festival American directors and critics started looking again to France for quality films and brilliant criticism. They found inspiration in France's preoccupation with cinema and the critic André Bazin, who offered a method for analyzing film (Graham 50-51). Since many New Wave directors were graduates of the *IDHEC (Institut des Hautes Etudes cinématographiques* founded in 1944) the interest in theory and criticism grew. Focusing on critics meant attention to journals, the most famous of which were the *Cahiers du cinéma* and *Point*. The French New Wave, therefore, made a name for the French film industry and renewed its international prestige.

New Wave cinema

Jean-Luc Godard's second film, *Le Petit Soldat*, embodies a curious paradox; it is an example of New Wave cinema and an anomaly within the movement. It was not shown until 1963 because it was banned by the French government for its sympathetic treatment of deserters during the Algerian war. Contrary to the New Wave aesthetics which focuses more on technique and less on social or political issues, it is one of only two New Wave films about the Algerian war, the other being the comedy, *Adieu Philippine.*

The film presents, in an ambiguous and incoherent fashion, the life of Bruno Forestier, a deserter from the French army working as a reporter-photographer in Geneva. Bruno is sponsored by the right-wing *OAS (Organisation de l'Armée secrète,* a secret army which seeks to undermine de Gaulle's negotiations for Algeria's liberation), for which he commits occasional political assassinations as needed. When he meets and falls in love with Véronica, who works for the opposing side, he decides that he does not want to comply with his handlers' request to assassinate a propagandist for the *FLN* (the Algerian National Liberation Front), a terrorist group fighting against the French and other Muslim groups. After much pressure from his sponsors Bruno relents and attempts the assassination, but fails. He is captured and tortured by the *FLN*, yet he reveals nothing. After a successful escape, he is tricked by his *OAS* superiors into completing his assigned assassination in exchange for passage for himself and Véronica to Brazil, only to learn that the group had already tortured and killed his lover.

Cosmopolitan themes manifest themselves as distance from screenplay content to technique, usually through irony. The film's most ironic contradiction is that the political backdrop of the film, the violence of the Algerian war, has been moved to an international setting far removed from all action, the city of Geneva. Geneva's apparent calm belies the sporadic violent clashes of the two extremist groups. Bruno describes himself as "fighting alone" in a struggle where both groups are equally removed from Bruno's ideals. Alienation is the hallmark of his personal and working relationships. The audience experiences this feeling of distance in the *film noir* characters' ambiguity, violence, unpredictability and unreliability (Deleuze 19). The technique reinforces the atmosphere with numerous jump-cuts and lacunae. Bruno's narration which introduces, concludes, and interrupts the narrative (all in the past tense) increases the feeling of distance (Le Sage 16-17). There is also double-voiced discourse in a mirror scene in which Bruno utters words that are mimetic language to Véronica, and possibly Godard's discourse on aesthetics to his audience, and in a later scene in which Bruno discusses questions of technique with Véronica as he takes her picture which could also be Godard's discussion of technique with his audience (Fell 2424).

The torture scenes, criticized for their scandalous nature, are the source of the most obvious irony. There is no blood and little screaming, yet Bruno is subjected to every kind of torture, from burning with matches to suffocation. Leading a banal existence, Bruno's tormentors go about their work as if they were in a factory. They socialize, run errands, joke about their daily problems and family obligations. The juxtaposition of their violent work and their bored attitude creates irony. The scene ends in an ironic twist. Bruno's leap out the window (to his death for all he knew) ends in a one-story bump at ground level and a route to "escape" which in turn leads him back to his obligations at the *OAS.*

Godard's statement that the subject of the film is really aesthetics explains why both political sides are painted unfavorably, as the director refuses to commit to either group. With the Algerian conflict as a back-drop, his aloof treatment of torture and his refusal to take sides earned the film headlines and inspired criticism. Godard applies universal values in his choice of locale and players — they are all outsiders. These decisions imply that aesthetics is more important than national issues. Because it showed a blatant disregard for any party's national interest and eschewed political commitment in favor of an aesthetic statement, it claimed a loft-ier, more cosmopolitan ideal, art.

Post-colonial France

France's colonial empire and old-world prestige were unraveling in the 1950s at the time New Wave directors and their French critics (in the *Cahiers du cinéma* and *Point*) received world attention for their experimen-tation and emphasis on aesthetics.

American critics studied both French film and its criticism because New Wave directors inspired semiotic critics who chose to write about film and were the first to claim to study film as artifact (Carroll 2-51). It was a perfect subject for critics like Roland Barthes who claimed inspira-tion from Saussure and Althusser. It is this taste for experimentation, the French public's interest in quality films, and the French intelligentsia's at-tention to the medium that enabled the French to continue their reputation for "quality" and "style."

In 1968, student revolts and social upheaval inspired directors like Godard and Marker to join collaborative filmmaking groups with political agendas, such as Dziga Vertov. The feminist movement inspired a de-mand for more women directors. The change in technology (lighter equip-ment) and the dominance of television influenced such experimentation as the *cinéma vérité* movement, inspired by Rauche, for example, who fo-cused on African immigrants (*Moi, un noir*) and on everyday life in poor neighborhoods (Armes 126-87). France continued to enjoy international prestige because of the influence of semiotic criticism and its attention to film. American critics read Christian Metz' *Essais sur la signification au cinéma,* and they also imitated Saussure, Althusser, and Barthes. In the 1980s after Mitterrand and the Socialists came to power, aid continued to go to film using the old formula of the *avance sur recettes*, and later, Jacques Lang, the Socialist Minister of Culture, awarded financial support to film projects that he considered worthy of increased subsidy. Concomitantly, French television was privatized, cable television flourished, and the audiovisual industry increased its offerings to the public and blurred the boundaries among traditional genres. France expanded its strategy of sponsoring coproductions to the Eastern block countries and Africa, and they continued to welcome foreign artists. Among foreigners working in France, Prédal lists a number of Chilean refugees from the 1970s, (the most famous of which is Raoul Ruiz), Chantal Akerman, a Belgian, and Robert Kramer, an American (755).

There are a number of reasons why France's interest in its colonies was conspicuous by its absence in film. The most obvious is that to value diversity might undermine the French policy of assimilation. Another is that only recently has it been practical, even feasible, to film on location because the equipment was so unwieldy. The colony that enjoyed the earliest film attention was Algeria, which inspired the film *Pépé le Moko* starring Jean Gabin. Africa was a second priority, inspiring such creditable films as Girod's *Etat sauvage* (1978), Tavernier's *Coup de Torchon* (1982), and Claire Denis'*Chocolat* (1988). Prédal asserts that African cinema would not exist without French support (755). French subsidies have helped its former African colonies to build a respected film industry, focusing world attention on great directors such as Sembene Ousmane, Desiré Ecaré, Ali Ghanem, Naceur Ktari, and Derri Bikani, to name only a few. Of all of France's former colonies, the least represented was Indochina.

The earliest treatment of Indochina was in the *Croisière jaune*, a project organized by Citroën during the 1930s and directed by André Sauvage. It followed a successful project on Africa, la *Croisière noire* (1924) by Léon Poirier (Comes et al. 32). The only director who consistently evoked Vietnam in his works was Pierre Schoendoerffer, a veteran from the war in Indochina, whose personal experience inspired the following films: *La 317ᵉ Section* (1965), *Le Crabe-Tambour* (1977) and the docudrama *Dien Bien Phu* (1992).[12] Apart from these works, one can name only two works on Indochina: *L'Amant* filmed on location in 1984 and Wargnier's *Indochine* in 1992.[13] The decision to film *Indochine* in Vietnam inspired a rapprochement between France and Vietnam, in part because Wargnier used local people in the film. Jacques Chirac's visit to Vietnam subsequent to the film was the first visit from a French head of state since the war (Worthy 32).

All three projects (except Schoendoerffer's) have a female protagonist framed in sensuous imagery. In her article, "Filmic Memorial and Colonial Blues," Panivong Norindr points out that recurrent in all contemporary rhetoric about Indochina is the metaphor of the "passionate romance or a stormy love affair."[14] Norindr has observed this lost lover metaphor repeated not only in recent films on Indochina, but in public comments and print references to this colony.[15]

Indochine is a film about the life of a French woman, Eliane, a rubber plantation owner's daughter, born and raised in Vietnam. After her father dies she manages her family's estate and adopts a young, orphaned Vietnamese princess. She raises this child loving her like her own daughter (an obvious and tired metaphor for colonialism). When her daughter grows into a young woman, she falls in love with Eliane's former lover (Jean- Baptiste) and becomes a revolutionary. After killing a naval officer in self-defense, she flees with Jean-Baptiste, bears his child, and is subsequently captured and imprisoned. When she is ultimately pardoned by the government, she opts to dedicate herself to her country's future, abandoning her son to Eliane. The film culminates with her son's acceptance of Eliane as his "real" mother.

Several reviewers note that the film implies a level of maturity for France looking at its imperialistic past. Indeed, implicit in the film is a self-serving comparison of French and American imperialism, which is more recent and military in nature. The serenity of the images and the female protagonists are in sharp contrast to the Americans' heavy-handed, unambiguous subject matter in the style of *The Green Berets.*[16] This implies that the U.S. handles the loss in Indochina in an immature way while France has "gotten beyond" its loss of Vietnam (Belles 189).

Although the French may have a point, the film drums this message into the viewer's consciousness with no subtlety. The film was conceived and written with Catherine Deneuve in mind, not the best way to produce an understated, ensemble cast masterpiece. It is full of melodrama, providing fertile ground for clichés to take root and crowd the viewer's consciousness. Stereotypical and worn-out metaphors are trotted out: the maternal image, the Joan of Arc topos, "the beneficent dictator," "the white goddess," "transformation in a savage world," "transformation through love," to name a few. Numerous reviewers have commented on the characters' lack of dimension. Indeed they seem to be figures in a pageant or characters in an allegory, personifying abstractions rather than showing the depth, ambiguities and contradictions of real-life characters. Some critics describe the work as "Hollywood" because of the eye-catching costumes, the lush cinematography, the linear plot, and the use of the protagonist as narrator.[17]

Feminists criticize the film's exploitative use of female characters as image and spectacle, not to mention the sexual exploitation and the manipulation of the ethnic female's image.[18] The extensive criticism notwithstanding, there was some positive critical reaction to the film. Albeit *Le Monde's* Jacques Siclier has a patriotic reason for praising *Indochine*, he sees the clichés as self-conscious strategizing on Wargnier's part (14). Some critics may see the use of a woman's story in Indochina as a rejection of the patriarchal systems in favor of "women's history," a necessary element to complete the picture of the past. For this study, *Indochine* is not of interest for its merits as a great film, but as an artifact that reveals French cultural values in the last decade of the 1990s and the image France would like to portray to the international community.

This film is a self-conscious effort to rewrite a soft-focused version of France's colonial history. If France cannot change the facts of its imperialistic past, it can project itself as viewing that past from a higher vantage point than other imperialists, which implies that it is the most cosmopolitan among that group. The cultural information conveyed here lies in the obvious effort to break patriarchal stereotypes and the inauthentic subtext apparent in how they are broken. The use of a female narrator to give a softened, more idealized version of France's colonial past is exploitative in that it uses the female image to its own end, to rewrite history and to control its judgment. In so doing, it exchanges one set of stereotypes for another. The choice of a woman protagonist with a personal story challenges the view that the film industry is sexist. Eliane is non-racist, non-imperialistic, mothering an ethnic child, raising her and her son as her own. She becomes a metaphor for the most idealized view of colonialism, the imperialist country as a mother figure. Eliane is a super woman, able to do a man's job, take over and run her family's rubber plantation and compete in a man's world of business, while she is gentle enough to be a mother and a lover.

Exchanging one set of stereotypes for another, France presents a cosmopolitan mask to its international audience, claiming to face its colonial past, yet trivializing it by using it as a back-drop in an actress-centered melodrama rather than a purely historical piece. The exhibitionism in the non-racist images of Eliane embracing the principles of diversity at every turn underscores an uneasy "protesting too much." As in all the films we have examined, the double-voiced discourse occurs again, this time revealing a vision of the colonized as "other." In the scene in which the Vietnamese rebel, one colonial says, "One day they will all rise up together . . ." The use of the pronoun "they" implies a European/ native dichotomy in spite of efforts to convey an image to the contrary. In other words, while the message is laudatory, its delivery is inauthentic.

Conclusion

If a snapshot could be taken today of the state of France's film industry it would reveal an embattled yet privileged institution which continues to fight hard in the international arena for its survival. French television co-sponsors some film productions, and films are watched increasingly on the *petit écran* while independent movie houses are on the wane. With the socialists in charge of the purse strings, films reflecting the French ideals of assimilation with works by Mathieu Kassovitz and Diane Kurys, received critical acclaim and financial support from the Minister of Culture (Lang) over and above the *avance sur recettes*. In the late 1990s most films paid lip-service to diversity. A film like *La Verité si je mens* (Gilou, 1996) depicts a French outsider breaking into a Jewish community, and *A l'autre côté de la mer* (Dominique Cabrera, 1997) tells the story of a *Pied Noir* who chose to remain in Algeria, and who, with his Arab friends, experiences racism from French and Arabs alike. Or, as in *Chacun cherche son chat* (Klapisch, 1995) and *Le Déménagement* (Doran, 1996), diversity is part of the "mix" in a cultural cocktail served to its viewers.

The French subsidy methods and co-production strategy have been successful and relatively unchanged since the *Libération*. After France's failure to protect its audio-visual industry during the GATT (General Agreement on Tariffs and Trade) talks, it has continued to view the American cultural and financial behemoth with concern. Many continue to wonder how France will accept American influence without losing its identity. It is clear that the sheer financial power of the United States will force the French into more co-productions, risking a loss of French identity to attract an international audience.[19] The French will also be pressured to join their American rivals in co-productions like *The Fifth Element*. This leads to another question: Will viewing French films become no different than a trip to the Wal-Mart, as these works' cultural identity is expunged to attract a more international audience? As a result of economic and political influences, the French concept of seeing a film will change. At this point the great concern to the French film industry is multiplex cinemas, an international phenomenon invented in the United States and imported to France via England and Belgium.[20] Multiplex cinemas with huge offerings in suburban malls are exerting pressure not only on the small independent theater owners, but on established businesses like Gaumont and Pathé.[21] Whatever the future of France's film industry, Malraux's statement is still true: "le génie de la France se retrouve dans le visage que lui donnent ses films" (Prédal 43).

Notes

[1] In *Le Cosmopolitisme* (Genève-Paris: Editions Slatkine, 1990), Muriel Augrey-Merlino provides a list of writers who used the word through the years as well as definitions from the nineteenth to late twentieth century: Rousseau, Balzac, Baudelaire, Barrès and Taine (221-224). See also: Simon Harel, "La Tentation cosmopolite," *Voix et Images* 41 (1989): 285-87; James Clifford, *The Predicament·of Culture* (Cambridge, Mass.: Harvard UP, 1988) 93; and Stephen Greenblatt, *Renaissance Self-fashioning: More to Shakespeare* (Chicago: U of Chicago P, 1980) 256.

[2] This is A. Peyrefitte's version of De Gaulle's quote in *C'était de Gaulle* (Paris: Fayard, 1994) 283. Also cited by Michel Winock, *Parlez-moi de la France* (Paris: Editions du Seuil, 1995) 250.

[3] In Catherine Bedarida's article, "Le Dixième congrès du Front National," *Le Monde,* le 29 mars, 1997, the *PIE (Parlement international des écrivains)* claims that the word "cosmopolitisme" is sufficient reason for the *Front National* to censor a book (7).

[4] The information to be gleaned from cultural signs in any artifact.

[5] See Margaret Mead, "Native Languages as Field-Work Tools." *American Anthropologist* 42.20 (1939): 189-205; Clifford Geertz, *The Interpretation of Cultures.* New York; Basic Books, 1973; Clifford 41.

[6] See Paul Ricoeur, "The Model of Text: Meaningful Action Considered as a Text," *Social Research* 38 (1971): 529-562; Clifford 41.

[7] Dudley Andrew, "France: Postwar French Cinema: Of Waves in the Sea," in *World Cinema Since 1945*, ed. William Luhr (New York: Ungar Pub. Co, 1987) 206.

[8] Thomas Hines, "War Crimes: Jean Renoir's *La Grande Illusion,"* *Crime in Motion Picture* (Kent: Kent State UP, 1986). See also Christopher Faulkner, *Jean Renoir: A Guide to References and Resources* (Boston: G.K. Hall & Co., 1979) 103-106.

[9] See Jeffery Alan Triggs, "The Legacy of Babel: Language in Jean Renoir's *Grand Illusion, "* *New Orleans Review* 15.2 (1988): 70-74.

[10] Jean-Claude Barreau summarizes the dichotomy in *La France va-t-elle disparaître?* (Paris: Grasset, 1997): "Il est assez facile de démontrer que la souveraineté du peuple, mythe fondateur et sacré de la République, ne peut s'excercer que dans le cadre de la nation (emphasis mine) . . . Pour les européistes, le véritable lieu civique n'est plus

la nation, c'est l'Europe. Il veulent en faire une supernation, n'accordant aux vieux Etats que les miettes du 'principe de subsidiarité' "(62).

[11] René Bonnell, *Le Cinéma exploité* (Paris: Edition du Seuil, 1978; Ramsay-Poche,1986). See also René Prédal, *50 Ans de cinéma français* (Paris: Nathan, 1996) 40-41.

[12] Guy Gauthier, "Indochine, Rêve d'Empire," *Cahiers du Cinéma* 482 (1992): 51-60. See also Yves Allon, "Entretien avec Pierre Schoendoerffer" *Cahiers du Cinéma* 480 (1992): 19-21.

[13] Although *L'Odeur de Papaya verte* was filmed in Vietnamese, it was shot entirely in a Parisian film studio.

[14] Panivong Norindr, "Filmic Memorial and Colonial Blues," in *Cinema, Colonialism, Postcolonialism: Perspectives from the French and Francophone Worlds.* ed., Dina Sherzer (Austin: U of Texas, 1996) 121.

[15] See Norindr's article (121) and her notes for a detailed list of references to Indochina. She quotes Bruno Masure, a television commentator, as describing the relationship between France and Indochina as a "vieille histoire d'amour" (France 2, 9 Feb. 1993). See also Jacques Siclier's review of *Indochine*, "Indochine, ton nom est femme," *Le Monde*, le 17 avril, 1992 p. 14. See also Didier Roth-Bettoni "Indochine: Le temps d'aimer, Le temps de mourir," *Cahiers du Cinéma* 481 (1992): 20-21.

[16] Mary E. Belles makes this point in her review, "*Indochine*," in *Magill's Cinema Annual 1993* (Englewood Cliffs: Salem P Inc., 1993) 189.

[17] See David Bordwell, "Classical Hollywood Cinema; Narrational Principles and Procedures," in *Narrative, Apparatus, Ideology*, ed. Philip Rosen (New York: Columbia UP, 1986) 18 (also cited by Norindr).

[18] See Norindr's article for an extensive list of the feminist issues raised by Wargnier's treatment of women in the film.

[19] See any of Woodrow Alain's articles in *Le Monde. i.e.* "Europe-Etats-Unis; La Nouvelle Guerre d'Indépendance," *Le Monde* le 23 février, 1987 p. 16.

[20] See the two-part article on multiplex cinemas by Carlos Pardo, "Multiplexes; opération danger 1" *Cahiers du Cinéma* 514 (1997): 60-69; "Multiplexes, opération danger 2" *Cahiers du Cinéma* 515 (1997): 58-66.

[21] Michel Huillard and Pascale Marcaggi, "Quand le documentaire vient au secours du cinéma . . ,"*Cahiers du Cinéma* 516 (1997): 47-51 describe the turn around of the Cinéma Saint André-des-Arts in the Quartier Latin.

References

Alain, Woodrow. "Europe-Etats-Unis; La Nouvelle Guerre d'Indépendance," *Le Monde* le 23 février, 1987 16.

Allon, Yves. "Entretien avec Pierre Schoendoerffer" *Cahiers du Cinéma* 480 (1992): 19-21.

Andrew, Dudley. "France: Postwar French Cinema: Of Waves in the Sea," in *World Cinema Since 1945.* ed. William Luhr. New York: Ungar Publishing Co., 1987 170-207.

Armes, Roy. *French Cinema.* New York: Oxford UP, 1985.

Augrey-Merlino, Muriel. *Le Cosmopolitisme.* Genève-Paris: Editions Slatkine, 1990.

Baecque, Antoine de. "Le Cinéma par la bande," *Cahiers du cinéma* 513 (1997): 37-48.

Bedarida, Catherine. "Le Dixième congrès du Front National," *Le Monde* le 29 mars, 1997.

Barreau, Jean-Claude. *La France, va-t-elle disparaître?* Paris: Grasset, 1997.

Barrès, Maurice. *Mes cahiers.* Vol. 2 Paris: Plon, 1901-02.

Belles, Mary E. "Indochine." *Magill's Cinema Annual 1993.* Englewood Cliffs: Salem P Inc., 1993.

Bonnell, René. *Le Cinéma exploité.* Paris: Seuil, 1978, reprinted by Ramsay Poche, 1986.

Carroll, Noël. *Mystifying Movies: Fads and Fallacies in Contemporary Film Theory.* New York: Columbia UP, 1988.

Clifford, James. *The Predicament of Culture.* Cambridge, Mass.: Harvard UP, 1988.

Comes, Phillippe de, Michel Marmin et al. *Le Cinéma français, 1930-1960.* Paris: Atlas, 1984.

Deleuze, Gilles. *Cinéma 2: Time and Image.* Trans. Hugh Tomlinson and Robert Galeta. Minneapolis: U of Minnesota P, 1989.

Edmiston, William F. and Annie Duménil. *La France contemporaine.* New York: Holt Rinehart and Winston/Harcourt Brace, 1997.

Faulkner, Christopher. *Jean Renoir: A Guide to References and Resources.* Boston: G.K. Hall & Co., 1979.

Fell, John L. "Le Petit Soldat," *Magill's Survey of Cinema.* Vol. 5 Englewood Cliffs: Salem P Inc., 1985.

Gauthier, Guy. "Indochine, Rêve d'Empire," *Cahiers du Cinéma* 482 (1992): 51-60.

Geertz, Clifford, *The Interpretation of Cultures.* New York: Basic Books, 1973.

Graham, Peter. *The New Wave.* New York: Doubleday, 1968.

Greenblatt, Stephen. *Renaissance Self-fashioning: More to Shakespeare.* Chicago: U of Chicago P, 1980.

Harel, Simon. "La tentation cosmopolite." *Etudes* 41 (1989): 281-293.

Hines, Thomas. "War Crimes: Jean Renoir's *La Grande Illusion*," in *Proceedings of the Fourth Annual International Film Conference.* Eds. Radcliff, Umstead, Douglas. Kent: Kent State UP, 1986.

Huillard, Michel, and Pascale Marcaggi. "Quand le documentaire vient au secours du cinéma . . . ," *Cahiers du Cinéma* 516 (1997): 47-51.

Johnson, Thomas. "*La Grande Illusion*," *Magill's Survey of Cinema.* Vol. 3. Englewood Cliffs: Salem P Inc., 1985.

Le Sage, Julia. *Jean-Luc Godard: a Guide to References and Resources.* Boston: G.K. Hall, 1979.

Mead, Margaret. "Native Languages as Field-Work Tools." *American Anthropologist.* 42.20 (1939): 189-205.

Metz, Christian. *Essais sur la signification.* Paris: Klincksieck, 1971.

Pardo, Carlos. "Multiplexes; opération danger 1," *Cahiers du Cinéma* 514 (1997): 60-69.

---. "Multiplexes, opération danger 2," *Cahiers du Cinéma* 515 (1997): 58-66.

Peyrefitte, Alain. *C'était de Gaulle.* Paris: Fayard, 1994.

Prédal, René. *50 Ans de cinéma français.* Paris: Nathan, 1996.

Ricoeur, Paul. "The Model of Text: Meaningful Action Considered as a Text." *Social Research* 38 (1971): 529-562.

Rosen, Philip., ed. *Narrative, Aparatus, Ideology.* New York: Columbia U.P., 1986.

Roth-Bettoni, Didier. "Indochine: Le temps d'aimer, Le temps de mourir," *Cahiers du Cinéma* 481 (1992): 20-21.

Sherzer, Dina, ed. *Cinema, Colonialism, Postcolonialism: Perspectives from the French and Francophone Worlds*. Austin: U of Texas P., 1996.

Siclier, Jacques. "Indochine, ton nom est femme," *Le Monde* le 17 avril, 1992 p. 14.

Triggs, Jeffery Alan. "The Legacy of Babel: Language in Jean Renoir's *Grand Illusion,* "
    New Orleans Review (1988): 15.2 70-74.

Winock, Michel. *Parlez-moi de la France* Paris: Seuil, 1995.

Worthy, Kim. " *Indochine,"* *Cinéaste* 20.1 (1993): 38.

16

New Cultural Spaces in France

Gregg H. Siewert
Truman State University

Public edifices are a lasting celebration of the political figures who build them and then leave them behind. Constructed on a vast scale (the Pharaohs' pyramids, the great hanging gardens), these monuments soon become part of a culture's collective memory. Such public places of commemoration are staples of French culture. Châteaux are tributes to lords, kings, and queens (and their friends), church architecture like Louis IX's *Sainte Chapelle* and monuments to capitalistic success such as Jacques Cœur's fine town houses in Bourges can also be considered institutionalized public spaces. The influence of Louis XIV on the cultural landscape of France is indelible. Napoleon's impact on Paris is also undeniable, witness the *Arc de Triomphe* and the church of *La Madeleine*. The modifications that his nephew Napoleon III and the prefect Haussmann brought to Paris (the boulevards and urban clearing) defined the capital for more than a century. Under de Gaulle, the *Maison de la radio* building project for the national radio and television studios was much decried when it opened in late 1963, but its circular architecture now seems tame.

The period 1975 to 1999 in France was little different, as it saw the implementation of a large number of important public spaces, particularly during the terms of office of President François Mitterrand, 1981-1995. Abbot Suger's proto-Gothic cathedral in Saint-Denis now competes for attention with the nearby *Stade de France* soccer stadium opened for the 1998 World Cup competition. The Seine riverfront will be known not only for Eiffel's Tower and the *Palais de Chaillot* but also the *Bibliothèque Nationale de France* in the Tolbiac area and the Ministry of Finance building and the multi-purpose sports and entertainment arena at Bercy on the opposite bank. These developments mark Paris and France for the ages in the same way previous great projects have done.

   This study proposes to examine briefly similar public cultural monuments, particularly in Paris, and demonstrate that this is not an isolated phenomenon in the capital, other building projects elsewhere in France are also discussed.[1] Where available, Internet Web addresses for these institutions are given;[2] many of these feature illustrations. These monuments include art museums and public buildings as well as public parks and public works projects. The great number of these projects is evidence of a forward-looking economy but also of a desire to leave a legacy of commitment to public art and architecture. Because tourism is France's most important economic resource, the conservators of its public image kept a close eye on museum construction and the government's role in the formation of collective memory. Such attempts may also be seen as a way to influence the future as well as to re-orient a public which became more and more accustomed to European and American television, sport, recreation, and other leisure entertainment. This examination of public spaces includes much of the museum construction in Paris[3] and in a few outlying regions, bearing in mind that regional and local civic governments played a great role in this endeavor as did the national government. Municipal gardens and major green spaces are included, along with mention of a few of the American-style commercial theme parks which utilize French themes and humor.

   The impetus for this study was the critical furor aimed at the construction of the new *Bibliothèque Nationale de France (BNF)* in the Tolbiac neighborhood of the thirteenth *arrondissement* on the right bank of the Seine opposite the more subdued *Palais Omnisports de Paris-Bercy (POPB)*. Inaugurated in 1995, and seen in the context of what future construction will surround the library, the building does not shock as much as when it was first proposed. Indeed, the institution underwent its official baptism of fire during the November 1998 work stoppage by library employees, an indication that it had become an everyday work place for French civil servants on the level of any other. In retrospect, it appears that for the *BNF* not to be criticized would have been the ultimate snub by the populace.

Initial outrage as a reaction to new public buildings is a French tradition. For example, I. M. Pei's glass pyramid entrance to the Louvre was attacked as discordant and unaesthetic in the mid-1980s, but the increased numbers of visitors who again crowd into the museum attest to the success of Pei's overall project. The *Grand Louvre* renovation project, with its boutiques, car parks, cafés, and such, did exactly what it set out to do in the late 1980s: refresh and increase the museum's exhibition space which has nearly doubled from 31,000 square meters to 60,000, and to revitalize an urban area that was losing city dwellers to the exurbs. Since the *Grande Pyramide* opened in 1989, it has almost become too successful, with it and its partner pyramids in the courtyard of the Louvre often difficult to distinguish among the lines of visitors awaiting admittance and the throngs of residents and tourists alike splashing in the easily accessible fountains. The *Musée d'Orsay* installation that opened in the refurbished train station in 1987 was also intensely questioned, but it too has weathered the protests.

Somewhat earlier, in the late 1960s and the early 1970s, much negative criticism was directed at the removal of the *Halles* market area in central Paris for the construction of the *Centre Georges Pompidou*. Despite virulent denunciations of the project, officially known as the *Centre National d'art et de culture Georges Pompidou*, the renovations introduced into that neighborhood solidified its place as the chic area in which to be seen. Since its opening in January 1977, the museum of modern art, the major occupant of the center that also includes the *Bibliothèque publique d'information* and the *Institut de recherches et de coordination acoustique-musique (IRCAM)*, acquired the status of most-visited monument in France, and just twenty years later, received a well-deserved restoration after hosting upwards of eight million visitors per year. Not all change was positive, of course. Still in the *Beaubourg* neighborhood, one can point to the *Forum des Halles* as an example of how quickly tastes change, as it was originally the site of high-price fashion boutiques and a Cousteau exhibit space but quickly became home to tourist attractions like a wax museum and to cinemas — an unsavory area that should be avoided at night by those fearing contact with bands of low-income adolescents and indigents. France has changed in many aspects, as even the groups of *clochards* formerly found beneath the bridges of central Paris are fewer, having been vigilantly removed to less visible shelters.

Another long and vitriolic debate involving architecture in Paris was the project to reconfigure the *La Villette* animal market area in the nineteenth *arrondissement*. From the moment that it was first proposed that the slaughterhouses be removed to the outskirts of Paris in 1955, there was much debate over what should be done with the site. In hindsight, the polemic that lasted well into the 1970s now seems risible, given the successful implantation during the 1980s of the *Cité des Sciences et de l'Industrie* in the former slaughterhouse building (inaugurated in 1986), and in the 1990s, the construction of a new *Conservatoire de Musique de Paris*, the new *Musée de la Musique* (it opened in 1996), the *Zénith* rock music hall auditorium, and other cultural spaces, including the popular public garden and play spaces that were created in the general *Parc de la Villette*. Because of the determination of the often-criticized architects and designers such as Fainsilber, Tschumi, Buren, and others who saw the project to completion, the entire *La Villette* neighborhood underwent renovation and re-evaluation as it added office space and hotels to accommodate visitors. Although long in completion, *La Villette* was transformed into a vibrant cultural community, welcoming more than three million visitors in 1997.

Lying nearly diagonally opposite from the *Parc de la Villette* in the northeast corner of Paris lies the new *Parc André-Citroën* along the Seine in the southwest corner of the fifteenth *arrondissement*. Built on the site of the former Citroën factories, these distinctive garden areas have given Paris another playful and festive park, quite unlike the severe *terrains de jeux* and *jardins publics* where *le petit Nicolas* was constantly in terror of the *gardien du square* or where fiercely protective *chaisières* patrolled the *Jardins du Luxembourg*. Indeed, just as a coin-operated *sanisette* replaced *Madame Pipi*, a new spirit in French public parks flourishes. Another area proposed for green space development is among the islands in the Seine at Boulogne-Billancourt near Sèvres. It will be interesting to watch what happens as the area's regional council decides how to employ the space of the former Renault factory buildings.

This same neighborhood on the left bank is home to the easy to use automated tramway line called *Val de Seine* (T2) which travels from Issy, not far from the *Parc Citroën*, looping around the river to its northwest terminus at one of the most dynamic of late twentieth-century Parisian neighborhoods, the *quartier de la Défense* at Puteaux. Although studies for a total design plan for the Défense neighborhood began as early as 1926 by

Le Corbusier, it was not until the construction in the late 1950s of the *CNIT (Centre National des Industries et des Techniques)*, a triangular avant-garde exposition hall of huge proportions, that this area became a focus for Paris's modern upward and westward expansion. Defenders of traditional Paris rationalized that erecting modern buildings within Paris itself would be too traumatic and too costly, and argued for development outside the city's limits. The *CNIT,* despite its huge scale, was not big enough and the interior was redesigned to house businesses and offices, a luxury hotel, restaurants, and shops, and these began opening in 1989. The architectural singularity of the *CNIT* gave way to the unusual *Grande Arche*, a controversial office cube with a window. As much an engineering challenge as a daring symbol, the arch was opened in 1989 to commemorate the bicentennial of the 1789 Revolution as well as to serve as a magnificent backdrop for the annual G-7 economic summit meeting of the leaders of the world's seven richest nations in 1989, hosted by President Mitterrand at the beginning of his second term of office. Ostensibly home to the *Ministère de l'Equipement*, office space in the *Grande Arche* also housed European Union information officials and other distinguished clients.

The *Grande Arche* and the dozens of other aluminum and glass buildings housing office complexes and corporate headquarters of France's and Europe's most prestigious companies were spectacular examples of modern construction technology and design. The thousands of employees using pedestrian walkways, shops, and plazas created an active new neighborhood in the *Défense*. Indeed, the polemic over the costs and the design of the arch had subsided by the late 1990s and it was just as fashionable and enjoyable to watch the comings and goings of pedestrians there, with most of the traffic funneled under the esplanades, as it was to sit in a café in St. Germain des Prés or on the Boulevard St. Michel.

Just over a hundred years before, the Eiffel Tower itself was the subject of tremendous vituperation by critics who claimed that it would disfigure Paris forever. The tower, built for the 1889 *Exposition Universelle* to commemorate the first centennial of the Revolution, endured years of ridicule until it firmly entered consciousness as the singular symbol of Paris. Its first slender rival which also elicited much criticism, the *Tour Montparnasse*, was completed in 1973, and given what followed in quick succession, the city came to terms with it quite easily, as well.

Modifying Hemingway's often-cited metaphor for Paris as a moveable feast, the city is indeed a changeable feast for the eyes. Points of contention move from neighborhood to neighborhood, and neighborhoods themselves change, but it often does seem the case that "*plus ça change, plus c'est la même chose.*"

The Eiffel Tower and the *Tour Montparnasse* represent major changes to Paris's landscape over a hundred-year period, but it can be just as enlightening to view more incremental changes in one particular portion of the city. The eastern half of Paris, where preservationists once feared the destruction of the *Place des Vosges* and the *Marais*, experienced numerous modifications in the last quarter of the century. Renovations in that part of the city were both moderate and radical. The Picasso museum, opened in 1985, managed to escape all critical disdain, most likely because it was housed in the beautifully renovated seventeenth-century *Hôtel Salé* in the fourth *arrondissement*. The quality of the interiors and exteriors of the restored façades and courtyards in the museum rival the work hanging on the museum's walls, and was one of the most outstanding examples of the successful marriage of the *ancien* and the *moderne*. Not far from the *Musée Picasso*, the *Maison Européenne de la Photographie* is another cultural monument that combined the old with the new. The city of Paris opened this "*musée du regard*" in 1996, preserving the 1706 architecture of the site's *hôtel particulier* while adding six levels of gallery and conservation space in modern additions in the adjacent lots.[4] These two buildings offer excellent examples of what could be achieved in restoration work and in accommodating new styles and up-to-date services in historically important monuments.

Perhaps the most important center for understanding Parisian space is the *Pavillon de l'Arsenal*, where the city developed its own museum of urbanism and development. The centerpiece of the exhibit space, an enormous multi-media scale model of the entire city, offers visitors an extraordinary panoramic view of Paris. The *Pavillon de l'Arsenal* also houses a research center for urban architecture called the *Centre d'Information, de Documentation et d'Exposition d'Architecture et d'Urbanisme de la Ville de Paris* and publishes an important series of volumes on public architecture called *Paris Projet: Aménagement, Urbanisme, Avenir.*[5] In the same neighborhood as the *Arsenal*, for those interested in the history of Paris and its urban development, the *Musée Carnavalet* and the *Hôtel de Sully*, the latter housing the *Caisse Nationale des Monuments Historiques et des Sites,* offer excellent archives and important permanent collections on the history of Paris, and both of these museums often offer interim exhibits about the Parisian landscape.

Not far from the *Pavillon de l'Arsenal*, however, is the *Opéra de la Bastille* which opened in 1989, and was yet another bicentennial building. Its bold curved walls and monumental exterior staircase cried out to be seen as at the cutting edge of design, but they soon appeared out-of-date. The aluminum tile façade peeled very quickly, not unlike what was occurring to the popular image of the Mitterrand years by the end of the 1990s. Innovative lighting in the *Opéra Bastille* allowed the interior to be seen from the outside at night producing an effect that has been interpreted as a metaphor for the transparency of the Left's attempts to dissolve social and cultural barriers. Nonetheless, the building's acoustical qualities and size (the main auditorium holds 2,700 spectators, where the *Opéra Garnier* building has only 1,996 seats), make up for many of its faults.[6] Placing the Opera building at the most sacred of France's revolutionary sites and in a proletarian neighborhood appeared a deliberate attempt by the Mitterrand regime to democratize the state's official home of classical opera, a noble endeavor perhaps, but as in other situations, the intentions were good and the results mixed. The elegant new opera building caused real estate prices in the neighborhood to increase and forced long-time residents to relocate, displaced by upscale shops, cafés, and restaurants.

The transformation of the *Avenue de Daumesnil* leading away from the Bastille towards the *Gare de Lyon* offers a small but telling example of the best intentions of imposing a new face on a tired and abandoned public space. The arcades beneath the former viaduct of the Vincennes rail line were transformed into new art galleries and boutiques on the street level, and consumers flocked to them. Very little in this neighborhood was left untouched, as the *Gare de Lyon* itself underwent transition, portions of it acquiring the ubiquitous glass and aluminum façade, although the well-known neo-rococo façade and the Train Bleu restaurant remained intact.

It was the Seine riverfront from the *Gare de Lyon* eastward that witnessed the most tremendous renovation in the last quarter of the century, due mainly to four large projects. First, the many offices in the *Ministère de l'Economie, des Finances, et de l'Industrie*[7] had to be removed from their longstanding location in the north wing of the Louvre to allow the completion of the final phases of the Grand Louvre project and the opening of new galleries in the *aile Richelieu*, completed in late 1996 after many delays. The Finance Ministry's relocation at the *Pont de Bercy* was linked to the *Météor* super-subway line that opened in October 1998 and travels from the Madeleine stop in the central Right Bank to the new library in Tolbiac.[8] Extending over the bank of the Seine, the new Finance Ministry's imposingly modern exterior acquired the requisite formidable security and anti-terrorist gates. However, below street level are small formal lawn spaces on which exquisite pieces of sculpture are visible from the windows of the ministry but not by unaware passersby. In the shadow of the Bercy building, the visitor has the impression of overlooking the dry moats of some medieval castle. The ministry may have been removed from the Louvre, but it retained some of its feudal privileges, as the lords and lackeys of finance within are the most important of modern bureaucratic functionaries, the keepers of the budget.

To the east of the Finance building lies the *Palais Omnisports de Paris-Bercy* (*POPB*), the third of the neighborhood's large construction projects but the first to be completed in the early 1980s. Its famous grass walls and rooftop are well seasoned after hosting many diverse events ranging from rock concerts to indoor sailing competitions by way of international tennis matches and equestrian shows. The wide pedestrian accesses to the arena provide rollerblading youths a good venue for their activity and the adjacent underground parking areas absorb the Finance Ministry's automobiles and the limousines that deliver star performers to the Holiday Inn-Bercy opposite it. Even though the *POPB* failed to bring Olympic competition back to Paris,[9] its radical architecture blends well with the quayside.

In the same neighborhood, a bit farther east, is the former American Cultural Center designed by Frank Gehry. Open only a brief time in the mid-1990s due to a lack of funding by the Americans, the building reverted to the French government and was then designated as the home of the expanded French Cinema Center, which needed new quarters after a 1997 fire damaged its original home in the *Palais de Chaillot*. This cultural space was not without its own polemic, as the various keepers of France's cultural patrimony were in considerable disagreement as to the contents and purposes of the cinema center. This neighborhood was also the focus of much interest in the radical *Parc de Bercy*, a green space housing a 2,500 space underground parking garage built on the site of the old wine warehouses along the Seine (Leloup 68-70).

The fourth and largest project in the area, on the opposite bank of the river, saw the installation of the national library, the *Bibliothèque Nationale de France*, François Mitterrand's prize construction project. Announcement of this project was made in the president's traditional 14 July televised speech in 1988, in symbolic timing just after his re-election. While there was much fear initially that the old Richelieu site in central Paris would be abandonned, traditionalists and preservationists of all stripes were relieved to learn that the marvelous reading room would be preserved for exhibits of large-format printed material such as posters, lithographs, broadsheets, artists' renderings, and the like. Dominique Perrault's architectural design was quickly selected, approved as much for its promises to incorporate new technology as for its romantic evocation of a cloister, garden, and forest which would have appealed to the nature-loving president. The construction of the building was hurried along to allow Mitterrand to inaugurate the building in the spring of 1995, just weeks before the end of his last term in office and only three months before his death.

Visitors to the new *BNF* are first impressed with the huge scale of the library's four corner towers and the enormous esplanade at the top of several dozen steps leading up from street level. Is this a pyramid to honor the president sometimes known as the Sphinx? Ascending the huge staircases to enter the building gives one time to think. Upon arriving at the top of the wooden deck with its views of the Seine and the Bercy park, one is surprised by the presence of yet more treetops inside the four corners of the rectangle delineated by the four right-angle towers of the library. One cannot look down into the secret courtyard where this garden is located; more decking prohibits access to the precipice. The trees seem to have been dropped into the midst of monolithic gray stone, weathered planks, and concrete from a Normandy forest glen. Only when one has descended the gently-sloped but high-walled pedestrian ramps into the main floor (the *haut-de-jardin* level) of the library can one access these secret trees.[10]

Once inside the library, unless visitors have paid the reader's fee, they have little access to the various reading rooms other than to glimpse them in passing, but they can enjoy the carpeted promenade, stop for a coffee at the library's cafés on the outdoor terrace, and visit the library's bookshop.[11] Although many have criticized the library's design and its serviceability, it has the potential to attract more users than before in its primary function as a library and as a home for quality temporary exhibits.

Another new building just west from the Bercy and Tolbiac areas that has not been without its own controversy is the *Institut du monde arabe (IMA)*. When the *Institut* opened in 1987, it represented quite a radical design in the neighborhood, thrusting its prow-like angle sharply at the Ile St. Louis. An engineering and architectural marvel, the glass and aluminum façades fit harmoniously into the building's narrow space along the left bank of the Seine as construction nearby continued in this style and familiar plane trees grew up around it. On the south façade, solar-driven panels open and close with the intensity of the sun, while the narrow entry way to the museum recalls the narrow streets in the urban centers of north African cities, where protection from the sun is an important concern. The building houses not only exhibit space but also a library, meeting spaces, a cinema, a good-sized specialized bookstore, two eating establishments for two distinct budgets, and a splendid rooftop terrace view of Notre Dame cathedral that rivals the perspective from the nearby Tour d'Argent restaurant windows.[12] The *IMA* was not the only project of this sort, as the creation of the *Maison du Japon* offered additional cultural views to Europe.

As a peripatetic architectural overview of contemporary Paris such as this could be nearly endless, it may be more instructive to view also other modern building sites in Paris and around France. The architectural firm that designed the *Institut du monde arabe* also designed the *Lycée du Futur* and several of the other buildings[13] at the site of the *Futuroscope* theme park outside of Poitiers. The *Futuroscope* venture is one of France's more bold regional projects, whose primary orientation is that of an image and technology-based theme park. It became a weekend getaway location for tourists from its opening in 1987, catering particularly to young people captivated by media and technology. In addition it provides a platform for business start-up opportunities and educational facilities such as a technology-oriented secondary school, expanded facilities for the local university, and is the major location since 1993 for France's distance learning institution, the *Centre National d'Enseignement à Distance (CNED)*. But why Poitiers, a relatively quiet provincial town, for this venture? The Poitou-Charentes region is home to René Monory, a cabinet-level minister during Mitterrand's presidencies, with roots in neighboring Loudun as its mayor and member of the regional council. Nearby Châtellerault is the adopted home of Edith Cresson, the government's Prime Minister in the early 1990s and European Commissioner. Cynics might suggest that such high-level influence had everything to do with selecting Poitiers. Although the long-term projects of *Futuroscope* were based on the exotic technology of the digitized universe, the short-term offer of much-needed local employment was quite down to earth. The city's location on the superhighway from Paris to Spain was another influence, as was the regular *TGV* (*Train à Grande Vitesse*) express train service which puts Poitiers only two hours away from Paris. Since opening in 1987, *Futuroscope*[14] has demonstrated a successful union of technology and marketing strategies by drawing more and more visitors each year, and because of its orientation towards the future, this high-technology amusement park has become much more than a public-works boondoggle.

Another cultural installation based on image and technology is that of the *Centre National de la Bande Dessinée et de l'Image (CNBDI),* located in the adopted home town of President Mitterrand, Angoulême. Although Angoulême was long a center of printing and paper mills, as described in Balzac's *Les Illusions perdues,* and was home to the companies whose presses printed most of the camembert cheese labels used in the first seventy-five years of the twentieth-century, the city most recently re-invented itself as the home to the French and Belgian illustrated narrative albums known as *la bande dessinée (BD or bédé),* and since the mid-1960s has hosted a huge international festival of these books every January. The *CNBDI* was first proposed in 1982 by Jack Lang, the Minister of Culture, during a visit to the book festival. Construction began in 1986 and the center was inaugurated in 1990. It became the official host of the comic book festival, and in a nod to Hollywood, the repository of many handprints in cement of the art's finest creators. The building itself is housed within the shell of an abandoned brewery, and features not only an interactive museum of the major developments in the history of *la bédé* but also a conservation facility, an archive, a library of all "comic book" albums printed and sold in France, and a center for the instruction of computer-aided imaging which is part of the city's University.[15] The Center is yet another example of an architectural attempt to make new without abandoning the old.

Outside of Paris, the southwest of France had no monopoly on museum construction, however. Perhaps the most moving of all the recent regional museums is *Le Mémorial de Caen*,[16] opened by President Mitterrand on June 6, 1988. Deliberately not referred to as a museum, the *Mémorial* commemorates not only the Normandy invasions of occupied France in 1944 but also serves as a *"centre de réflexion"* on war and armed conflict. While offering an outstanding museum experience that probes the rise of fascism and Europe's response to it, the foundation also hosts colloquia on peace and aims to invite all Nobel Peace Prize winners to come to Caen for debates and programs. Since its opening, the entire neighborhood around the museum in the north part of Caen has undergone important economic revitalization. Born out of a need to recreate a collective memory for Caen, since seventy-five percent of the city center had been obliterated by Allied bombing raids during World War II, the *Mémorial* succeeds brilliantly in its historical aims but has also boosted the local economy. It is one of the most moving cultural spaces in France outside Paris.

There are many other cultural spaces in France developed in the 1990s that deserve discussion. Also in Normandy, the installation of Queen Mathilde's embroidered tapestry in Bayeux within a proper museum space gave new life to one of the town's former convents. Computer and graphics technology improve the wait for admittance to the tapestry and several rooms of dioramas, a dramatic slide show projected onto drakkar-like sails, and a short video film all improve the visitor's understanding of these celebrated panels. Closer to Paris, the restoration of Claude Monet's house and gardens at Giverny have deservedly put the Seine River region around Vernon on the list of popular sites for international tourists. At the other end of the touring scale, a clever museum celebrating camembert cheese near the tiny market town of Vimoutiers in the Orne opened in 1996.[17]

One unconventional tourist site that rose up just north of Paris in the suburb of Saint-Denis is the *Stade de France*, the focus of much world attention as the principal venue for the 1998 World Cup championship. The construction project was an amazing public works project but with the French victory in the finals, the stadium became a site of pilgrimage for

French sports fans; guided tours of the Camelot of French football were made available, even after the matches were long completed. The soccer stadiums in Marseille, Nantes, and elsewhere were extensively and expensively refurbished for the 1998 World Cup competition. Lyon, in addition to upgrading its stadium, completed its new *Opéra de Lyon*. The city of Lille[18] and the regional government actively sought an Olympic season; its sports installations were renovated, while at the same time its refurbished art museum garnered great praise. Despite claims to an inactive economy, there has been growth in the public sector in France, and cultural spaces have contributed greatly to it.

In addition, although four French theme parks went bankrupt in the mid-1990s (*Schtroumpfland*, the *Parc Cousteau*, *Mirapolis*, *Le Triton*), French taste for these *parcs de loisirs* remains strong, given the advent of the 35-hour work week and improved transportation. Not only are there the well-known theme parks like *le Parc Astérix* and *Disneyland Paris* in Marne-la-Vallée,[19] any number of water parks and roadside museums, municipal museums and cultural spaces and *médiathèques* were opened, all of which attempted to respond to the growing demand for cultural as well as general entertainment.

Many of the new cultural spaces discussed here clearly have political origins, although not all of them derive from the Mitterrand administrations. There is little doubt that the cityscape of Paris underwent a great number of transformations in the last twenty years of the century. Even the tradition of the great royal patrons of culture (François Ier, Louis XIV) persists in a project such as Mitterrand's *BNF,* in which this avid reader, writer, and bibliophile created a strong sense of his place in French history as a defender of her great literary tradition in a sober but large-scale fashion, accompanied by Romantic touches of gardens and forests. In a similar vein, the development of the *CNBDI* validated a maverick but peculiarly francophone literary art form, fostering not only the aesthetics of the *bédé* but its commerce as well. For sheer panache, the *Grande Arche* flaunts its open structure among the solid rectangles at *la Défense*, a monument of the Left asserting a *contestataire* presence among the more traditional headquarters of late twentieth-century giants of capitalism. The *Opéra de la Bastille* may be seen as an attempt to bring classical opera out of its ornate museum into a modern setting but in the end tickets remained as difficult as ever to obtain. The buildings at *La Villette* and at Poitiers's *Futuroscope* portend that the future will embrace all types of music, science, industry, and technology. In a way, these new cultural spaces encouraged users to look to the future with a sense of optimism and adventure. Their designs, especially in the case of the *Grande Pyramide du Louvre*, radically challenged the status quo, a philosophical legacy that Mitterrand would probably not disavow.

This period of renovation and "modernization" did open new venues of art and culture in all corners of France, with the implicit goal of asserting France's leadership in cultural tourism. At the end of the century, however, many still argue that the astronomical expenses incurred for the building of these "monuments" are not altogether justified, as the original objective to make culture more available to the general public has not yet been achieved (Delarue).

In this overview of new cultural spaces developed in France from 1975 to the end of the century, it is clear that the lines of demarcation between "Culture" and "culture" have become quite transient. Cultural mores have changed, for where once it was forbidden to walk on the grass in French parks, it is now encouraged. In fact, those who refrain from walking on the grass may well be left behind as France embraces a new cultural environment. Although the principle of inscribing the new with the old remained strong, French public architecture, both in Paris and in outlying regions, took in the last decades of the century new, bold steps into the third millennium with innovative programs that reaffirmed the importance of public cultural space.

Notes

[1] Indispensable histories of architecture in Paris and France are those by Norma Evenson and Anthony Sutcliffe. The latter's chapter 9 is particularly useful for background on the 1980s and early 1990s. While Evenson's illustrations are in black and white, most of Sutcliffe's visual documents are in color. Cohen and Fortier's volume contains brief descriptions, renderings, and photographs of all the monuments cited in this study.

[2] The advent of Internet sites offers the opportunity to remain current without extensive travels to France. The most useful is the official site of the *Ministère de l'Equipement, du Logement, des Transports et du Tourisme* which oversees all public works projects: <http://www.equipement.gouv.fr>. The site's "musée retrouvé" of earlier *Travaux Publics* provides particularly interesting visuals that document the social importance of these projects. Another source of information on the life of museums in France is the site maintained by the *Ministère de la Culture* at <http://www.culture.gouv.fr>. One

more gauge of opinion is available at <http://www.mygale.org/02/gauzolle>, a site known as "Critiques d'Espaces," organized by students and teachers of the professional architectural community.

³ The *Mairie de Paris's Guide des musées de Paris* (1996) gives practical information and numerous illustrations as well as an excellent summary of each of the 134 museums it covers. Composed by the city's *Direction des affaires culturelles,* it is difficult to obtain, being available only at the city hall offices of each *arrondissement.* Some of the same information is available in Kaplan's *Little-Known Museums in and around Paris.* Information on architectural details of individual structures in Paris is available from White, with commentary about almost all monuments and houses in Paris, arranged by neighborhoods, streets, and *arrondissements.* There is no place-name index, as the proper-name index is devoted primarily to architects and designers.

⁴ The *Maison Européenne de la Photographie's* Web site at <http://www.mep-fr.org> provides numerous documents illustrating the harmonious incorporation of old and new into the museum.

⁵ Although ten of the first twenty issues (many are double-numbered) are out of print, a glance at the featured topics of the monographs is like reading a summary of Parisian headlines from the late 1960s through the 1980s, and these volumes are well worth seeking out. For example, Issue 29 (1990) titled "L'Aménagement du Secteur Seine Rive Gauche" treats the area near the new library on the abandoned rail lines behind the Austerlitz station (the Tolbiac neighborhood) and on the opposite bank (the former wine warehouses of Bercy) where much new construction in Paris occurred in the 1990s.

⁶ The *Opéra de Paris* Internet site at <http://www.opera-de-paris.fr> includes a descriptive visit of the nineteenth-century *Opéra Garnier* building as well as insights into the new building at the Bastille.

⁷ The name of this ministry having become impossibly long, the press has abbreviated it to Bercy, in the manner of referring to the official residence of the President of France as the Elysée and the Prime Minister's office as Matignon.

⁸ *Météor* represents the second and most recently completed of the *grands travaux* in the area, and can best be accessed at the *RATP's (Réseau Autonome des Transports Parisiens)* fascinating Internet site, <http://www.ratp.fr>.

⁹ This was a long-time goal of the Chirac and the Tibéri mayorships, and an Olympic host proposal was put forward for 2008, bolstered by the success of hosting the 1998 World Cup championship.

¹⁰ Blasselle and Melet-Sanson, 96-111, provide excellent photos and a clear overview of the controversy surrounding the *BNF.*

¹¹ The *BNF's* Web sites are <http://www.bnf.fr> and <http://gallica.bnf.fr>.

¹² The *Institut's* Web site at <http://www.imarbe.org> provides views and descriptions of the façades, good diagrams of the interior space, and other useful services such as programming information and access to the bookstore where purchases can be made on-line.

¹³ The site <http://www.architecture-studio.fr> offers extensive views of some twenty major projects dating back to 1986. It provides a fascinating visual tour of their projects, showcasing the designers' most important and breath-taking endeavor, the new European Parliament buildings in Strasbourg.

¹⁴ See<http://www.futuroscope.fr>. The architectural firm of Denis Laming, responsible for most of the other buildings at *Futuroscope* (originally entitled *le Parc Européen de l'Image*) has a large photo archive of projects at <http://www.laming.com>.

¹⁵ The Center's Web site at <http://www.cnbdi.fr> offers a virtual visit of all the floors of the center and excellent background information on its history and economic

structure. Given its educational mission of expanding the use of images, it is very well maintained.

[16] The on-line site at <http://www.unicaen.fr/collectivite/memorial/> is quite extensive, with numerous illustrations.

[17] See <http://giverny.org> and <http://www.camembert-country.com>.

[18] Longtime mayor of Lille, Pierre Mauroy, was President Mitterrand's first Prime Minister, 1981-1984.

[19] See their Web sites at <http://www.parcasterix.fr> and <http://www.disneylandparis.fr>.

References

Atelier Parisien d'Urbanisme. *Paris Projet: l'Aménagement du Secteur Seine Rive Gauche.* Paris: Centre d'Informations, de Documentation et d'Exposition d'Architecture et d'Urbanisme de la Ville de Paris, 1990.

Blasselle, Bruno and Jacqueline Melet-Sanson. *La Bibliothèque nationale de France; Mémoire de l'avenir.* Paris: Gallimard, 1996.

Cohen, Jean-Louis and Bruno Fortier. *Paris: La Ville et ses projets; A City in the Making.* Paris: Editions Babylone, 1992.

Delarue, Marie. *Un Pharaon républicain: les grands travaux de Mitterrand.* Paris: Grancher, 1999.

Durussel, Arnaud and Thierry Follain. *Le Guide La Défense, Quartier d'affaires 1998.* Paris: Agence Newport Edition, 1997.

Evenson, Norma. *Paris: A Century of Change, 1878-1978.* New Haven: Yale UP, 1979.

Kaplan, Rachel. *Little-Known Museums in and around Paris.* New York: Harry Abrams, 1996.

Leloup, Michèle. "Les métamorphoses de Bercy." *L'Express* 3 Dec. 1998: 68-70.

Laushway, Ester. "Not one for the books." *Europe* May 1999: 38-9.

Mairie de Paris. *Guide des musées de Paris.* Paris: Direction des Affaires Culturelles de la Ville de Paris, 1996.

Meyer, Philippe. *Paris la Grande.* Paris: Flammarion, 1997.

Sutcliffe, Anthony. *Paris: An Architectural History.* New Haven: Yale UP, 1993.

White, Norval. *The Guide to the Architecture of Paris.* New York: Charles Scribner's Sons, 1991.

V. Perceptions of France from the United States -

Perceptions américaines de la France

17

La France et ses rapports diplomatiques avec les États-Unis vus par la récente presse américaine

Michel Sage
West Chester University

Avec l'effondrement du système Est-Ouest, les États-Unis se sont imposés comme gardien de l'ordre mondial. Rien ne se fait sans eux, de l'Europe au Proche-Orient, de la Chine à l'Afrique des Grands Lacs. Pour le moment, la tâche est relativement simple: les crises sont d'ampleur limitée et la diplomatie américaine est minimaliste: promotion du libre-échange et de la démocratie; maintien en l'état des dispositifs existants (Alliance atlantique, traité de sécurité avec le Japon, protection de la péninsule arabique); désamorçage des situations les plus explosives (Inde/Pakistan, conflit israélo-arabe, Irak); dialogue constant avec la Russie et la Chine. Enfin, l'intervention de l'OTAN au Kosovo en mars 1999 a permis d'établir une force multinationale de paix dans la région et de montrer que, lorsque l'essentiel est en jeu, c'est la solidarité transatlantique qui prévaut. Or, une fois le calme rétabli dans un monde où semblent se stabiliser les grands jeux géopolitiques, une voix de dissension se fait à nouveau entendre dans le camp occidental — celle de la France. Et même si le plus souvent il ne s'agit que d'une opposition de principe à l'égard des États-Unis, plus par la forme que par le fond, la France irrite. Elle est, en temps de paix et par tradition, l'allié « difficile », le pays « trublion » par excellence.

En effet, à en juger par la récente presse américaine et après un bref répit pendant le conflit kosovar, il y a au moins un sujet politique sur lequel opinion et gouvernement sont en accord. C'est l'indifférence générale à la détérioration des rapports franco-américains depuis dix ans et très probablement depuis l'affront d'avril 1986 — date de l'interdiction de survol du territoire français lors du raid américain mené en Libye. C'est ainsi que le *New York Times* et le *Washington Post*, sans contredit les deux journaux les plus influents des États-Unis, adoptent à peu près la même attitude — condescendance et douce compréhension envers un interlocuteur un peu caractériel mais avec qui il convient de ménager l'avenir. L'*International Herald Tribune* cite le *Post* dans son éditorial du 17 décembre 1996: « S'il faut admettre que le gouvernement américain puisse agir avec maladresse vis-à-vis de ses alliés, il ne cherche pas la dispute. En revanche, le gouvernement français paraît à l'affût de petits conflits un peu partout dans le monde » [Les traductions des citations sont de l'auteur]. Même reproche de la part de Roger Cohen du *New York Times*: « Jacques Chirac [...] et ses alliés politiques se comportent de manière irascible envers la plus grande partie du reste du monde et en particulier à l'égard des États-Unis ».

L'attitude des États-Unis vis-à-vis de la France peut se résumer par un mélange d'agacement et d'exaspération envers un allié qui prend un peu trop systématiquement le contre-pied des positions américaines sur la scène mondiale. La France est accusée de tous les torts — même ceux communément pardonnés par le « politiquement correct » américain. Non sans humour, le *Washington Post* reconnaît « que nous les Américains, dans notre élan pour la diversité culturelle, sommes prêts à être tolérants à l'égard de toutes les nations et tous les groupes ethniques de la planète — sauf les Français ».

La fréquence d'articles ayant trait à la France et à sa culture par rapport à d'autres pays européens est en soi significative. Sans aucun doute, la France compte, même et surtout si l'on écrit le contraire — et c'est souvent le cas. De l'insignifiant au sérieux, du dangereux au risible, la presse anglo-saxonne se déchaîne à l'occasion des accords du GATT, de l'intégration de la France dans le dispositif de commandement de l'OTAN, des rapprochements de la France avec Cuba et l'Iran et, plus récemment, de sa position un peu trop complaisante à l'égard de l'Irak. Sachons qu'en politique internationale, la grande presse américaine, sous le couvert d'impartialité, s'aligne le plus souvent sur la position du Département d'État. D'autre part, cette tension permanente entre les deux pays vient de l'ambiguïté qui marque le statut particulier de la France, perçue à la fois comme un allié et comme un ennemi culturel puisque présentée dans la grande presse comme une nation profondément hostile aux valeurs américaines. Il n'est pas dans nos intentions d'analyser ici tous les griefs échangés entre les deux capitales ces dernières années mais de faire le bilan de ces querelles à travers des tendances confirmées par une lecture régulière de la presse de réflexions américaine.

Si les Américains aiment la France, c'est qu'ils veulent y trouver un pays délicieusement désuet et passéiste, plus épris de haute culture que de haute technologie. Bref, une France qui garde son rang et surtout son silence. Or la nation dérange un peu trop systématiquement les intérêts américains et proclame un peu trop haut son droit à la différence. Aux yeux de l'Amérique, la France est empêtrée dans une insoluble contradiction car, malgré son nationalisme provocateur, elle s'est enchaînée aux États-Unis par un sentiment d'amour-haine qui la condamne à vivre dans leur sillage. En effet, le pays qui a inventé les quotas d'importation de produits culturels et l'Académie française a pour capitale la ville la plus américanisée d'Europe. Du « Macdo » au « franglais », la presse américaine savoure ces perles de contradictions et ne manque pas de brosser le tableau d'un pays fier de sa gloire passée et de son bagage culturel mais incapable de faire face aux idées et techniques nouvelles. Au-delà des simplifications, les idées qui sous-tendent l'argumentation résument une conception de la France très répandue aux États-Unis: un pays fort en gueule qui compense la diminution de son rôle sur la scène mondiale par de grands gestes diplomatiques.

L'ampleur des préjugés, des exagérations et des incompréhensions de part et d'autre de l'Atlantique montre que les rapports franco-américains ne laissent jamais indifférents. Ils sont singuliers, uniques et passionnels; un curieux mélange d'admiration, de reconnaissance, de mépris, de rancœur, d'amour et de haine. La France... on aime ou on déteste. Aux États-Unis, la francophilie semble parfois aussi excessive que la récente vague de francophobie popularisée sous le nom de « French bashing ».

Peu d'autres pays de taille équivalente inspireraient à *Newsweek* une section spéciale annoncée en couverture ou au *New York Times* une page entière d'analyse, avec une amorce à la une sans qu'une telle attention fût justifiée par un événement majeur. Malheureusement, ces reportages sont largement dépréciatifs; la couverture de l'hebdomadaire annonce la gloire déclinante du pays et la première page du quotidien de New York, « La déconfiture de l'image et de l'esprit de la France ».

> Certes, la France reste un pays riche, aux infrastructures soignées, où le savoir-vivre et l'art de la table contribuent à donner une impression d'opulence et de tradition. Mais, à l'instar des statues dorées ornant les ponts de Paris qui distraient le regard du touriste et lui évitent le spectacle des sans-abri dormant sous les arches, l'émouvante beauté de ce pays masque des abîmes de désespoir (Cohen, 11 février 1997).

L'avenir du pays apparaît plus sombre encore:

> La France perçoit l'innovation comme une menace, pour son économie comme pour son identité. Il suffit aujourd'hui de se rendre à Londres ou à Berlin pour constater à quel point Paris est devenu fade et sans énergie. L'impression de vivre dans un musée est de plus en plus tangible. [...] Le pays hésite à faire des choix et, visiblement, s'enfonce (ibid.).

En soulignant l'immobilisme de la classe politique, des syndicats et des « technocrates » français, Roger Cohen présente la France comme un anti-modèle et conclut que « son caractère original n'a plus beaucoup d'écho à l'étranger ». Bien entendu, pour le reporter basé à Paris, il s'agit tout autant de rassurer le lecteur américain sur le bon fonctionnement de son propre pays que de relever les erreurs de cet « anti-modèle » que représentent l'éli-tisme et l'étatisme français. La rhétorique moralisatrice est à peine déguisée. En effet, cette enquête sur le désarroi économique, social et politique d'un pays réputé pour sa folie des grandeurs est bien le bilan de crise d'un modèle de société jugée à l'aune des critères de la réussite américaine. « Alors que d'autres pays se sont mis à l'heure de l'esprit d'entreprise et de la mondialisation, poursuit Roger Cohen, la France voit son économie et son identité menacées par l'innovation. [...] La crise est une crise d'identité politique et culturelle ». Économiquement, « le sentiment d'avoir perdu ses repères se traduit par la résistance à la nouveauté ». Le quotidien de New York souligne enfin la passivité française face à l'Internet et à l'informatique en évoquant une fois de plus l'anecdote mainte fois reprise dans les jour-naux américains d'un Jacques Chirac tout étonné de découvrir pour la pre-mière fois une « souris » d'ordinateur ... au grand Salon de l'Informatique![1] Au passage et à juste titre, le journal ne manque pas de rappeler les vingt ans de succès du Minitel en France mais aussi son incapacité à s'imposer sur le marché international et sa pauvreté face à l'Internet. Six mois plus tard, dans un article au titre particulièrement caustique — « France's Alle-giance: To Things French, Like Hypocrisy », le même journaliste qualifiait le pays de « basket case », c'est-à-dire de « cas désespéré » (« France has become America's favorite European basket case ») et le comparait au Ti-tanic en plein naufrage avec son piano qui persiste à jouer: «it is the Ti-tanic-with-piano-still-tinkling adrift on a sea of global competition » (Cohen, 24 août 1997).

Il est à noter que si la presse américaine s'acharne sur le pays, c'est parce que, plus que tout autre et de tous temps, celui-ci a fait de l'État la pierre angulaire de son fonctionnement. Or c'est bien à propos du rôle du gouvernement dans l'économie d'un pays que se situe le plus grand clivage France/États-Unis. Journalistes et commentateurs sont perplexes devant l'attachement des Français au rôle de l'État à tous les niveaux, et cela en pleine difficulté économique. Sous la forme d'un petit conte à la manière de Voltaire, le *Business Week* du 10 février 1997 imaginait Bill Gates, le fondateur et Président directeur général de Microsoft, arrivant en France avec l'intention d'y fonder une nouvelle entreprise. Après tout, relève l'hebdomadaire, « l'idée n'est pas si saugrenue, puisque les compétences technologiques abondent en France ». Mais face à l'immobilisme, au fonctionnariat, au syndicalisme et à la lourde législation du travail, sans compter les grèves, les jours de congés et la perspective d'une semaine de 35 heures, Bill va vite déchanter. À bout de patience, il s'écrie: « Sortez-moi de là! ... C'est le Titanic des entrepreneurs! » En effet, malgré ses nombreux avantages — l'excellence de son infrastructure, la qualification et le niveau de productivité de sa main-d'œuvre, la qualité de ses bureaux de recherches, sa situation géographique — les chiffres du Département du commerce américain restent décevants; en 1998, la France n'était que la septième destination des investisseurs américains.

Pourtant, c'est dans le domaine de la politique internationale que la stéréotypie dépréciative est la plus sensible. Il suffit que la France soit en désaccord avec les États-Unis pour que certains poncifs apparaissent, et en particulier celui de l'héritage du général de Gaulle qui, à lui seul, semble encore incarner l' « arrogance » française. La presse américaine n'a pas manqué d'évoquer le spectre du gaullisme pour condamner les huit essais nucléaires français effectués dans le Pacifique entre septembre 1995 et mai 1996, moins sur le plan militaire, stratégique ou même scientifique mais comme la dernière et futile tentative d'une nation à la conquête de son ancien prestige. Avec humour, le *New York Times* dénonçait les « fantaisies gaulliennes » de Jacques Chirac au nom du principe néocartésien: « J'appuie sur le bouton, donc j'existe ». Ainsi, le cliché d'une France en mal de gloire réapparaît chaque fois que le pays affiche son indépendance vis-à-vis de la communauté européenne ou cherche à se démarquer de la mouvance américaine. La fréquence des titres de presse à ce sujet est tristement révélatrice: « The Fading Glory of France », « The Glory that was France », « Liberté, Égalité, Médiocrité - The Glory is Gone » ou même en français dans le texte: « Le Jour De Gloire Est Passé » [2].

Parmi d'autres, l'exemple de l'affaire du commandement sud de l'OTAN a montré l'ampleur des malentendus franco-américains. En 1996, la France décidait de rejoindre le commandement intégré de l'Alliance atlantique, l'OTAN que la France du général de Gaulle avait quittée en 1966, mais dont elle demeurait toujours membre. Or une véritable campagne de presse, visiblement inspirée par le Département d'État, a battu son plein sur l'affaire du « flanc sud » en laissant entendre que la France souhaitait prendre le contrôle de la sixième flotte américaine en Méditerranée. L'accusation était, bien entendu, grotesque. En réalité, le ministre des Affaires étrangères français avait rappelé qu'il existait des solutions pratiques pour le commandement et que les craintes sur le « démantèlement » du commandement sud, agitées par la presse américaine, étaient infondées. Dans cet incident, la diplomatie française n'avait pas fait preuve de légèreté et d'inconscience comme voulait le faire croire la presse américaine mais avait, tout au contraire, adopté une voie réaliste et volontariste; réaliste de comprendre que la construction d'une identité européenne de sécurité et de défense passait par une clarification des relations françaises avec l'Alliance atlantique; volontariste par la définition ambitieuse de ce que devait être une Alliance rénovée qui ferait sa place à l'Europe dans son fonctionnement et dans ses structures. Certes, il était naturel que les États-Unis défendent leurs intérêts au sein de l'OTAN et éprouvent des réticences à voir entamer leur prééminence; ce qui l'était moins, était le rôle réducteur et partisan de la presse américaine qui dramatisait et exacerbait les passions inutilement. Finalement, en juin 1997, le nouveau Premier ministre, Lionel Jospin annonçait qu'il ne jugeait pas réunies les conditions d'intégration et le projet était abandonné. Pour Hubert Védrine, son ministre des Affaires étrangères, la question n'avait pas été traitée « entre alliés, mais à Washington, entre la Maison Blanche, le Pentagone, le Département d'État, le Congrès et les médias » (« Défense: l'Europe sous tutelle »). Les détails de l'incident importent peu à présent mais ce qui paraît plus grave, c'est l'incompréhension et le manque de jugement qui ont conduit la presse américaine à laisser entendre que le retour des Français dans certains rouages militaires de l'OTAN avait pour but de vouloir y diminuer le rôle des États-Unis. En fait, la question qui se posait à Washington était de savoir dans quelle mesure la France entraînait dans son sillage ses alliés européens car, en principe, lorsque ceux-ci sont unis et solidaires, les États-Unis sont obligés de composer. Là où la France se trouve seule, ses objections sont largement ignorées. A ce jour, la France et les États-Unis restent en désaccord sur la réforme des structures de l'Alliance, sur les modalités de son élargissement et sur le degré d'autonomie de l'OTAN par rapport à l'ONU. Les États-Unis plaident pour étendre le rôle de l'Alliance atlantique dans la gestion des crises hors de son territoire et dans la lutte contre la prolifération nucléaire, bactériologique et chimique; la France qui redoute une sorte de « gendarme planétaire » dominé par les Américains souhaite que toute intervention de l'OTAN, hors du territoire de ses membres, soit autorisée au préalable par le Conseil de Sécurité de l'ONU. Des deux côtés de l'Atlantique, la lutte est engagée. Alors que la presse américaine relève l'excessive partialité française à l'encontre d'Israël, sa trop grande complaisance à l'égard de l'Iran ou son trop grand silence sur les dangers du programme militaire irakien, la presse française souligne les dangers à long terme que pose la présence d'une « hyperpuissance » américaine qui s'affirme, sans rivale ni contrepoids, dans tous les domaines des relations internationales.

En général, les reproches qui apparaissent régulièrement dans les colonnes et les éditoriaux de la presse américaine suivent quatre grandes tendances: un nationalisme mal placé, une présence internationale disproportionnée, un pessimisme injustifié et, enfin, un rayonnement culturel surévalué.

L'image de la France qui persiste dans la presse américaine est celle d'une nation fière sinon prétentieuse, voire arrogante et ingrate. Elle vit au-dessus de ses moyens et semble toujours motivée par une cyranesque ambition de grandeur. Or la France n'a plus les moyens de ses ambitions et, même si son « modèle de société » montre des signes de redressements conjoncturels, son secteur public et sa politique industrielle sont dépassés et doivent s'adapter à la victoire du libéralisme et aux progrès de la mondialisation. Pour les Français, cette forme de nationalisme n'est pas synonyme de xénophobie; il s'agit du désir de tenir son « rang », d'exalter des valeurs différentes, de défendre, au-delà de ses intérêts spécifiques, un point de vue indépendant avec l'ambition de jouer un rôle d'arbitre sur la scène internationale. Dans un monde dominé par la puissance américaine, la France doit garder les moyens de faire entendre sa voix et de peser sur les grands événements.

Directement liée à la notion d'identité nationale est celle de présence internationale et, sur ce point, la grande presse américaine partage l'opinion générale; le rôle de la France dans le monde est disproportionné. En effet, compte tenu de la taille de son territoire et du modeste pouvoir de son économie, le pays est surévalué dans sa culture, sa civilisation, son Histoire, sa cuisine, son art et surtout dans le rôle international auquel il prétend. Pour les États-Unis, il s'agit de faire ce que l'on appelle en économie boursière une « correction » ou une réévaluation entre pouvoir réel et pouvoir estimé. Les Français, eux, estiment que taille et puissance ne sont pas synonymes de sagesse — ils iraient même jusqu'à penser le contraire. La France n'est pas forcément anti-américaine de nature mais elle refuse le modèle américain en tant que modèle unique.

Sur le plan psychologique, les Français sont perçus comme d'incorrigibles pessimistes et qualifiés de « bourrus, aigris et étroits d'esprit » (Waxman). Aux yeux de la presse américaine, ce pessimisme est injustifié et ne fait que confirmer l'esprit négatif des Français. La France a tout pour réussir et, pourtant, elle déprime; on parle de marasme, de morosité ou encore de « blues à la française ». En fait, le pessimisme est de bon ton et c'est le contraire qui surprend. Dans sa « lettre de Paris » intitulée « C'est inhabituel, les Français sont contents! », William Pfaff reprend le titre du *Monde* (« Quand la France s'amuse... ») et annonce que cette nouvelle seule mérite une page à la une! Car en temps normal, « exprimer de l'optimisme pour la conjoncture et l'avenir de la France et de la fierté pour ses réalisations passées, serait de la vantardise digne des Américains à qui il manque le sérieux d'un peuple mature! » Le comble, ironise le journaliste, c'est que lorsque les correspondants étrangers publient leurs articles négatifs, les Français se plaignent qu'un « complot anglo-saxon » (en français dans le texte) cherche à dénigrer le pays. Pour la presse, le pays pèche par excès d'individualisme: les Français ne s'unissent que pour faire grève, râler ou manifester et confondent volontiers solidarité et corporatisme. Contrairement aux pays anglo-saxons qui ont, eux, le sens de la collectivité, la France est une société qui a bâti sa logique sur la méfiance de l'autre et la protection du clan. Dans son article intitulé « What's Ailing France *Now?* » qu'accompagne le dessin d'une étiquette de grand cru où figurent les mots « Château D'Ysfunction — Produit de France — 1998 », Eugen Weber, journaliste au *New York Times,* écrit que « la France est une société bloquée dans laquelle les droits acquis s'annulent mutuellement, une démocratie où la liberté de critiquer entrave la liberté d'entreprendre ». Selon les commentateurs, la « grosse déprime » des Français tient à la fin des certitudes des « Trente Glorieuses », mais aussi à ce sentiment que la culture française n'exerce plus la même influence, n'offre plus la même densité créatrice qu'auparavant. Le danger, toujours selon la presse, est qu'on passe vite de l'humeur mélancolique à la fièvre patriotique et la montée du Front National semble confirmer cette tendance.

Enfin, la presse américaine estime que l'apport culturel français est surévalué. Sur le plan artistique et intellectuel, les Français se répètent et ont perdu confiance dans leur esprit créatif. Les penseurs, en particulier, ne méritent plus le prestige des années passées: les philosophes Serres-Derrida-Baudrillard enseignent à l'étranger et s'endorment sur des fonds de structuralisme. Dans leurs ouvrages, Alan Sokal et Jean Bricmont s'en prennent à Lacan, Deleuze, Guattari et dénoncent leurs « impostures intellectuelles ». Seul le cinéma semble encore capable de promouvoir la culture française à l'étranger. Dans son article « French Kiss-off », la journaliste Sharon Waxman du *Washington Post* explique les raisons de cet épuisement culturel:

> Les Français supposent leur supériorité dans tous les domaines: des arts à la philosophie, de la cuisine aux droits de l'homme. Mais même cela n'est pas suffisant pour entretenir le mythe d'une gloire nationale. Les Français veulent être les premiers en tout ou du moins participer: des armes nucléaires au rap, de la politique africaine à l'art du graffiti. Je ne suis pas certaine que cela soit une mauvaise chose en soi, mais c'est exiger beaucoup d'un peuple de 53 millions (sic) seulement.

En proclamant ainsi l'infériorité du modèle « républicain » français face au modèle « démocratique » américain, il semble que l'Amérique se fasse le champion de l'éclectisme culturel face à l'élitisme social. Précisément parce qu'il se pose en tant que « modèle », chaque pays se perçoit dans un rôle historique dominant et se voit investi d'une mission de portée universelle[3]. Nées de leurs révolutions sœurs de la fin du dix-huitième siècle, les deux nations sont idéologiquement en concurrence — la France plus que les États-Unis puisque puissance oblige. La France se veut fille des Lumières, de 1789, de la Déclaration des droits de l'homme. Elle est la nation libératrice qu'ont aimée les intellectuels africains et les élites d'Asie ou du monde arabe, le pays qui incarne la liberté, la souveraineté, l'humanisme, la paix et, au-delà de tout, une culture fortement imprégnée d'identité nationale. Les États-Unis, eux, se sentent aux avant-postes du combat pour la démocratie et la liberté, le progrès et la consommation, l'individu et la culture de masse. D'un côté, les États-Unis veulent façonner le monde à leur image, de l'autre la France se considère comme le dernier bastion contre le colosse planétaire qui menace l'Europe. Si les autres pays européens ont choisi, pour diverses raisons, de s'associer et de composer, la France, elle, a choisi de s'opposer. Les points de vue des deux pays semblent irréconciliables; l'un est la première puissance du monde; l'autre un État moyen qui entend rester un « grand ». L'un exerce naturellement son « leadership », que l'autre lui conteste. L'un entend répandre sans obstacle sa culture de masse; l'autre tient à défendre la sienne propre. Il faut constater que les principaux points de friction entre Américains et Français ne proviennnent pas de conflits d'intérêts directs, mais souvent de politiques menées envers des pays tiers. Reste aussi à préciser que lors des prises de position diplomatiques françaises qui ont récemment irrité les Américains — qu'il s'agisse de l'OTAN, du Proche-Orient, de l'Afrique centrale ou de Cuba — la France n'a pas tant cherché à se singulariser qu'à défendre des positions européennes. Le malheur veut que, face au mutisme timoré de ses partenaires européens, la France exprime un peu trop fort le droit de l'Europe à la différence.

Faut-il s'offusquer de la déferlante d'articles négatifs dont la presse américaine a gratifié la France ces derniers temps? Aucun autre pays n'inspire autant d'éditoriaux ou de sections spéciales, à l'exception de la Russie et du Japon. Le pari du Général de Gaulle, celui d'une France qui compte, même en irritant, semble être gagné. Même négatifs, les articles sur la France sont le plus souvent perçus comme un signe de vitalité. Malheureusement, la France n'intéresse la presse américaine que dans la mesure où elle confirme certains stéréotypes. L'influence artistique, culturelle et politique de la France touche essentiellement une élite; pour l'homme de la rue, le prestige du pays se résume toujours à trois mots: « Food, Wine, and Fashion ». Quant aux motivations derrière les évidents partis pris de certains éditoriaux, celles-ci viennent très certainement d'une volonté de remettre la France à sa place. Il s'agit souvent d'une réaction à l'anti-américanisme d'une grande partie de l'intelligentsia française. Derrière leur objectivité de façade, ces articles ressemblent souvent à des règlements de comptes à la petite semaine. Comme tout phénomène médiatique, les critiques arrivent et repartent. Il est donc inutile de trop noircir le tableau et de tomber dans le même piège, d'autant plus que l'atmosphère entre les deux pays s'est améliorée depuis la participation militaire française au Kosovo — même si celle-ci a été pratiquement occultée par la presse anglo-saxonne. La presse américaine a également reconnu que la position de la France à l'égard de l'Iran était largement partagée en Europe et qu'en l'occurrence, c'étaient les États-Unis qui s'étaient isolés. Il en était de même à propos de la loi Helms-Burton et de l'embargo sur Cuba, où l'Europe et le Canada faisaient front commun. Signalons aussi que tous les journalistes américains ne sont pas hostiles au « modèle français » . Diane Johnson, journaliste au *New York Times*, estime que les élections législatives de juin 1997, largement remportées par la gauche, correspondaient à un choix de société. « Les électeurs français ont rejeté en bloc le capitalisme de style américain et la société violente et dégradée qu'il engendre à leurs yeux [...] Nous aurions avantage à regarder leurs succès au lieu — nation de Protestants que nous sommes — d'y voir l'enfer »[4]. Dans le même quotidien, le professeur Ronald Tiersky, explique que la France a une fonction diplomatique spéciale à remplir: « Les Français jouent leur rôle habituel: celui d'une voix indépendante contre les plus grandes puissances. Qu'elle ne soit pas guidée par les Américains ne signifie pas qu'elle soit hostile ». Enfin, toujours en novembre 1997, lors de la dernière crise irakienne, le *Wall Street Journal* ouvrait ses colonnes à un chercheur de l'American Enterprise Institute qui, lui aussi, prenait la défense de la « perfide » France. Michael Ledeen signalait que « la supposée amoralité de la France n'était que la marque d'une conception différente de l'intérêt national » et que « les Français n'éprouvaient pas le besoin de draper chacune de leurs actions dans des justifications moralisantes ». Selon lui, les États-Unis « feraient bien d'apprendre des Français, plutôt que de dénoncer leur supposée perfidie, car ils ont visé juste; plus de Machiavel, moins de Cecil B. De Mille ». Mais avouons que ces commentaires sont rares.

Passionnelle et paradoxale, la relation franco-américaine est sans doute l'un des plus curieux exemples de couple stratégique de l'époque moderne; un mélange d'irrationnel et de partis pris où se mêlent fascination et incompréhension. La presse anglo-saxonne parle de « love/hate relationship », de « frères ennemis », ou encore de « vieux couple chamailleur ». Jean Guisnel intitule sont dernier ouvrage sur les relations franco-américaines : « Les pires amis du monde ». Bref, la France est devenue le pays souffre-douleur, « l'ennemi en temps de paix » — « the country people love to hate ». Mais de manière à ne pas laisser une trop mauvaise impression de la France, la presse américaine adoucit systématiquement le ton en fin d'article. Elle ne manque pas de rappeler la profonde solidarité qui existe entre les deux plus anciens alliés de l'histoire américaine, la communauté de leurs idéaux démocratiques, et le sentiment de s'être toujours trouvés ensemble du même et bon côté des conflits du siècle. Chacun des deux pays semble renvoyer à l'autre l'image de ses contradictions, de ses difficultés mais aussi, parfois, de sa propre grandeur. Les causes des mésententes sont diverses mais ont toutes ce point en commun: l'origine du message. En effet, les « signaux » envoyés de part et d'autre de l'Atlantique ne sont pas toujours bien perçus ni toujours émis consciemment. La France porte une grande part de responsabilité dans l'image qu'elle donne d'elle-même à l'étranger et surtout aux États-Unis.

Notes

[1] Cas exceptionnel, le 27 janvier 1997, la France se trouvait à la une du *Los Angeles Times* dans un article intitulé « Why the French Hate the Internet ». Le constat

était sans nuance: la France est « l'un des rares bastions qui refusent de se joindre au grand « love-in » planétaire des technologies de l'information. [...] Les branchés high-tech y sont considérés comme des ringards. Les intellectuels écrivent des diatribes contre le réseau mondial. Les cyber-cafés font faillite, les fournisseurs d'accès ne trouvent pas d'abonnés ».   Selon le journal de Los Angeles, plusieurs raisons expliquent cette aversion pour l'Internet: le mode de vie national, la peur d'une « polution culturelle » puisque la France résiste à tout ce qui peut « diluer » sa culture et enfin « la destruction de la langue française, donc l'identité de la nation ».   Dans son article, Amy Harmon ne manque pas de faire le parallèle entre l'attitude de la France face à Internet et l'attitude du général de Gaulle face à l'OTAN.

Dans un article particulièreement acerbe, Scott Sullivan de *Newsweek,* brocarde la folie des grandeurs des Français: « Ce n'est pas le succès ou l'échec qui parle au cœur des Français, c'est la grandeur elle-même. Les Français continuent de révérer Louis le Grand le prodigue, Robespierre le fanatique et Napoléon le monomaniaque. Et c'est cette même dynamique qui est à l'œuvre dans la politique étrangère de la France ».

L'universitaire américain, Richard Kuisel, parle du « narcissisme démesuré » de ces deux pays: « deux grands narcissismes — les deux seules cultures au monde qui croient être investies d'une mission civilisatrice et croient que leur modèle est applicable universellement », cité par Charles Trueheart dans *l'International Herald Tribune* du 15 juillet 1997.

Dans son article « Liberty, Equality, Bon Appétit », Diane Johnson établit un parallèle entre le célèbre « French paradox » alimentaire et le système économique français: « Les Français ne semblent pas avoir de problème de morale. Ils savent manier le paradoxe. [...] Nous pouvons, à notre manière, railler les utopies mais, jusqu'à présent, les Français ont plutôt bien géré leur utopie à fort cholestérol ». De même, dans son article « France Must Be Doing Something Right », William Pfaff écrit: « Le défi que la France (et l'Allemagne) lance actuellement à la doctrine américaine est d'ordre éthique et politique, soutenant que maximiser les bénéfices n'est pas le but de l'existence, même dans le domaine économique ».

Références

Cohen, Roger. « For France, Sagging Self-Image and Esprit », *New York Times* 11 Feb. 1997: A1+.

---. « France's Allegiance: To Things French, Like Hypocrisy », *New York Times* 24 Aug. 1997: E3.

---. « Lacking Barricades, France Is in a Funk », *New York Times* 29 Dec. 1997: E2.

Edmondson, Gail. « Once Upon a Time, Bill Gates Came to France... », *Business Week* 10 Feb. 1997: 56.

Guisnel, Jean. *Les pires amis du monde.* Paris: Éditions Stock, 1999.

Harmon, Amy. « Why the French Hate the Internet », *Los Angeles Times* 27 Jan. 1997: A1+.

Hoagland, Jim. « Le Jour De Gloire Est Passé », *Washington Post* 22 July 1990: C1+.

Johnson, Diane. « Liberty, Equality, Bon Appétit », *New York Times* 8 June 1997: E2.

Kornheiser, Tony. « Pardon my French », *Washington Post* 26 Feb. 1995: F1+.

Ledeen, Michael. « In Defense of 'Perfidious' France , *Wall Street Journal* 28 Nov. 1997: 1+

Lightfoot, Warwick. « The French Miracle », *Wall Street Journal* 6 Oct. 1994: 1+.

McGrory, Mary. « Chirac's Green Cheese Diplomacy », *Washington Post* 18 June 1995: C1.

Morrison, James. « French Stereotypes », *Washington Times* 6 Nov. 1995: A18.

Pfaff, William. « France Must Be Doing Something Right », *Sun* [Baltimore, MD] 22 June 1998: 11A.

---. « Unusually, the French Are Happy », *The National Interest* Winter 1998/99: 52-59.

Riding, Alan. « The French Funk », *New York Times Magazine* 23 Mar. 1994: 25+.

---. « Where is the Glory That Was France? » *New York Times* 14 Jan. 1996: Section 2.

Sokal, Alan et Jean Bricmont. *Impostures intellectuelles*. Paris: Seuil, 1996.

Stanger, Theodore et Marcus Mabry. « Liberté, Egalité, Médiocrité », *Newsweek* 20 June 1994: 50.

Sullivan, Scott. « The Glory That Was France », *Newsweek* 9 May 1994: 18-19.

Tiersky , Ronald. « France Plays its Part », *New York Times* 11 Nov. 1997: A27.

Trueheart, Charles. « Resisting Global Currents, France Sticks to Being French », *International Herald Tribune* 15 July 1997: 1+.

Védrine, Hubert. « Défense: l'Europe sous tutelle », *Le Point* le 12 avril 1997.

Vinocur, John. « The Political Lesson: Forward To The Past », *International Herald Tribune* 2 June 1997: 1+.

Walsh, James. « The Search for a New France », *Time* 15 July 1991: 8-9.

Waxman, Sharon. « French Kiss-Off », *Washington Post* 30 Oct. 1995: E1+.

Weber, Eugen. « What's Ailing France *Now?*» *New York Times* 2 Apr. 1998: D4.

18

Hollywood Remakes of French Films: Cultural and Cinematic Transformation

Colette G. Levin
University of Pittsburgh at Greensburg

During the course of its history Hollywood cinema has often sought inspiration in films created by French filmmakers. As early as 1945 Fritz Lang based his *Scarlet Street* on *La Chienne* , a film directed by Jean Renoir in 1932. Since then adaptations of French films have appeared on the screen from time to time. In recent years, however, the practice has become widespread in Hollywood, so much so in fact that those who follow the progress of French cinema on the international scene acknowledge that remakes have become a cinematic trend. An article entitled "Hollywood remakes: a feeling of déjà vu" states that "for many years now, the American film industry has been inspired by French cinema. All the giants of American cinema have been caught up in translations of French originals, and today French films account for 90 percent of films remade by Hollywood" (4).

The decision by a Hollywood filmmaker to remake an original French film is usually based on pragmatic considerations. In the motion picture industry "a film's success (its ability to fly) is based not on predictable constants like the laws of physics and aerodynamics but on the unpredictable and whimsical laws of human likes and dislikes. Remakes and sequels bring at least a degree of predictability to the marketplace" (Boggs 394). Indeed, remakes of motion pictures that have already met with success in France represent a sound financial investment. Coline Serreau's *Trois Hommes et un couffin* (1985) is a case in point. This was "one of the greatest domestic box-office hits of recent French cinema. Over ten million people saw the film in the year of release, rising to twelve and a half million within three years, making it by far the most popular French film of the 1980s" (Austin 89). The remake, *Three Men and a*

Baby, on the other hand, was to gross over 158 million (Waxman C6). It is, indeed, clear that a filmmaker who commits himself to remaking a French film aims to make use of a proven motion picture which has been well received in its country of origin and to remake it into an even more successful film to be distributed widely in the United States and abroad. The exploitation of French films by Hollywood has been noted by French critics:

> On sait d'ailleurs que les Américains pratiquent délibérément le remake fondé sur le remaniement des modèles scénaristiques d'origine. Les films européens leur fournissent des intrigues, des idées, des personnages intéressants, mais des dialogues et des schémas narrativo-dramatiques jugés inadéquats pour le public. On assiste alors à des transformations typiques de modèle moderne en modèle classique (Vanoye 152).

Indeed, the Hollywood filmmakers' general practice involves selecting those elements from the original that they wish to imitate and transforming or eliminating those that they believe will not appeal to American viewers. Although each remake is unique and although there are many variations in the creative decisions adopted by filmmakers, a detailed analysis of the original films and their Hollywood remakes leads to general observations not only about the process used in film adaptation but also about the similarities and contrasts found in the French and Hollywood cinemas.

One of the most common practices among filmmakers involves acknowledging openly and immediately the source upon which their own film is based. This is done most often by retaining the initial title as in *Diabolique* or using a title that comes close to the original. *Three Men and a Baby* and *Breathless* are near direct translations of titles used in French films. If a translated title is not deemed acceptable, then one which is reminiscent of the original is chosen. This is the case for *Birdcage,* the remake of *La Cage aux folles.* Another way for a Hollywood director to acknowledge his debt to his French source is to use the names of the original protagonists. In *Three Men and a Baby* Pierre, Michel and Jacques become Peter, Michael and Jack. In *Breathless* the heroine, an American girl named Patricia, is replaced by Monica Poiccard, a French girl whose last name is that of the hero in *A Bout de Souffle.* In general, though, names are changed only if and when the originals are not commonly used within the geographical location or during the times in which the action of the remake takes place. In *Diabolique* all French names are dropped in favor of more American sounding names. The only exception is Nicole Horner, which, when pronounced appropriately, can pass as an American name.

In general, the practice of Hollywood filmmakers is to retain as much of the original as possible as long as the material does not present any perceived roadblock to viewers' interest and approval.

This holds true as well for the handling of the plot. Typically the remakes exploit the plots found in French films expanding them only when, in order to meet viewers' expectations, it is deemed desirable to include contemporary social issues and action-filled episodes in the story line. *Le Grand Chemin,* for example, offers the story of a young Parisian boy left by his mother in the care of a couple living in a quiet, provincial village. While Louis stays with Marcelle and Polo, "diverses épreuves l'attendent [...] aux côtés d'une petite fille figurant le guide et l'initiatrice" (Vanoye 216). The plot outlines both young Louis' traumatic passage from childhood to adolescence and the important role he plays in the reconciliation of Marcelle and Polo, long separated after the accidental death of their own son. Mary Agnes Donoghue attracted by the originality and freshness of this plot makes use of it in her remake, *Paradise,* modifying it by incorporating a detailed exploration of the plight of children of divorce in contemporary society. Willard, the young boy who yearns to meet his own absentee father, forms an alliance with Billy, his playmate, and stands by her as she confronts the father who abandoned home and family years earlier.

Another French film, *Les Diaboliques,* offers an interesting plot that involves a diabolical plot fomented by the headmaster of a French school and his mistress to get rid of his wealthy, sickly wife by frightening her and inducing a heart attack. Jeremiah Chechick exploits the original plot and, in a further effort to capture his audience's interest, causes the action to rebound dramatically. The headmaster's wife, who in the French film dies as the result of the murderous machination, survives in the remake. She lives on to wage a courageous fight along with the redeemed ex-mistress against the tyrannical abuse of their respective husband and ex-lover. Together the two women triumph dramatically over their evil master, supported in their fight by a private female detective with anti-sexist attitudes whose words convey the overall feminist message found at the heart of the revamped plot.

The plot of *Trois Hommes et un couffin* is similarly incorporated in its remake, *Three Men and a Baby.* It involves the portrayal of the psychological transformation which occurs when three young men are forced to take responsibility for the care of a baby left on their doorstep. The director of the remake, convinced that the original focus on psychological development is insufficient to hold the interest of American viewers, bolsters a minor episode involving protagonists, police, and drugs and gives it a new, inflated dramatic importance by adding action-filled adventures and suspenseful episodes. Thus, if one examines how Hollywood filmmakers handle the French plots that they borrow, one comes to the conclusion that in general they imitate the originals faithfully and that, even when incorporating additional episodes meant to meet their viewers' cinematic expectations, they find the basis for their inspiration in the French plots themselves.

Typically, the French film provides the remake not only with its plot but also with its major characters and their personality traits. This is especially apparent when actors with physical appearances similar to those of the original actors are cast in the remake. In *Diabolique* Nicole Horner played by Sharon Stone presents the tall, blond appearance of the earlier incarnation by Simone Signoret and the short, round-faced Mia Baran played by Isabelle Adjani is highly reminiscent of Vera Clouzot's Mme Delasalle. It is only when the Hollywood filmmakers suspect that the physical appearance of a character might not be appealing to their viewers that they bring some modifications to the original model. *Paradise* introduces Billy, the nine-year old playmate of a ten-year old boy named Willard who has come from the city to the country to stay with his mother's friend, Lilly. Billy's appearance contrasts sharply with that of Martine, the ten-year old playmate of eight-year old Louis in *Le Grand Chemin*. While Martine is tall, sloppy-looking and unattractive, Billy is short, with a pretty face and long blond hair. The change is brought about by the wish to present a more attractive portrait of the young girl and to have her relate as an equal partner to the boy as, unlike Martine, she offers support and concern rather than confrontation.

In general, attitudes, values and beliefs expressed by the French characters are echoed by their American counterparts. Thus, love and commitment to family values find expression in both *Trois Hommes et un couffin* and *Three Men and a Baby* as both sets of protagonists are allowed to grow emotionally. The Hollywood director, however, introduces minor changes in the characterization in order to eliminate or modify certain elements which might be offensive to prospective American audiences. Thus, the image of motherhood in *Trois Hommes et un Couffin* is modified in *Three Men and a Baby*. In the French film, Jacques, upon realizing that he is responsible for the care of a baby, immediately seeks the help of his mother. Arriving with a cradle in hand, he finds much to his surprise that his mother, although very much taken with the baby and very warm in her welcome, has plans of her own that she will not give up. Her explanations indicate that, left very much to her own devices, she has built a new lifestyle which involves the pursuit of pleasure. "There is no third age anymore," observes Pierre. In the remake motherhood is portrayed in different terms. Jack's call to his mother to enlist her help in taking care of the baby is answered promptly. His mother, assessing the situation with clarity and intelligence, arrives at the decision that she will not come to her son's rescue. Her decision is not dictated by any conflicting need of her own, but rather out of a desire to have her son learn responsibility. Her didactic and moralistic stand is in keeping with the American view of what is appropriate behavior for a mother. The remake consistently attempts to offer a positive image of motherhood. Sylvie, unlike her French counterpart whose motivation is to get even with the baby's father for his indifference towards her, leaves her daughter at Jack's door because she cannot cope with taking care of her and with making a living as an actress. It is interesting to note that this act of abandonment is not that of an American but rather that of an English mother. Her claim that she cannot cope is amply supported by the fact that it takes the three men's combined efforts to deal with the responsibilities for the baby's care. She is, furthermore, exonerated by her youth and inexperience, by her expressed worry that she is not providing what her daughter needs, and by the honest acknowledgment of her own personal needs and hopes. Her final acceptance of the responsibility of motherhood supports the aura of morality established by the more mature mother in the American remake.

Sometimes personal hopes and aspirations affecting relationships between men and women in the French films are altered in the remakes and the alteration has much to do with the filmmakers' efforts to eliminate anything that they perceive as offensive to their audience. *Trois Hommes et un Couffin* portrays a society whose main goal is the pursuit of pleasure and the rejection of emotional commitment. We learn early in the film that the three male protagonists share an apartment which serves as a safe haven from unwelcome long-term involvement with women. A certain misogyny is apparent as the men perceive women merely as sex objects. Although some specific relationships are mentioned, they are not sufficiently developed to convey the impression of meaningful and lasting commitment. In the remake, on the other hand, the presence of Rebecca, a character created for the sole purpose of providing a girlfriend for Peter, softens the overall view of the society at play. Involved in an open relationship with Peter for five years, Rebecca is keeping her feelings in check because Peter is uncomfortable with sentimentality and disinterested in commitment. She shows patience and restraint in the hope that Peter will eventually grow up. Her presence and that of Jack's mother serve to call attention to the three bachelors' youth and to soften the portrayal of their immature lifestyle.

The same concern not to portray values that might not find approval with American viewers is evidenced as well in *Cousins.* This remake rejects the original premise found in *Cousins, Cousines* which shows a long suffering wife throwing herself with complete abandon to feelings of joy and happiness in an affair with a cousin by marriage. The remake, reluctant to deal with a married woman who, although justified, feels absolutely no guilt about an extra-marital *liaison,* replaces her with a female character who struggles to conciliate responsibilities and personal desires. This modification is typical of the practice of Hollywood filmmakers who adopt the models presented by their French sources, but who, in their vigilance to eliminate values and behavioral patterns that might prove shocking to the American viewers, alter the original characterization to include traits that will find easy acceptance.

Characters in the French films function in a world deliberately created to convey an aura of verisimilitude. A number of "accessoires et décors sont amenés à être vus" (Vanoye 63) in order to provide an authentic cultural background for the action in the film. Thus, the *mise en scène* in *Trois Hommes et un couffin* depicts a way of life popular among successful, professional types in Paris in the 80s. The remake, *Three Men and a Baby,* aiming at creating an appropriate background for its action as well, is mindful of the geographical displacement to the United States. Cultural contrasts in the *mise en scène* of both films are highly visible. For example, comparing the French and American living quarters shared by the three protagonists results in an interesting view of cultural divergences. The spacious, luxurious apartment in which the American men live is very different from the Paris habitat which is more sedate, more classical but equally luxurious by French standards and tastes. Such diverse activities as birthday parties and jogging exercise reflect faithfully the contemporary way of life of many Americans while the public gardens where people are seen, walking, sitting, and reading the daily paper give a truthful representation of how the French spend their leisure hours.

Like their French counterparts, Hollywood filmmakers incorporate in their remakes elements that help to define the times in which the action occurs. *Les Diaboliques* is a mystery suspense film which takes place in a boarding school of a small French town in the 1950s. The recent remake places the action in a small American town in the 1990s. Authentic details pertaining to the spartan living conditions that existed forty years ago contrast with those found in a small American town today. Each film presents a completely autonomous portrayal of a lifestyle reflecting the location and the time in which the action takes place.

In the French film the selection of elements for the *mise en scène* is also dictated by the dramatic needs of the action. "Le vraisemblable n'est ni le vrai, ni le réel, ni même la représentation globale qu'on peut se faire de ce qui arrive le plus communément dans la vie. Le vraisemblable découle du nécessaire, c'est-à-dire d'un ensemble d'enchaînements logiques agencés par l'auteur" (Vanoye 24). In *Le Retour de Martin Guerre,* for example, an historically authentic device used by shoemakers in sixteenth-century France helps to cast doubt on the identity of the impostor by showing that his shoe size does not match that of the real Martin. *Sommersby,* in a similar effort to show that suspicions about the hero's identity are solidly grounded, provides its own authentic means for casting doubt on the impostor. Thus, the analysis of the *mise en scène* in both original film and remake reveals that the patterns established by the French film are observed by the Hollywood filmmaker who adapts to geographical, temporal and dramatic exigencies in this own selection of elements to be used in the remake. Interesting cultural contrasts can be observed as viewers note the *mise en scène* of both films.

The French film offers Hollywood filmmakers patterns of narration which they can edit and modify to suit the Hollywood classical style of filmmaking which over the years has proven to be popular with American film viewers. The original usually opens with an exposition that can be quite explicit and detailed. For example, in *Le Retour de Martin Guerre* the disembodied voice of a narrator relates at length the early history of Martin Guerre and his wife, Bertrande de Rols. In the remake the expository beginnings are presented in a more concise form. *Sommersby* opts for a montage-sequence offering information on Jack Sommersby's trials as a soldier during the Civil War. In a similar curtailment of the original exposition, the credits sequence of *Trois Hommes et un couffin* which, together with scenes of a party in progress, provide the viewer with the preliminary information necessary to the understanding of the storyline, is replaced by a superimposed series of cartoons offering a concentrated commentary on the three male protagonists and their lifestyle.

The French narration is sometimes reticent about revealing information that is unecessary to the comprehension of the plot. In *Le Grand Chemin* Marcelle who has been and is still grieving the loss of her young child after two years expresses her grief in a cold, unresponsive attitude toward her husband Polo. The psychological foundation for her inconsolable grief and for her excessively harsh reaction to her husband remains unexplained and is left for the viewer to interpret. On the other hand, American viewers, traditionally accustomed to clearly-delineated situations are known to frown upon this lack of precise communication. The Hollywood director, therefore, steps in to lift the veil of silence in *Paradise* and to provide the psychological basis for the continued depression and lasting grief. Lily, in a confrontation with her husband Ben, blurts out that she is overwhelmed by intense feelings of guilt resulting from her failure to respond to her child's cries sometimes before he died. A similar attempt to clarify ambiguities present in the original occurs in *Sommersby*. At the beginning of *Le Retour de Martin Guerre* we are made to believe that Bertrande, a young woman, whose husband has been absent for many years, recognizes her mate and welcomes him back upon his return. It is only much later that we come to realize that the man claiming to be Martin Guerre is actually an impostor and even then, we are not sure whether Bertrande is aware of the imposture. The American viewer lacks enthusiasm for this kind of ambiguity traditionally tolerated by the French. Therefore, early in *Sommersby* we hear Laurel uttering "Who is this man sitting in my kitchen?" revealing that she is not deceived by the impostor but is willing to make herself an accomplice to the deception of others in the community. There is no ambiguity in her attitude and there is no ambiguity in the viewer's mind. Thus, while both the French and the Hollywood films provide objective accounts of the events in the plot, the French narration is sometimes less open than its Hollywood counterpart.

Interestingly, however, in some cases the narration of the Hollywood film is called upon to conceal or to detract attention away from unpleasant realities. Since American viewers, unlike their French counterparts, traditionally show very little tolerance for unhappy endings, *Le Retour de Martin Guerre* which shows the hero put to death for having taken on the identity of another man , is less than a satisfactory model for the Hollywood filmmaker. He, therefore, calls on his film's narration to solve the impact of such an ending on his public. As the protagonist is about to be put to death for a crime he committed in his youth, the filmmaker deliberately tempers with the perceptions of his viewers by skillfully shifting their attention away from the gallows to what ultimately becomes a celebration of the love shared by Jack and Laurel. At the very moment that the man we know as Sommersby is about to be hanged for murder, the image of the young wife fighting her way through the crowd to reach her husband in time builds a crescendo of suspense which draws our attention away from the impending death. The viewers begin to share in the wife's efforts to join her husband in spite of all kinds of impediments thrown in her way and, as she finally reaches him, the audience becomes totally involved in the film's triumphal closure.

In summary, the analysis of French original films and their Hollywood remakes leads to the realization that French cinema is an important source of inspiration for Hollywood. The noticeable increase in the number of remakes in the last decade testifies to the interest in French storylines. Moreover, the process of adaptation used by Hollywood filmmakers betrays a constant preoccupation with every facet of the original film practice which serves as the basis from which creative decisions concerning the remake emerge. The French film as well as its Hollywood remake present to their respective viewers an authentic reflection of their own culture. Motion pictures created on both sides of the Atlantic Ocean are, indeed, important repositories of cultural materials. It is important, therefore, to engage in a serious comparison of both cinematic content and cinematic form as a means to gather information on the similarities shared by both cultures and on the contrasts which characterize French and American cultures at the end of the twentieth century.

References

Austin, Guy. *Contemporary French Cinema.* Manchester and New York: Manchester
    University Press, 1996.
Boggs, Joseph M. *The Art of Watching Films.* Mountain View, California: Mayfield
    Publishing Company, 1996.
"Hollywood remakes: a feeling of déjà vu." *News from France* . Washington, D.C.:
    French Embassy Press and Information Service, 12 Jul. 1996. 4.
Vanoye, Francis. *Scénarios Modèles, Modèles de Scénarios.* Paris: Nathan, 1991.
Waxman, Sharon. "A Matter of Déjà View." *Washington Post.* July 15, 1993.

Film Index

A bout de souffle. Dir. Jean-Luc Godard. Perf. Jean-Paul Belmondo, Jean Seberg, and
    Daniel Boulanger. SNC, 1960.

Birdcage. Dir. Mike Nichols. Perf. Robin Williams, Nathan Lane, Gene Hackman, and Dianne Wiest. United Artists, 1996.

Breathless. Dir. Jim McBride. Perf. Richard Gere and Valerie Kaprisky. Miko, 1983.

La Cage aux folles. Dir. Edouard Molinari. Perf. Ugo Tognazzi and Michel Serrault. United Artists, 1979.

La Chienne. Dir. Jean Renoir. Perf. Michel Simon, Janie Marèze, and Georges Flamant. Braunberger, 1931.

Cousins. Dir. Joel Schumacher. Perf. Ted Danson, Isabella Rossellini, Sean Young, and William Petersen. Paramount, 1989.

Cousins, Cousines. Dir. Jean-Charles Tacchella. Perf. Marie-France Pisier, Marie-Christine Barrault, Victor Lanoux, and Guy Marchand. Gaumont, 1975.

Diabolique. Dir. Jeremiah Chechick. Perf. Sharon Stone, Isabelle Adjani, Charles Palminteri, and Kathy Bates. Warner, 1996.

Les Diaboliques. Dir. Henri-Georges Clouzot. Perf. Simone Signoret, Vera Clouzot, Charles Vanel, and Paul Meurisse. Filmsonor, 1954.

Le Grand Chemin. Dir. Jean-Loup Hubert. Perf. Anémone, Richard Bohringer, Antoine Hubert, and Vanessa Guedi. Warner, 1987.

Paradise. Dir. Mary Agnes Donoghue. Perf. Melanie Griffith, Don Johnson, and Elijah Wood. Touchstone, 1992.

Le Retour de Martin Guerre. Dir. Daniel Vigne. Perf. Gérard Depardieu, Nathalie Baye, Sylvie Meda, and Maurice Barrier. Palace, 1982.

Scarlet Street. Dir. Fritz Lang. Perf. Edward G. Robinson, Joan Bennett, and Dan Duryea. Universal, 1945.

Sommersby. Dir. Jon Amiel. Perf. Richard Gere and Jodie Foster. Warner, 1993.

Three Men and a Baby. Dir. Leonard Nimoy. Perf. Tom Selleck, Steve Guttenberg, and Ted Danson. Touchstone, 1987.

Trois Hommes et un couffin. Dir. Coline Serreau. Perf. Roland Giraud, Michel Boujenah, André Dussolier, and Philippine Leroy Beaulieu. UKFD, 1985.

Conclusion

19

Bibliographic Essay on Contemporary France

Rosalie Vermette
Indiana University-Purdue University Indianapolis

Another "fin de siècle" has arrived. This one, like the last, marks in France the end of a period of rapid change. Despite phenomenal advances in science and technology, many of the basic underlying social and cultural questions and preoccupations of the French are still the same. Immigration remains a burning issue with all of its attendant ramifications of competition for jobs and threat to national cohesion. In the post-colonial era of the late twentieth century, the populations migrating to French cities come not from the distant French countryside as they did a hundred years ago, but from the Maghreb, Subsaharan Africa, and the Caribbean. This new wave of immigrants has rapidly and profoundly changed the social fiber of France, the culture and complexion of French society, and the demands on France's social and political institutions, as several of the works discussed below indicate.

Uncertainty and malaise are palpable sensations among the French on the eve of the twenty-first century. In the wake of the influx of immigrant populations in the last three or four decades, the beginnings of a new European economic and political order, and the globalization of industry, communications, and culture, France is preoccupied with the fear of losing its national identity, its unique *civilisation.* Since the post-war years of the 1950s, France has been struggling to hold on to its cultural identity in the face of what the French perceive as an American invasion (see in particular Carolyn Durham's *Double Takes* and Richard Kuisel's *Seducing the French,* reviewed below). Remaining an old and revered traditional civilization while becoming a modern society has caused much consternation for the French.

In the last decades of the nineteenth century, Paris underwent an enormous period of urban renewal, initiated by Baron Haussmann during the Second Empire and completed by the end of the century under the Third Republic. Paris became a modern city, yet significant monuments belonging to its cultural heritage were preserved. The last decades of the twentieth century have seen Paris undergo another face lift, another round of modernization, affirming France's recommitment to progress and modernity. *Les grands travaux* of President Mitterrand thunder the praises of a strong Fifth Republic. The Opera at the Bastille, the Ministry of Finance complex at Bercy, the Grande Arche at the Défense, the new Bibliothèque Nationale on the banks of the Seine, the Musée d'Orsay in a former train station, the new science and technology park at La Villette on the site of the former slaughterhouses of Paris, the *Parc Citroën* on the site of a former automobile plant, and — most notably and most controversially — I.M. Pei's glass pyramid in the courtyard of the Louvre, all attest to France's will to merge the past with the present, to hold on to traditional forms while transforming them into emblems of the present.

This respect for tradition coupled with a fascination with the present and a hope for the future is a central trait of the national character of France. In light of the important changes taking place currently inside the country and on the wider European and international stages, France is preoccupied once again with its national identity, as Alistair Cole in *French Politics and Society* and the contributors to *Aspects of Contemporary France* conclude (discussed below). The French are reexamining their Frenchness, trying to find out who they are, as Edward Knox's excellent article in a recent issue of the *French Review* demonstrates. Within a twenty-month period, between November 1995 and July 1997, the French produced no less than thirty book-length studies of who they are (Knox 98-101). Evidently, a similar need to know who the French are has also become an American (and a British) preoccupation in the last two decades of the century, if the abundance of popular and scholarly works coming out of the United States (and England) is any indication (Knox 96-98).

What follows is an annotated review of a limited and selective list of books, periodicals, and electronic resources to help those interested in learning more about contemporary France. The items are presented alphabetically by author within categories that correspond to those used to organize the chapters in this volume. This bibliography is intended to complement both Knox's article and the references that accompany each chapter presented in this volume. Works already referred to in individual chapters and in Knox's article will generally not appear in this bibliography. Almost all of the studies reviewed below were published in the

1990s, more precisely in the second half of the decade, and many of them trace the history of current social situations in France to their roots in the nineteenth century. This bibliography, therefore, presents up-to-date and current French, American, and British views of France at the dawn of the third millennium.

I. Politics

Jean-Paul Brunet's edited work, *Immigration, vie politique et populisme en banlieue parisienne (fin XIXe-XXe siècles)* (Paris: L'Harmattan, 1995) furthers our understanding of the different waves of immigration to France over the last one hundred years and the integration, or non-integration, of these immigrants and their progeny into French society. The development of a "red belt" around Paris, along with the history and role of populism and the *Parti Communiste Français (PCF)* in these areas, is the major theme running through this work. The sudden and surprising rise in popularity of the *Front National* party in these heavily working-class areas, especially to the north of Paris, in the late 1980s and 1990s is of great concern to the authors.

Alistair Cole's *French Politics and Society* (London/New York: Prentice Hall, 1998) is a study of the Fifth Republic from 1981 through 1995. This work by a British specialist in European and French politics aims to be a textbook for undergraduates or a reference work for non-specialists. Cole's central theme is the steady erosion over the last two decades of France's claim to "exceptionalism," the idea that France is somehow not like other countries. This weakening of French exceptionalism, Cole argues, is the result of both internal (societal changes, a *dirigiste* economy, immigration, integration, and growing cultural diversity) and external (European Union) pressures on the French political system. A valuable reference section on French politics concludes the book.

Christopher Flood and Laurence Bell's *Political Ideologies in Contemporary France* (London/Washington, DC: Pinter, 1997) examines the various ideological responses to the major social, economic, and political changes that have been reshaping France in the last three decades of the century. Edited by two British specialists in French politics, this book outlines a range of competing ideologies — communism, socialism, Gaullism, national populism, ecologism, feminism, multiculturalism — important to French political life. Renowned specialists such as Alec Hargreaves and Máire Cross writing on multiculturalism and the feminist ideology respectively make this a valuable collection of studies on contemporary social as well as political France.

John T.S. Keeler and Martin A. Schain have edited the book, *Chirac's Challenge: Liberalization, Europeanization, and Malaise in France* (New York: St. Martin's Press, 1996) which examines the first year of Jacques Chirac's presidency. The authors detail how major concerns of French voters in 1995 — unemployment, social welfare, immigration, and the plight of the excluded, or homeless — are all sources as well as manifestations of the general malaise that marked France as the march toward a unified Europe progressed. These concerns, as well as such diverse social and political issues as education policy, sexual harassment in the workplace, health care policy, and the challenges of belonging to the European Union are analyzed in thirteen articles.

Maurice Larkin's *France since the Popular Front: Government and People, 1936-1996* (Oxford: Clarendon, 1997, 2nd edition) is a history of modern France by one of the leading British scholars in the field. This study provides a comprehensive and authoritative examination of a pivotal sixty-year period leading up to France at the end of the twenty-first century. A vast amount of information and analysis is contained in this highly readable and solid contribution to French history by an outside observer. Events and historical figures are placed in an international context and examined from a comparative point of view. The French economy, welfare benefits, education, disabilities of women, patterns of religious observance, and the role of the church are a few of the issues studied. An extensive annotated bibliography concludes the book.

Ronald Tiersky's *France in the New Europe: Changing yet Steadfast* (Belmont. CA: Wadsworth, 1994) is an enlightening essay by an American specialist in French political history. Tiersky's book situates major political and social themes in the changing French cultural landscape of the early 1990s, on the eve of European integration. Major figures who influenced events and ideas leading up to the final decade of the century are examined in this work designed for students new to the study of France. Immigration and the fear of loss of national identity, the New Europe and the perplexing question of national sovereignty are among the themes examined. A substantial list of suggested readings is included.

II. Social issues

The French Welfare State (New York: New York UP, 1991), edited by John S. Ambler, contains chapters by seven American and French academics, all political scientists with the exception of one sociologist. This mix explains the study's focus on examining the role of political ideologies in matters of French social policy. The topics treated in the different chapters include the social policies of the French welfare state during the Fifth Republic, family policy, housing policies, and social insurance. Substantive lists of references are included at the end of each chapter.

Jacqueline Ancelin's *L'action sociale familiale et les caisses d'allocations familiales: Un siècle d'histoire* (Paris: Association pour l'Étude de l'Histoire de la Sécurité Sociale, 1997) is written by a former director of the *Action sociale à la Caisse Nationale des Allocations familiales*. In spite of this, Ancelin examines honestly and objectively the century-long history of the welfare services instituted to assure the well-being of children and their families in France. This study is designed to be a reference work for those interested in social policy, health care, and family life in France. The twenty appendices include the texts of relevant legal and governmental decrees, circulars, and laws.

In *La France imaginée: Déclin des rêves unitaires?* (Paris: Fayard, 1998), Pierre Birnbaum, a specialist in the political history of late twentieth-century France, poses a number of questions: Have the long-time rivals, Republicanism and Catholicism, abandoned their disparate views on unity and reached a conciliatory position within the framework of an improbable liberalism? Has the church, like the state, put aside its arrogant stance and learned the arts of dialogue and coexistence? The France described here is a nation hesitant to adopt a pluralistic society, hesitant to invent a national identity in which race and ethnicity would play new roles. This work is a valuable effort to situate the origin and development of those French cultural attitudes that have culminated in the agenda of the National Front.

Robert Castel's *Les Métamorphoses de la question sociale: Une chronique du salariat* (Paris: Fayard, 1995) is a comprehensive study of France's workers, written from a sociological perspective. Castel examines the plight of France's underclass (the long-term unemployed, the residents of the *banlieues*, the underprivileged, youth looking for work, and those receiving minimum benefits from the state) and finds that the situation in the 1990s is altogether different, more dangerous and precarious, than it had been in the past.   The study is presented as an historical chronicle, Castel's purpose being to situate France's current wage earners, and wageless earners, with reference to the past.

Bleddyn Davies, José Fernández, and Robin Saunders have written a comparative overview of home care for the elderly in France and England, *Community Care in England and France: Reforms and the Improvement of Equity and Efficiency* (Aldershot, England/Brookfield, USA: Ashgate, 1998). Financed by *La Fondation de France*, this study reflects an increasing awareness in France of the need for greater government intervention in the care of the elderly. An informative list of references pertinent to the study of these health care issues in France and England is included.

The thirty-four short articles that constitute *Parallel Views: Education and Access for Deaf People in France and the United States* (Washington, DC: Gallaudet UP, 1994) form an enlightening comparative study of education and the deaf cultures in France and the United States.   The articles were originally presented at a French-American colloquium in Paris in 1991, sponsored by the Franco-American Foundation, and cover a wide-range of topics relevant to the issue, revealing much about French attitudes towards deaf people, their right to equal educational opportunities, and access to traditional careers.

Pierre Guillaume's *Histoire sociale de la France au XXe siècle* (Paris: Masson, 1993) is an informative social history offering an important evolutionary perspective on the society and culture of late-century France. Guillaume identifies the major social changes that have marked the last century and a half and examines the impact of each on the lives of various groups of society, from the age-old peasant population to the more modern managerial class. Among the themes explored are health care, leisure and cultural activities, education, crime, social conflict, the changing role of women, and social legislation.

The Graying of the World: Who Will Care for the Frail Elderly? (New York: Haworth P, 1994), edited by Laura Katz Olson, examines the social and health care situation of the aging population in eleven countries of the world. Chapter 8, co-written by a French economist and a French sociologist and translated into English, looks at the social policies that deal with the aged and frail segment of the contemporary French population. The book shows that the situation is unfortunately becoming more critical each year. A short list of references in French is included.

Christian Poiret's *Familles africaines en France: ethnicisation, ségrégation et communalisation* (Paris: L'Harmattan, 1996) provides useful information about the social conditions of Subsaharan African populations living in France. Poiret, a sociologist, questions the evolution of French society since the 1970s and offers insights into the French propensity to ethnicize historical and social realities. Included in the issues discussed by Poiret are the struggles of the *sans-papiers* and the homeless, the social stigma of polygamy practiced by some Subsaharan Africans, segregation and discrimination, and the marked "foreignness" of these immigrant populations.

Jean-Pierre Willems's *Vocational Education and Training in France* (Berlin: European Center for the Development of Vocational Training, 1994) is part of a series aimed at describing the vocational training systems of the twelve member states of the European Center for the Development of Vocational Training. Willems's report provides information about the French educational system, and current and future trends of employment in France and within the new European community. Diagrams and statistical charts abound to illustrate this informative study. Appendices, including a useful bibliography of French sources on aspects of the subject provide additional information.

III. Identity

Alec G. Hargreaves's *Immigration, "Race" and Ethnicity in Contemporary France* (London/New York: Routledge, 1995) is an analysis of the complex issues of immigration and integration that have been such major concerns of French public life since the early 1980s. Calling into play numerous social science disciplinary approaches, including cultural and political analyses, Hargreaves argues that the descendants of immigrants identify closely with France's majority population, but that it is the French majority — and French government policies — that form the strongest barriers against integration. In addition to providing an excellent scholarly analysis of the situation, Hargreaves also provides a comprehensive bibliography on the subject.

Juliette Minces, in her *La Génération suivante* (Paris: Éditions de l'Aube, 1997), a work originally published in 1986, examines the problem of the integration of the children of North African immigrants into French society since the 1970s. Considered "unassimilable" by many, these children face strong cultural, economic, and legal barriers to integration. The growth of unemployment and the fear of a loss of national identity has fueled anti-immigrant fervor and inspired French laws, notably those passed in the 1990s (see her postscript to the 1997 edition), that underscore France's xenophobia and racism. This work is also very helpful as background for the study of *Beur* literature.

Aspects of Contemporary France (London/New York: Routledge, 1997), edited by Sheila Perry, is a collection of essays in which ten British scholars of French studies discuss such issues as higher education in France, television, women, the Catholic Church, secularism and Islam, film, and the French consumer's influence on the development of the retail trade. Each chapter provides an in-depth and up-to-date examination of a social theme viewed from a particular disciplinary perspective. The questions of cultural identity, or "Frenchness," and nationhood are central to each of these studies. A helpful chronology of events leading up to each particular issue's manifestation in the mid-1990s is provided at the end of each chapter, along with a bibliography.

Sheila Perry and Máire Cross's edited work, *Voices of France: Social, Political and Cultural Identity* (London/New York: Pinter, 1997), consists of a selection of papers originally presented at a conference in England in 1995. The fifteen papers are divided into three broad areas: "People's Voices," from opinion polls, surveys, and television programs; "Cultural Voices," from the working class, ethnic minorities, and youth; and "Alternative Voices," from the margins of society. The wide range of topics covered includes many that are not usually treated by scholars: mass culture, popular music forms (hip-hop, reggae), newspapers of the homeless, social suffering. Relevant bibliographies follow each essay.

The authors who contributed to *Identity Papers: Contested Nationhood in Twentieth-Century France* (Minneapolis: U of Minnesota P, 1996), edited by Steven Ungar and Tom Conley, share the premise that French studies represents the interplay of language, literature, ideas, and history. The book's fourteen essays examine French social attitudes and issues of the 1990s as direct progeny of the social conditions of the 1930s. From a study of literature and film dating from the Paris *Exposition Universelle* of 1937 through an analysis of Mitterrand's *grands travaux*, the contributors attempt to shed light on the on-going debate about national identity in France. Extensive notes follow each article.

Michel Wieviorka's *La France raciste* (Paris: Seuil, 1992) gives a cross-section of urban France the chance to express their fears, frustrations, and concerns about the number of immigrants, especially North African immigrants, moving into their cities and the effect this is having on the social order in France, on French culture, and on national identity. The individuals interviewed live in five urban working class areas (Roubaix, Mulhouse, Marseille, and the Parisian *banlieues* of Montfermeil and Cergy) and include politicians and militant union members, policemen and social workers, teachers and magistrates.

IV. Culture

Carolyn A. Durham's *Double Takes: Culture and Gender in French Films and their Hollywood Remakes* (Hanover, NH: UP of New England, 1998) is an insightful examination of the cinema art form termed "le remake." Durham, a professor of French and French studies, produces a revealing intercultural study about film and cultural attitudes towards gender and cultural identity. This study — grounded in post-modernist and feminist theory — points out the inherent conflict that exists with Hollywood's remaking of French films, especially when practiced by the Disney Corporation's film studios. This conflict is between France's belief in its mission to civilize and the United States's practice of cultural imperialism. A comprehensive bibliography plus a surprisingly long list of some seventy films concludes the volume.

Alec G. Hargreaves and Mark McKinney have edited *Post-Colonial Cultures in France* (London/New York: Routledge, 1997), in which fifteen essays focus on the "post-colonial condition" that marks French culture at the end of the twentieth century. The essays, written by British, American, and French researchers, are divided into five sections: an "Overview" where immigration and the post-colonial problematic in France are examined; "Mass Media" or the representation of immigrant minorities in the media; "Music" where the impact of world music in France and forms of immigrant music are discussed; "Visual Arts" in which the *métissage* of post-colonial comics and gaps in ethnic representations are reviewed; and "Literature" where *Beur* literature and post-colonial women writers are discussed. Extensive lists of references are provided.

Diana Holmes's *French Women's Writing, 1848-1994* (London/Atlantic Highlands: Athlone, 1996) is part of the series *Women in Context* which examines women writers from different countries against the backdrop of the significant literary and social issues and events that both defined and influenced their writing. Both literary and non-literary French women writers — chiefly those whose works can be found in translation — are included. By embracing non-literary writers of a country in this way, more women (feminist and non-feminist alike) are brought out of the margins and a wider variety of techniques and strategies for expressing female reality are explored. The concluding chapter presents an enlightening essay on the state of women's writing in France at the end of the twentieth century.

The Handbook of French Popular Culture (New York/Westport: Greenwood P, 1991), edited by Pierre Horn, is a collection of articles examining various aspects of contemporary French daily life and popular culture. Among the subjects are advertising, comics, detective and spy fiction, cartoons, film, food and wine, leisure, love, newspapers, magazines, feminine press, popular music, radio and television, science fiction, and sports. American and French writers offer revealing insights into the culture and the national character of late twentieth-century France. Extensive lists of references on each topic provide useful resources for learning more about the history of French popular culture.

Richard F. Kuisel's Seducing the French: The Dilemma of Americanization (Berkeley: U of California P, 1993) seeks to understand postwar French anti-Americanism, on the one hand, alongside French fascination with American culture and cultural artifacts, on the other. As a cultural historian, Kuisel is interested in the love-hate relationship of the French with Americans and what this reveals about the French as a nation, in particular about their fear of losing their identity to the cultural invader. Kuisel's conclusion is that "Plus ça change, plus c'est la même chose," that is, as France has become more like America in the last thirty years it has in reality suffered no significant loss of its own unique cultural identity.

Gilles Lipovetsky's The Empire of Fashion: Dressing Modern Democracy (Princeton: Princeton UP, 1994), translated from the 1987 French edition by Catherine Porter, offers a subtle, if not oblique, look into twentieth-century French culture (and world culture) through the eyes and the mind of a contemporary French philosopher and social thinker. Choosing to investigate the issue of individualism — a central character trait of the French — through the unorthodox and usually marginalized subject of fashion, and more particularly of clothing and its accessories, Lipovetsky provides an original key to an understanding of modern French culture. The epilogue, written for the English translation, provides an updated analysis of the concept of individualism.

Pierre Maillot's Les Fiancés de Marianne: la société française à travers ses grands acteurs (Paris: Editions du Cerf, 1996) is a convincing study examining film heroes as documents to reveal France's collective sense of its cultural identity. Over the past sixty years film has replaced literature as the embodiment of French social reality and the male movie star has come to represent the social ideal. As such each major male film star embodied characteristics which, as the fiancé of Marianne (the feminine representation of *la République*), he offers the nation at a particular moment in time. This interesting thesis examines Jean Gabin, Jean Marais, Gérard Philippe, Alain Delon, Jean-Paul Belmondo, and Gérard Depardieu against the political, social, historic, and cultural realities that surround their particular Mariannes.

Clyde Thogmartin's *The National Daily Press of France* (Birmingham, AL: Summa Publications, 1998) is an enlightening study of journalism in France from the early seventeenth century through the end of the twentieth century. A comparative examination of French and American newspapers and newspaper readers offers unique insights into the national characters of both cultures. Among the areas of major difference between the two groups are the level of general knowledge of each readership, the role of ideological positions in the reporting of the news, and the "look" of newspapers in each country. An extensive list of references concludes the work.

V. Perceptions of France

Raymonde Carroll's *Cultural Misunderstandings: The French-American Experience* (Chicago: U of Chicago P, 1988) is a trail-blazing study of intercultural misunderstanding. Translated by Carol Volk from *Évidences invisibles* (1987), Carroll's book provides an insightful and often humorous ethnographic examination of cross-cultural behavior. A French anthropologist married to an American, Carroll uses an innovative methodology to explore obvious and not-so-obvious patterns of thought and behavior that all too often lead to hurt feelings, and worse. Carroll's work underscores the importance of cultural competence as a prerequisite for effective and empathic intercultural exchange.

Colin Gordon's *The Business Culture in France* (Oxford: Butterworth-Heinemann, 1996) forms part of a series that examines business cultures in the major countries of the European Union. The underlying premise of the works in the series is that an understanding of the culture of a country is more important than an understanding of the language of that country when trying to set up markets or to expand corporately into that country. Individual chapters in the France volume focus on determinants of the business culture thought to be significant for France.

The French Way: Aspects of Behavior, Attitudes, and Customs of the French (Lincolnwood, IL: Passport Books, 1995) by Ross Steele is a concise "dictionary" of eighty-four major French cultural traits organized alphabetically. As such, the book helps American readers gain a greater awareness of the similarities and differences between their cultural traditions and those of the French. This dictionary provides a brief but incisive look into the French way of thinking, living, and interacting among themselves which, in turn, sheds light on how the French interact with non-French both inside and outside the Hexagon (see p. 44 for a definition of *Hexagon*).

Sally Adamson Taylor's *Culture Shock! France: A Guide to Customs and Etiquette* (Portland, OR: Graphic Arts Center Publishing, 1997) offers a perceptive look at the national identity of France, focusing on those invisible cultural realities which make France a unique nation. Taylor's goal is to encourage and to assist in the development of cultural fluency and multicultural expertise through an examination of specific cultural behaviors. The book contains an extensive bibliography of works on French identity and of guides for understanding the French and life in France.

Laurence Wylie and Jean-François Brière's *Les Français* (Englewood Cliffs, NJ: Prentice Hall, 1995, 2nd edition) was written originally in 1970 as a textbook on French culture for Americans. Using a methodology borrowed from cultural anthropology, Wylie and Jean-François Brière, his collaborator in the second edition, examine French society, its social patterns and institutions, its symbols and structures, its rituals and industries as ways of knowing the French people, their attitudes and behaviors, their values and beliefs. The comparative approach used so deftly by these investigators helps American students gain a better understanding of the French. Reflective questions and critical exercises are provided for each chapter.

VI. General

Newspapers, in which France — unlike the United States — is still exceedingly rich, are one of the best ways to keep abreast of developments in contemporary French culture and civilization. The problem of French newspapers arriving out-of-date in North America has been partially solved with the development of newspaper Web sites. FranceLink <www.francelink.com/hotlinks/news/france/news-fr.html> provides easy links to the Web sites of over forty French newspapers and other news sources, including national papers such as *Libération* and *Le Monde* and regional papers such as *Nice-Matin* and *Dernières Nouvelles d'Alsace.* Two United States newspapers published in French, the weekly *France-Amérique* (New York: Le Figaro) and the monthly *Le Journal Français* (San Francisco) also offer Web access <www.france.com/france-amerique> and <www.journalfrancais.com>. FrancePress, the publisher of *Le Journal Français,* produces in addition a bi-monthly newsmagazine, *France Today.*

Weekly newsmagazines published in France offer valuable insights into contemporary French life. *L'Express* <www.lexpress.fr> and *Le Nouvel Observateur* <www.nouvelobs.com> are commonly available in academic and larger public libraries in North America. Several popular magazines published in the United States or Great Britain focus on contemporary French culture. *France: A Quarterly Review of la Vie Française* is published in Britain by Centralhaven, Ltd. *France Discovery Guide,* which covers news and information of particular interest to casual visitors to France, is published annually by the French Government Tourist Office in New York. Another valuable French government publication is *France Magazine,* issued quarterly by the French Embassy in Washington, D.C.

Academic journals that provide information and analysis on contemporary France include, especially, *The French Review,* published by the American Association of Teachers of French. *The French Review* carries articles on such topics as pedagogy and film as well as literature. In addition each issue has a special book review section devoted to discussing recent books relating to French "Society and Culture." Other academic journals which feature examinations of contemporary French life include *L'Année politique, économique et sociale en France* (Paris: Editions du Moniteur; annual); *Contemporary French Civilization* (Montana State University-Bozeman; semi-annual); *French Cultural Studies* (Chalfont St. Giles, England: Alpha Academic; three issues per year); *French Politics and Society* (Cambridge, Mass.: Harvard University; quarterly); *Modern & Contemporary France* (Abington, England: Association for the Study of Modern & Contemporary France; quarterly); and *Sites: The Journal of Twentieth-Century/Contemporary French Studies* (Chur, Switzerland: Gordon and Breach; semi-annual). The ten issues a year of *Regards sur l'actualité,* a government-sponsored periodical published by *La Documentation Française,* provide useful in-depth as well as general coverage of current events with a special emphasis on politics, public affairs, and socio-economic conditions.

Quid (Paris: Robert Laffont; annual) is an always up-to-date almanac of French life. Edited by Dominique and Michèle Frémy, *Quid* is a handy, comprehensive, and hefty (1800 pages plus) source of a variety of statistical information relating to everything French, from cinema to economics to sports.

Among works of general interest, the following four titles are noteworthy: John Ardagh's *Cultural Atlas of France* (New York: Facts on File, 1991), written with the assistance of Colin Jones, provides a stunning textual and pictorial, as well as cartographical, overview of the culture of France. The first part of the atlas focuses on France's varied and fruitful geography, while the second and third parts deal with the historical France and the France of today. The final section of the atlas is a detailed portrait of France, region by region. For example, four pages are devoted to contemporary Brittany, with a general map of the region and seven color illustrations. The *Cultural Atlas of France* is an extremely helpful reference tool for anyone concerned with understanding France and the French.

Frances Chambers's *Paris* (Oxford/Santa Barbara: Clio Press, 1998), Vol. 206 of the World Bibliographical Series, is an annotated bibliography providing a handy guide to a wide body of published materials on the city of Paris. The 430 separate entries deal with the history, geography, economy, and politics of the French metropolis. In addition, the volume provides a guide to studies on the people of Paris, their culture, customs, social organization, and current living conditions. The separate author, title, and subject indexes provide easy access to the books and articles cited in this useful bibliography.

French Cultural Studies: An Introduction (Oxford: Oxford UP, 1995), edited by Jill Forbes and Michael Kelly, is a cultural analysis of the one hundred and twenty-five years that stretch from the Prussian defeat of France in 1871 and the early 1990s. Fifteen British specialists of French cultural studies work collaboratively to examine major social and political themes and events, historical moments, and elements of traditional as well as popular culture. National identity and the effects of changing perceptions brought about by technological advances, decolonization, the rise of a broad Francophone culture, changing social and cultural alignments, and the post-war threat of the Americanization of French culture and the potential loss of France's "Frenchness" are the subjects of the eight chapters of the work. The volume concludes with a useful chronological outline of France's major political, economic, cultural, and social milestones between the 1870s and the 1990s.

Rounding out this survey of resources available for the study of French culture is the *Encyclopedia of Contemporary French Culture* (London/New York: Routledge, 1998), edited by Alex Hughes and Keith Reader. A multi-dimensional, cross-disciplinary collection of articles on broadly defined aspects of French culture, this reference book is an overview of post-World War II France. Written by British and American academics for a general audience, this book contains over 700 entries of varying length. The wide-ranging list of subjects covered includes cinema, political institutions, social policy, gender-based studies, critical theory, literature, and popular culture (sports, media, fashion, food, detective fiction), both in France and, to a limited extent, other Francophone countries. In summary, this is an essential and vital reference tool for anyone looking for ready information about contemporary French culture.

Reference

Knox, Edward. "Regarder la France: une réflexion bibliographique." *The French Review* 72 (1998): 91-101.

Authors' Biographies – Biographie des auteurs

Marc Bertrand is Professor of French Studies at Stanford University. Using a socio-critical approach, he has written many books and articles on contemporary authors (Claude Simon, Jean Cayrol, Nathalie Sarraute) as well as Jean Prévost, Sartre, Beauvoir, Camus, and Flaubert. He has also worked on contacts and relationships between popular traditions and learned culture from the seventeenth to nineteenth centuries.

Douglas Daniels is Associate Professor of French and Head of the Department of Modern Languages and Literatures at Montana State University-Bozeman. Fulbright and NEH Fellow, co-founder (with Bernard Quinn) and currently Managing Editor of *Contemporary French Civilization,* his scholarly interests include contemporary French politics, popular culture, and French media.

Claud DuVerlie (1941-2000) was a Professor of Modern Languages & Linguistics at the University of Maryland Baltimore County. For ten years, he directed the *France-TV Magazine* project. His scholarly interests included contemporary France and the European Union, France's audio-visual policies and practices, and modern French cinema. An important focus of his research was the utilization of media and telecommunication technologies in foreign language learning and intercultural communication.

Michel Gueldry is Associate Professor of French and European Studies and Chair of the French Department at the Monterey Institute of International Studies in California. He is currently completing a manuscript on the impact of European integration on France in the 1990s (Greenwood, 2000). His scholarly interests include modern and contemporary French history and politics, the European Union, religion and spirituality, business French, and environmental policy in France.

Alain Kimmel teaches at the Centre international d'études pédagogiques (CIEP) in Sèvres, France and was formerly at the Institut d'études politiques in Paris. Former Editor in Chief of *Echos,* he is currently in charge of the section "L'air du temps" on the CIEP web site. He is a regular contributor to *Le Français dans le Monde* and the author of three books: *Certaines Idées de la France, Vous avez dit France?,* and *Le Nouveau Guide France.*

Jeri DeBois King is the Anne Morrison Chapman Distinguished Professor of Modern Languages at Converse College where she teaches French and Spanish and coordinates the Anne Morrison Chapman Endowment which funds visiting professors and student scholarships for study abroad. She is the author of *Paratextuality in Balzac's 'La Peau de chagrin'* (Edwin Mellen Press, 1992).

Edward C. Knox is College Professor of French and Director of the European Studies Program at Middlebury College. The author of books and articles on French literature and civilization, his recent publications and research interests concern the image of France and the United States in the French and American press. He currently chairs the Commission on Universities for the American Association of Teachers of French (AATF).

Colette G. Levin is Associate Professor of French at the University of Pittsburgh at Greensburg. She is currently involved in an on-going project to create an inventory of cultural components pertaining to the representation of French and American cultures in original French films and their Hollywood remakes. Her scholarly and pedagogical interests include French cinema, world cinema, film theory, French for the professions, the eighteenth-century French novel, and contemporary French civilization.

Chris Pinet, Editor in Chief of *The French Review*, teaches French at Montana State University-Bozeman. He has published widely on literature and contemporary French society in the *Stanford French Review, French Review, Contemporary French Civilization, Modern and Contemporary France, Canadian Modern Language Review, and Journal of Language for International Business*. His current research is on the Parisian Red Belt.

Michel Sage is Associate Professor of French at West Chester University in Pennsylvania. He is the author of articles on French and European literature in the seventeenth and twentieth centuries and foreign-language pedagogy. He is currently working on a manuscript on the French and American press. His scholarly interests include French history and politics, business French, phonetics, and the development of distance education on the Internet.

Gregg H. Siewert is currently Associate Professor of French at Truman State University in Kirksville, Missouri, and teaches business French, literature, and language. He has presented research on topics such *as le Tour de France,* Maurice Chevalier, and the semiology of camembert cheese illustrations. He has been an NEH Fellow several times and is currently working on Raymond Queneau.

Roland Simon is Associate Professor of French at the University of Virginia. He is the recipient of the Gilbert Chinard Prize in Criticism for his *Orphée Médusé: Autobiographies de Michel Leiris* (L'Age d'homme, 1984) and the author of many articles on French culture and literature. Co-editor with R. T. Denommé of a collection of essays, *Unfinished Revolutions: Legacies of Upheaval in Modern French Culture* (Penn State Press, 1998), he has taught at the Taft School, Stanford University, Middlebury College, and Princeton University.

Alan J. Singerman is currently Professor of French at Davidson College, where he teaches French language, literature, civilization, and film. His scholarly interests focus on the eighteenth-century French novel, film, and contemporary French society. He has authored many books and articles and edited the first volume prepared by the AATF Commission on Cultural Competence.

Alice J. Strange is Associate Professor in the Department of Foreign Languages at Southeast Missouri State University. Her professional interests include the teaching of French language and literature and the study and teaching of contemporary French society and culture. She is an active member of the American Association of Teachers of French, a regular participant in its conferences, and contributor to its publications.

Jacqueline Thomas is Professor of French in the Department of Language and Literature at Texas A&M University-Kingsville. She is the author of the Testing Program to accompany McGraw-Hill's *Rendez-vous* (1998) and her latest article "Beckett's Happy Days: A Rescript of *Lady Chatterley's Lover*," recently appeared in *Modern Drama*. Her scholarly interests include metalinguistic awareness in second and third language learning.

Fred Toner is Associate Professor of French at Ohio University where he is Coordinator of elementary French and Supervisor of the graduate teaching assistants. He teaches undergraduate and graduate courses on foreign language methodology, contemporary French civilization and culture, focusing on the minority voice, and an upper-level course on the interrelationship of the arts, studying the juncture of text and music. He has authored a textbook and several articles.

Rosalie Vermette is Professor of French and former chair of the French Department at Indiana University-Purdue University Indianapolis. A member of the Commission on Cultural Competence of the American Association of Teachers of French, her scholarly interests include medieval French hagiographic and Romance literature, modern and contemporary French culture, and the relationship between geography and literature.

Ann Williams-Gascon is Professor of French at Metropolitan State College of Denver, where she teaches courses in language, literature, and culture. She has received several excellence in teaching awards and is a frequent presenter at regional, national and international language conferences. She has co-authored two college-level French textbooks as well as articles and reviews. She is an active member of the AATF Commission on Cultural Competence.